U·X·L
ENDANGERED SPECIES

3RD EDITION

U·X·L
ENDANGERED SPECIES

3RD EDITION

VOLUME 1

MAMMALS

Julia Garbus
Noah Berlatsky
Kathleen J. Edgar, Project Editor

U·X·L
A part of Gale, Cengage Learning

GALE
CENGAGE Learning·

Farmington Hills, Mich • San Francisco • New York • Waterville, Maine
Meriden, Conn • Mason, Ohio • Chicago

U•X•L Endangered Species, 3rd Edition

Julia Garbus and Noah Berlatsky

Project Editor: Kathleen J. Edgar

Acquisitions Editor: Christine Slovey

Contributing Editor: Elizabeth Manar

Rights Acquisition and Management: Amanda Kopczynski and Ashley Maynard

Composition: Evi Abou-El-Seoud

Manufacturing: Wendy Blurton

Product Design: Kristine A. Julien

For product information and technology assistance, contact us at **Gale Customer Support, 1-800-877-4253.**
For permission to use material from this text or product, submit all requests online at **www.cengage.com/permissions.**
Further permissions questions can be emailed to **permissionrequest@cengage.com**

Cover photographs: © Orangutan by Stephen Meese, © Rothschild's Starling by Nagel Photography, and © Grand Cayman Blue Iguana by Frontpage, all Shutterstock.com.

While every effort has been made to ensure the reliability of the information presented in this publication, Gale, a part of Cengage Learning, does not guarantee the accuracy of the data contained herein. Gale accepts no payment for listing; and inclusion in the publication of any organization, agency, institution, publication, service, or individual does not imply endorsement of the editors or publisher. Errors brought to the attention of the publisher and verified to the satisfaction of the publisher will be corrected in future editions.

LIBRARY OF CONGRESS CATALOGING-IN-PUBLICATION DATA

Names: Garbus, Julia, author. | Berlatsky, Noah, author. | Edgar, Kathleen J., editor. | Gale (Firm)
Title: U X L endangered species / Julia Garbus, Noah Berlatsky ; Kathleen J. Edgar, project editor.
Other titles: Endangered species.
Description: 3rd edition. | Farmington Hills, MI : U-X-L, A part of Gale, Cengage Learning, 2016. | Includes bibliographical references and index.
Identifiers: LCCN 2015037374 | ISBN 9781410332981 (vol. 1 : alk. paper) | ISBN 9781410332998 (vol. 2 : alk. paper) | ISBN 9781410333001 (vol. 3 : alk. paper) | ISBN 9781410332974 (set : alk. paper)
Subjects: LCSH: Endangered species--Juvenile literature.
Classification: LCC QL83 .G37 2016 | DDC 591.68--dc23
LC record available at http://lccn.loc.gov/2015037374

Gale
27500 Drake Rd.
Farmington Hills, MI 48331-3535

978-1-4103-3297-4 (set)
978-1-4103-3298-1 (vol. 1)
978-1-4103-3299-8 (vol. 2)
978-1-4103-3300-1 (vol. 3)

This title is also available as an e-book.
978-1-4103-3296-7
Contact your Gale sales representative for ordering information.

Printed in China
1 2 3 4 5 6 7 20 19 18 17 16

Table of Contents

VOLUME 2: ARACHNIDS, BIRDS, CRUSTACEANS, INSECTS, AND MOLLUSKS

Arachnids

Birds

VOLUME 3: AMPHIBIANS, CORALS, FISH, PLANTS, AND REPTILES

Amphibians

Corals

Fish

Plants

Reptiles

Reader's Guide

U•X•L Endangered Species, 3rd Edition, presents information on endangered and threatened mammals, birds, reptiles, amphibians, fish, corals, mollusks, insects, arachnids, crustaceans, and plants. Its 242 entries were chosen to give a glimpse of the broad range of species currently facing endangerment. While well-publicized examples such as the polar bear, tiger, and giant sequoia are examined, so too are less conspicuous—yet no less threatened—species such as the Ganges River dolphin, Knysna seahorse, and golf ball cactus.

The entries are spread across three volumes and are divided into sections by classes. Within each class, species are arranged alphabetically by common name.

Each entry begins with the species' common and scientific names. A fact box containing classification information—phylum (or division), class, order, and family—for that species follows. The box also lists the current status of the species in the wild according to the International Union for Conservation of Nature and Natural Resources (IUCN) and the U.S. Fish and Wildlife Service (USFWS, which administers the Endangered Species Act). Finally, the box lists the country or countries where the species currently ranges.

Locator maps outlining the range of a particular species are included in each entry to help users find unfamiliar countries or locations. In most entries, a color photo provides a more concrete visualization of the species. Sidebar boxes containing interesting and related information are also included in some entries.

Each entry is broken into three sections:

- The information under the subhead **Description and biology** provides a general description of the species. This includes physical dimensions, eating and reproductive habits, and social behavior.

- The information under the subhead **Habitat and current distribution** describes where the species is found today, its preferred habitat, and, if available, recent estimates of its population size. Research studies are not conducted at regular intervals for some of these species, so 10 or more years may pass before new estimates become available.

- The information under the subhead **History and conservation measures** relates, if possible, the history of the species and the factors currently threatening it. Conservation efforts to save the species, if any are underway, are also described.

Included in each volume of *U•X•L Endangered Species, 3rd Edition*, is an overview of the history and current state of endangerment and its causes. It is followed by an explanation of the fact boxes and classifications used in the set and then a discussion of the International Union for Conservation of Nature and Natural Resources (IUCN) that includes a brief history of the organization, its current focus, and a brief explanation of the status categories in which the IUCN places imperiled species. The next section focuses on the Endangered Species Act (ESA), briefly examining its passage, purpose, implementation, status categories, and current state. A look at the changes in species' status from the 2nd to 3rd edition follows. Each volume also includes a **Words to Know** section that provides definitions of words and terms used in the set.

At the back of each book is a selection of **Critical Thinking Questions** that encourage reflection on the causes of endangerment and human efforts to protect wildlife. A **Classroom Projects and Activities** section follows, offering ideas for discussion and collaborative problem-solving.

A **Where to Learn More** section lists books, periodicals, websites, environmental organizations, and other resources such as movies and apps. The book listing is annotated. The environmental organizations list—a selected catalog of organizations focusing on endangered species—contains contact information and a brief description of each organization.

Finally, the volumes conclude with a cumulative index providing access to all the species discussed throughout *U•X•L Endangered Species, 3rd Edition*.

The scope of this work is neither definitive nor exhaustive. No work on this subject can be. The information presented is as current as possible, but the state of endangered species changes almost daily.

A note about the 3rd Edition

Since the publication of *U•X•L Endangered Species, 2nd Edition*, in 2004, the endangered or threatened status of many of the species included in these volumes has changed. Through the efforts of conservationists (people who work to manage and protect nature) and legislators, some of these species have recovered or have been assigned a less-threatened status (known as downlisting). The bald eagle, for example, listed as threatened under the ESA at the time of the *U•X•L Endangered Species, 2nd Edition*, has been removed from the list entirely and downlisted to "Least Concern" by the IUCN. The bald eagle population had plummeted, in part, because the powerful pesticide DDT weakened the shells of the birds' eggs. Listed as endangered in 1967, the U.S. national bird recovered after DDT was banned, its habitat was protected, and captive breeding programs were instituted. Other successes include the grizzly bear, the American bison, the black-footed ferret, and the Steller sea lion in the United States; the Iberian lynx in Europe; the African elephant; the markhor, a wild goat that is Pakistan's national animal; and three monkey species from Central and South America.

Along with successes, there have been serious setbacks. Other species previously listed have declined to the very brink of extinction. Several are familiar, such as the gorilla, endangered because of hunting and disease, and the northern white rhino, of which only three are known to remain. But less well-known or beloved species suffer equally, especially if their populations have always been small. For example, the mongoose lemur, a monkey-like animal native to several islands near the coast of Africa, has dropped from vulnerable to critically endangered status due to the destruction of its forest habitat for agriculture. Some more developed countries with stable, strong governments, such as the United States and Australia, may have ample resources to devote to conservation, whereas less economically developed and less stable countries and regions often lack such tools. Of the 24 species described in this book that have moved to a more threatened status since 2004, more than half are from such areas, including many from war-torn or impoverished regions of Africa.

U•X•L Endangered Species, 3rd Edition, cannot cover all threatened species worldwide, but 38 new species have been included in this edition to ensure that the situations of animals and plants worldwide—as they stand 12 years after the publication of *U•X•L Endangered Species, 2nd Edition*—are represented. New species described include the most familiar butterfly in the United States, the monarch, which is under consideration as an endangered species by the USFWS. The vibrant black-and-orange insect feeds on milkweed plants, which are becoming rare because of pesticide use. The new species presented reflect the diversity of the world's endangered creatures. There are mammals such as the okapi, birds such as the African penguin, arachnids such as the peacock tarantula, crustaceans such as the vernal pool tadpole shrimp, insects such as the Morrison bumblebee, mollusks such as the freshwater pearl mussel, amphibians such as the axolotl, fish such as the great hammerhead shark, plants such as the whitebark pine, and reptiles such as the bog turtle. Corals are included for the first time. These ocean invertebrates, animals without backbones, are moving toward extinction more rapidly than other animals such as amphibians, mammals, and birds.

Conservationists today face similar concerns to those described in *U•X•L Endangered Species, 2nd Edition*, many with more urgency. Some species described in this book, such as the saiga, the gray and Indiana bats, and the Wyoming frog, have declined in number because of disease. Scientists are working hard to understand the illnesses and develop ways to prevent them. The biggest reason for endangerment, however, continues to be habitat loss. Species as diverse as the Grand Cayman blue iguana, the giant catfish, the peacock tarantula, and Chapman's rhododendron, a flowering plant, have become endangered because people have logged forests, planted crops, grazed animals, built homes, dammed rivers, and engaged in other activities that destroyed these species' habitats. Habitat fragmentation, when development results in animals' living areas being broken up into smaller, separated areas, has threatened species such as the maned wolf, pygmy hippopotamus, and California tiger salamander.

The problem of commercial exploitation has nearly doomed some species included in these volumes. Animals such as the long-tailed pangolin and the great hammerhead shark are captured illegally and are then sold for food or because their bodies are thought to have medicinal properties. In the oceans, overfishing continues to threaten such species as the southern bluefin tuna. Bycatch—being caught by mistake in nets intended for other animals—threatens other species such as sea turtles and sawfish. Laws and treaties protecting species can help preservation efforts, as can educating local communities about the importance of species that share their environment. However, laws and education may not stop people driven by hunger from eating endangered animals, or those driven by poverty from capturing and selling them. Conservationists say that one of the best ways to conserve threatened species is to help local communities find new ways of surviving that do not endanger wildlife.

Since *U•X•L Endangered Species, 2nd Edition*, was published in 2004, scientists, authors, and the media are using new terms to describe the effects of human activity on the environment, although the changes these terms describe have been ongoing for many years. First, scientists have begun referring to our era as that of a sixth great extinction. All species become extinct eventually, at a natural rate of several species per year. Before the era of humans, the planet experienced five periods of mass extinctions, when most living species disappeared. But since 1900, extinctions have increased to more than 100 times the natural rate. This sixth wave, unlike the earlier five, is human-caused. The **Endangerment and Its Causes** section discusses the different ways human actions threaten animal and plant species. Another change in terminology is that since 2004, climate change has become increasingly evident and increasingly discussed. Several animal species described in this book, such as polar bears and corals, have already been harmed by climate change. Scientists predict that if people continue burning fossil fuels (oil, gas, and coal) at the current rate, many more species will be at risk of extinction by the end of the 21st century.

Since 2004, the realities of climate change and the sixth wave of extinction have demonstrated even more strongly than before that the fates of humans and other living species are inextricably interwoven. It is possible to take measures that rescue endangered species from the edge of extinction, prevent others from becoming threatened, and improve people's lives at the same time. These measures, however, require more than intense efforts to save particular animals. They call for people to reflect on how their actions affect not only other humans, but also the species with which we share our planet. And then these reflections must turn into actions that will improve not only the situations of today's people, animals, and other species, but the lives of those that will come in the future.

Acknowledgments

Special thanks are due for the invaluable comments and suggestions provided by the *U•X•L Endangered Species* advisory board:

Ela-Sita Carpenter, Museum Educator, Maryland Science Center, Baltimore, Maryland

Adam J. Eichenwald, Neighborhood Nestwatch Researcher; Atlanta Representative at Smithsonian Migratory Bird Center, Atlanta, Georgia

Martha N. Mather, 6th grade science teacher, Kennewick School District, Kennewick, Washington

Carrie Radcliffe, Restoration Coordinator and Safeguarding Database Manager, Atlanta Botanical Garden, Atlanta, Georgia; Mountain Bog Project Coordinator, Georgia Plant Conservation Alliance, Athens, Georgia; Consulting Botanist, Georgia Department of Natural Resources and U.S. Forest Service Southern Region

The U•X•L staff would also like to offer its profound thanks to Cinqué Hicks, Director, and Jamie Vidich, Operations Manager and Content Development Lead, of Bookbright Media for their invaluable contributions to this set. Their vision, skill, and enthusiasm are much appreciated.

Comments and suggestions

Cengage Learning welcomes your comments on *U•X•L Endangered Species, 3rd Edition*, and suggestions for species to be included in future editions of this work. Please write: Editors, *U•X•L Endangered Species, 3rd Edition*, 27500 Drake Rd., Farmington Hills, MI 48331-3535; call toll-free: 1-800-877-4253; fax: 1-877-363-4253; or send an e-mail via www.gale.com.

Endangerment and Its Causes: An Overview

Living organisms have been disappearing from Earth since the beginning of life on the planet. Most of the species that have ever lived on Earth are now extinct. Extinction and endangerment can occur naturally as a normal process in the course of evolution or as the result of a catastrophic event, such as the collision of an asteroid with Earth. Scientists believe some 65 million years ago, an asteroid struck near Mexico's Yucatán Peninsula, bringing about the extinction of almost 50 percent of plant species and 75 percent of animal species, including the dinosaurs. Scientists have identified five great extinction episodes in Earth's history before humans appeared on the planet. Although these five periods were marked by widespread, rapid extinction, species are continually disappearing; species become extinct at a rate of one to five species a year due to disease, competition among species, or natural climate change.

When humans became the dominant species on the planet, however, the extinction rate of other species began to increase dramatically. Especially since the 17th century, technological advances and an ever-expanding human population have changed the natural world as never before. At present, scientists believe extinctions caused by humans are taking place at 100 to 1,000 times nature's normal rate between great extinction episodes. Species are disappearing faster than they can be created through evolution. Therefore, the planet has entered a sixth wave of mass extinction that scientists believe is caused by human activity.

Because scientists have described and named only a small percentage of Earth's species, it is impossible to measure the total number of species endangered or going extinct. At least 1.9 million animal species and 450,000 plant species have been identified, but scientists say that possibly millions more have not yet been discovered. According to the International Union for Conservation of Nature and Natural Resources (IUCN), amphibians and corals are the animal groups at highest risk of extinction, with about 40 percent of each group threatened. About 25 percent of mammals and 13 percent of birds are at risk. Since 1980, birds and mammals as a whole have become slightly more endangered, the status of amphibians has dropped more sharply, and the outlook for corals has plummeted.

Humans are endangering species and the natural world primarily in three ways: habitat destruction, commercial exploitation of animals and plants, and the introduction of nonnative species into a habitat. Human activity has also accelerated climate change, which already threatens some species. Some experts state that if climate change continues at its current level, 25 percent of all species could be at risk by 2050.

Habitat destruction

The destruction of habitats all over the world is the primary reason species are becoming extinct or endangered. Houses, highways, dams, industrial buildings, and ever-spreading farms now dominate landscapes formerly occupied by forests, prairies, deserts, scrublands, and wetlands. For instance, 46,000 to 58,000 square miles (119,000 to 150,000 square kilometers) of forest each year are destroyed worldwide, the equivalent of 36 football fields each minute. Tropical rain forests, home to 50 percent of all animal and plant species, once occupied 6 million square miles (15.5 million square kilometers) worldwide. Now, only 2.4 million square miles (6.2 million square kilometers) remain.

Habitat destruction can be obvious, or it can be subtle, occurring over a long period of time without being noticed. Pollution, such as sewage from cities and chemical runoff from farms, can change the quality and quantity of water in streams and rivers. To species living in a delicately balanced habitat, this disturbance can be as fatal as the clearcutting of a rain forest.

When remaining habitats are carved into smaller and smaller areas or fragments, species living in those smaller areas suffer. The fragments become crowded, with increased competition for scarce resources and space. Access to food and water may become limited. In search of such resources, animals may be killed while crossing roads or may venture into areas inhabited by people, causing conflicts with them. And, very importantly, habitat fragmentation limits access to mates. A smaller pool of mates reduces a species' genetic diversity, the number of different genes in a population. Genetic diversity plays a key role in the evolution and survival of living things, allowing a species a greater chance of adapting to changing environments and resisting disease.

Commercial exploitation

Animals have long been hunted by humans, not only for their meat but also for parts of their bodies that are used to create clothing, medicines, love potions, trinkets, and other things. Overhunting has caused the extinction of many species and brought a great many others to the brink. Examples include some species of whales, slaughtered for oil and baleen; the black rhinoceros, which is killed for its horns; and bluefin tuna, which are prized as a delicacy in Asia. Species that people find attractive or interesting, such as certain corals and arachnids, may become threatened in the wild as they are collected or captured for the pet or hobby trade.

Although international treaties outlaw the capture and trade of many endangered or threatened species, these laws are difficult to enforce, especially in countries that lack resources or a stable government. The smuggling of endangered species is a huge international business, estimated to be worth $10 billion to $20 billion a year. One reason people may hunt, capture, and trade endangered species is because they feel they have little economic alternative. So they may eat endangered animals for protein or capture and sell them as a livelihood.

Introduced species

Native species are those that have inhabited a given biological landscape for a long period of time. They have adapted to the environment, climate, and other species in that locale. Introduced or exotic species are those that have been brought into that landscape by humans, either accidentally or intentionally. In some cases, these introduced species may not cause any harm. They may, over time, adapt to their new surroundings and fellow species, becoming "native." Most often, however, introduced species seriously disrupt ecological balances. They compete with native species for food and shelter. Often, they prey on the native species, which may lack natural defenses against the intruders. They may also carry diseases that infect the native species or may take the resources that native species require for survival. When introduced species cause or are likely to cause harm to an environment, they are called invasive species. In the last 500 years, introduced plants and animals, including insects, cats, pigs, and rats, have caused the endangerment or outright extinction of hundreds of native species. In fact, more than 40 percent of threatened or endangered species are at risk because of invasive species.

Climate change

When humans burn fossil fuels, carbon dioxide is released into the air. This gas in the atmosphere creates a layer of insulation that stops Earth's heat from going into space. The more carbon dioxide in the atmosphere, therefore, the warmer Earth becomes. Since the 19th century, when the Western world became industrialized, the levels of carbon dioxide in the atmosphere have increased by 33 percent. Earth became 1.5°F (0.8°C) warmer from 1901 to 2012. Scientists estimate that Earth could warm anywhere from 0.5 to 8.6°F (0.28 to 4.78°C) over the next 100 years. This trend is referred to as global warming. A related term, climate change, refers to all major, long-lasting changes in climate, including global warming but also encompassing longer, more severe heat waves and changes in rainfall that lead to floods or droughts. These heat waves and rainfall changes are linked to increased levels of carbon dioxide and other gases in the atmosphere.

Climate change threatens many species in many ways. Warming temperatures in polar regions threaten animals that live or hunt on ice, such as polar bears. As melting sea ice causes sea levels to rise, these rising waters could engulf areas near the shore where animal and plant species live. Warmer ocean temperatures kill or weaken corals, while warmer temperatures on land can force animals to move to cooler areas or wake animals too early from hibernation. Droughts threaten many animals, especially amphibians, and plants. The effects of climate change on species can be direct; for example, the endangered Australian ant only emerges in cool weather. Or it can be indirect, threatening a species by disturbing the web of life in which the species exists. The blue whale, for instance, eats small sea animals called krill, which feed on algae that grow under sea ice. Rising temperatures have melted sea ice, reducing the algae population. This reduction in food supply has decreased the krill population by as much as 80 percent, which in turn could threaten the blue whale. Some scientists state that climate change has already contributed to the extinction of one species: the golden toad, a small, bright orange amphibian from Central America.

U•X•L Endangered Species *Fact Boxes and Classification: An Explanation*

Each entry in *U•X•L Endangered Species, 3rd Edition*, begins with a shaded fact box that contains the common name of the species, followed by its scientific name. The box lists the classification information for that species: phylum (or division), class, order, and family. It also lists the current status of that species in the wild according to the International Union for Conservation of Nature and Natural Resources (IUCN; see page xxix) and the Endangered Species List compiled under the U.S. Endangered Species Act (ESA; see page xxxi). (Note: For a listing of species whose status has changed since the publication of the 2nd edition, see page xxxv.) Finally, the box lists the countries or regions where the species is currently found and provides a locator map for the range of the species.

Classification

Biological classification, or taxonomy, is the system of arranging plants and animals in groups according to their similarities. This system, which scientists around the world currently use, was developed by 18th-century Swedish botanist (a scientist who studies plants) Carolus Linnaeus. Linnaeus created a multilevel system or pyramid-like structure of nomenclature (naming) in which living organisms were grouped according to the number of physical traits they had in common. The ranking of the system, going from general to specific, is: kingdom, phylum (or division for plants), class, order, and family. The more specific the level (closer to the top of the pyramid), the more traits shared by the organisms placed in that level.

Scientists currently recognize six kingdoms of organisms: Animalia (animals, fish, humans); Plantae (plants, trees, grasses); Fungi (mushrooms, lichens); Protista (bacteria, certain algae, other one-celled organisms having nuclei); Eubacteria (bacteria, blue-green algae, other one-celled organisms without nuclei); and Archaea (one-celled organisms found only in extreme environments such as hot or highly acidic water).

Every living organism is placed into one of these kingdoms. Organisms within kingdoms are then divided into phylums (or divisions for plants) based on distinct and defining characteristics. An example would be the phylum Chordata, which contains all the members of the kingdom Animalia that have a notochord (a rod, such as a backbone, that runs up an animal's back to support its body). Organisms in a specific phylum or division are then further divided into classes based on more distinct and defining characteristics. The dividing continues on through orders and then into families. Organisms that share a family often have the same behavioral patterns.

To further define an organism, Linnaeus also developed a two-part naming system—called binomial nomenclature—in which each living organism was given a two-part Latin name to distinguish it from other members in its family. The first name—italicized and capitalized—is the genus of the organism. The second name—italicized but not capitalized—is its species. This species name is an adjective, usually descriptive or geographic. Together, the genus and species form an organism's scientific name.

How similar organisms are separated by their scientific names can be seen in the example of the white oak and the red oak. All oak trees belong to the genus *Quercus*. The scientific name of white oak is *Quercus alba* (*alba* is Latin for "white"), while that of the red oak is *Quercus rubra* (*rubra* is Latin for "red"). In the past, scientists mainly took account of physical characteristics and behavior to group species together and give them scientific names. Now that scientists are able to compare species' DNA sequences, they also use this genetic information to classify species.

Each species or organism usually has only one scientific name under binomial nomenclature, which enables scientists worldwide who do not speak the same languages to communicate with each other about the species. However, as scientists learn more about species, they sometimes reclassify them based on new information. In such cases, a species will have a former name and a new name. Species can also end up with more than one name when scientists disagree about how they should be classified, with some scientists using one name and others preferring another. Alternate scientific names for a species are called "synonyms."

The scientific names provided for the species in *U•X•L Endangered Species, 3rd Edition*, are those used by the IUCN and the Endangered Species List. The Endangered Species List draws its taxonomic information from the Integrated Taxonomic Information System (ITIS). ITIS has also been consulted as a source for *U•X•L Endangered Species, 3rd Edition*, to determine accuracy of species' scientific names and taxonomies.

International Union for Conservation of Nature and Natural Resources (IUCN)

The International Union for Conservation of Nature and Natural Resources (IUCN), one of the world's oldest international conservation organizations, is a worldwide alliance of governments, government agencies, and nongovernmental organizations. It was established in Fontainebleau, France, on October 5, 1948. Working with scientists and experts, the IUCN tries to encourage and assist nations and societies around the world to conserve nature and to use natural resources wisely. As of December 2015, IUCN members represent 89 governments, 127 government agencies, and more than 1,000 nongovernmental organizations.

The IUCN has six volunteer commissions. The largest and most active of these is the Species Survival Commission (SSC). The mission of the SSC is to conserve biological diversity by developing programs that help save, restore, and manage species and their habitats. One of the many activities of the SSC is the production of the IUCN Red List of Threatened Species.

Available online, the IUCN Red List website has provided the foundation for *U•X•L Endangered Species, 3rd Edition*. The list presents scientifically based information on the status of threatened species around the world. Species are classified according to their existence in the wild and the current threats to that existence.

IUCN Red List categories

The IUCN Red List of Threatened Species places threatened plants, animals, fungi, and protists (organisms such as protozoans, one-celled algae, and slime molds) into one of nine categories:

- **Extinct:** A species that no longer exists anywhere around the world.

- **Extinct in the wild:** A species that no longer exists in the wild, but exists in captivity, in cultivation, or in an area well outside its natural range.

- **Critically endangered:** A species that is facing an extremely high risk of extinction in the wild.

- **Endangered:** A species that is facing a very high risk of extinction in the wild.

- **Vulnerable:** A species that is facing a high risk of extinction in the wild.

- **Near threatened:** A species that currently does not qualify as critically endangered, endangered, or vulnerable, but is close to qualifying or may qualify in the near future.

- **Least concern:** A species that has been evaluated but does not qualify as critically endangered, endangered, vulnerable, or near threatened because it is widespread or abundant.

- **Data deficient:** A species on which there is little information to assess its risk of extinction. Because of the possibility that future research will place the species in a threatened category, more information is required.

- **Not evaluated:** A species that has not been evaluated for inclusion on the list.

The IUCN updates its Red List assessments at least once per year, giving a new version number to each update. The trends shown in the 2015 report were not encouraging. As of its version 2015.2 Red List, the IUCN listed 11,877 threatened animals, 10,896 threatened plants, and 11 threatened species from the fungi and protist groups. Threatened species are those classified by the IUCN as critically endangered, endangered, or vulnerable. The number of threatened species on the IUCN Red List in 2015 is more than twice the number listed in 2000. However, many new species have been evaluated since 2000, which accounts for part of the increase. Cycads (palmlike plants found in tropical and subtropical regions) and amphibians are the two groups with the greatest percentage of threatened species in 2015. It is estimated that 63 percent of all cycads are threatened and 41 percent of all amphibian species are threatened.

Endangered Species Act

The Endangered Species Act (ESA) was passed by the U.S. Congress in 1973 and was reauthorized in 1988. The purpose of the ESA is to recover species around the world that are in danger of human-caused extinction. There are three basic elements to the ESA program: the creation of a list of endangered animals and plants (the Endangered Species List), the formulation of recovery plans for each species on the list, and the designation of critical habitat for each species listed. Through this program, the act seeks to provide a means of conserving those species and their ecosystems.

The U.S. Fish and Wildlife Service (USFWS), a part of the Department of the Interior, is the federal agency responsible for listing (or reclassifying or delisting) endangered and threatened species on the Endangered Species List. The National Marine Fisheries Service is responsible for many species that live in the oceans. The USFWS website hosts the Environmental Conservation Online System (ECOS), which lists all the species on the Endangered Species List as well as related scientific reports. ECOS has provided crucial source material for *U•X•L Endangered Species, 3rd Edition*.

The decision to list a species is based solely on scientific factors. Once a species is placed on the list, the USFWS is required to develop a plan for its recovery and to designate critical habitat for the species. Critical habitat is an area that has been deemed essential to the physical and biological needs of the species, either in their original range or an area similar to it. The designated critical habitat must provide appropriate space for population growth and normal behavior so that a species may recover. Critical habitat designation does not prohibit human activity or create an isolated refuge for the species in the chosen area. Once it has been established, however, any federal agencies planning to build on that land (a highway, for example) must seek the permission of the USFWS. Any other activities requiring federal permits must go through the USFWS as well. Private landowners are not affected, except that the designation alerts the public to the importance of the area in the species' survival. The ESA explicitly states that the economic interests of the human community must be given ample consideration in designating critical habitats and requires the balancing of species protection with economic development.

When a species is placed on the Endangered Species List, it is positioned in one of two categories:

- **Endangered:** A species that is in danger of extinction throughout all or a significant part of its range.
- **Threatened:** A species that is likely to become endangered in the foreseeable future.

The ESA outlaws the buying, selling, transporting, importing, or exporting of any listed species. Most important, the act bans the taking of any listed species within the United States and its territorial seas. "Taking" is defined as harassing, harming, pursuing, hunting, shooting, wounding, cutting, trapping, killing, removing, capturing, or collecting. The taking of listed species is prohibited on both private and public lands.

Violators of the ESA are subject to heavy fines. Individuals can face up to $100,000 in fines and up to one year's imprisonment. Organizations found in violation of the act may be fined up to $200,000.

On November 2, 2015, there were 2,246 species on the Endangered Species List. This total included 1,345 animals and 901 plants. The total also included 1,592 species found on U.S. territory or in U.S. waters, while the remaining 654 were species found in other countries.

Since its passage in 1973, the ESA has been continually targeted by its many opponents. Some of those opponents believe the ESA prohibits human progress, placing the rights of other species ahead of the rights of humans. There are many interest groups who lobby against the ESA: building and real estate development associations oppose the ESA because it could present some federal impediments to the large financial gains to be made in constructing new communities or facilities. Loggers, oil companies, farmers, fishers, hunters, fur traders, and others whose means of making a living are affected are also heavily represented in anti-ESA activism. Politicians, even those who nominally support the ESA, do not often find it politically advantageous to provide the necessary support and funding to rescue little-known animals or to oppose large and powerful companies.

In 1995 many Texans became upset on hearing news reports that said the USFWS might designate millions of acres of Texas land as critical habitat for the golden-cheeked warbler, an endangered bird. Designation of critical habitat is a required step for every species listed under the ESA. As a result of public outcry, U.S. senator Kay Bailey Hutchinson, a Republican from Texas, helped pass legislation that halted the USFWS's activities in the entire United States. The USFWS was prevented from designating new endangered or threatened species or designating critical habitat for existing species for a year. According to the USFWS, far less land was being proposed as critical habitat than news reports suggested, and critical habitat designation has no effect on private landowners anyway, a fact that the public often overlooks. When the moratorium (suspension of activity) was lifted in 1996, the agency faced delays and a backlog of proposed species to address.

In 2011 the nonprofit Center for Biological Diversity (CBD) concluded 10 years of lawsuits against the USFWS. The CBD had argued that the government agency was acting too slowly in listing new species. Under the eight years of President George W. Bush's administration (2001–2009), only 62 new species were listed, compared to 522 listed under the previous eight years during President Bill Clinton's administration (1993–2001). Meanwhile, the list of proposed species was getting longer as the USFWS took its time in making decisions. When the CBD and the USFWS made a settlement in 2011, the government agency agreed to decide on the backlog of 757 candidate species by 2018.

As recently as 2015, President Barack Obama's administration proposed making major changes to the ESA that would give states a larger role in the process of proposing new species for the ESA. It would also require that species be proposed only one at a time, rather than in bunches, which is currently done and saves time and steps. Opponents say that these changes will make it harder for citizens and organizations to propose new species as endangered.

Some of the species included in *U•X•L Endangered Species, 3rd Edition*, are losing the last few acres, streams, caves, or hillsides they require to survive; others stand only a few individual animals away from extinction. In the meantime, government agencies, wildlife organizations, politicians, and individuals often disagree on how best to balance the needs of humans and endangered species. Human activities are frequently the cause of endangerment, and human interests often conflict with those of other species. However, there are many examples in *U•X•L Endangered Species, 3rd Edition*, that illustrate how human efforts, including the protections of the ESA, can be critical in bringing species back from the verge of extinction.

Changes in Status from the 2nd Edition

Key: PE = Proposed Endangered; OFF = Delisted because of recovery;
LR–CD = Lower Risk, Conservation Dependent; TH = Threatened;
R = Rare (no longer used); NT = Near Threatened; VU = Vulnerable;
EN = Endangered; CE = Critically Endangered;
EW = Extinct in the Wild

Species that moved to a less threatened status, 2004–2016

Mammals

Armadillo, giant: EN to VU (IUCN)

Bat, gray: EN to NT (IUCN)

Bison, American: EN to TH (ESA)

Bison, European: EN to VU (IUCN)

Elephant, African: EN to VU (IUCN)

Ferret, black-footed: EW to EN (IUCN)

Lynx, Iberian: CE to EN (IUCN)

Markhor: EN to NT (IUCN); EN to TH (ESA)

Marmoset, white-eared: EN to VU (IUCN)

Monkey, Central American squirrel: EN to VU (IUCN)

Panda, red: EN to VU (IUCN)

Rat, giant kangaroo: CE to EN (IUCN)

Sea lion, Steller: EN to NT (IUCN)

Tamarin, golden lion: CE to EN (IUCN)

Birds

Booby, Abbott's: CE to EN (IUCN)

Cormorant, Galápagos: EN to VU (IUCN)

Eagle, bald: TH to OFF (ESA)

Macaw, Lear's: CE to EN (IUCN)

Magpie-robin, Seychelles: CE to EN (IUCN)

Parakeet, golden: EN to VU (IUCN)

Plover, piping: VU to NT (IUCN)

Warbler, Kirtland's: VU to NT (IUCN)

Woodpecker, red-cockaded VU to NT (IUCN)

Crustaceans

Shrimp, Kentucky cave: EN to VU (IUCN)

Insects

Dragonfly, Hine's emerald: EN to NT (IUCN)

Mollusks

Mussel, fat pocketbook pearly: CE to VU (IUCN)

Plants

Cypress, Saharan: CE to EN (IUCN)

Reptiles

Turtle, leatherback sea: CE to VU (IUCN)

Viper, meadow: EN to VU (IUCN)

Species that moved to a more threatened status, 2004–2016

Mammals

Fox, island gray: LR-CD to NT (IUCN); PE to EN (ESA)

Gazelle, dama: EN to CE (IUCN); PE to EN (ESA)

Gorilla: EN to CE (IUCN)

Hippopotamus, pygmy: VU to EN (IUCN)

Lemur, mongoose: VU to CE (IUCN)

Marmot, Vancouver Island: EN to CE (IUCN)

Mink, European: EN to CE (IUCN)

Numbat: VU to EN (IUCN)

Oryx, scimitar-horned: PE to EN (ESA)

Possum, mountain pygmy: EN to CE (IUCN)

Birds

Duck, Laysan: VU to CE (IUCN)

Ground-dove, purple-winged: EN to CE (IUCN)

Honeycreeper, crested: VU to CE (IUCN)

Kestrel, Mauritius: VU to EN (IUCN)

Murrelet, marbled: VU to EN (IUCN)

Pelican, Dalmatian: LR–CD to VU (IUCN)

Amphibians

Frog, Goliath: VU to EN (IUCN)

Fish

Catfish, giant: EN to CE (IUCN)

Sawfish, largetooth: EN to CE (IUCN)

Plants

Cactus, Tamaulipas living rock: VU to EN (IUCN)

Cycad, Natal grass: R to VU (IUCN)

Reptiles

Gharial: EN to CE (IUCN)

Tortoise, angulated: EN to CE (IUCN)

Turtle, Central American river: EN to CE (IUCN)

Words to Know

Adaptation: A genetically determined characteristic or inherited trait that makes an organism better able to cope with its environment.

Alpine: Relating to mountainous regions.

Arid: Land that receives very little rainfall annually and has a high rate of evaporation.

Biodiversity: The entire variety of life on Earth.

Biologist: A person who studies living organisms.

Botanist: A scientist who studies plants.

Brackish: A mixture of freshwater and saltwater; briny water.

Browse: A method of grazing in which an animal eats the leaf and twig growth of shrubs, woody vines, trees, and cacti.

Canopy: The uppermost spreading, branchy layer of a forest.

Captive breeding: A practice by which biologists (people who study living organisms) help a species reproduce in a controlled environment, such as a zoo, aquarium, or captive-breeding facility. Humans carefully select mating partners based on the individuals' genetics, behavior, and age, to find a match that will produce the healthiest offspring.

Carapace: A shell or bony covering on the back of animals such as turtles, lobsters, crabs, and armadillos.

Carnivore: An animal that eats mainly meat.

Carrion: The decaying flesh of dead animals.

Cetacean: An aquatic mammal that belongs to the order Cetacea, which includes whales, dolphins, and porpoises.

Chaparral: An ecological community of shrubby plants adapted to long, dry summers and natural forest-fire cycles, generally found in southern California.

Clear-cutting: The process of cutting down all the trees in a forest area at one time.

Clutch: A number of eggs produced or incubated at one time.

Competitor: A species that may compete for the same resources as another species.

Conservation: The management and protection of the natural world.

Conservationist: A person who works to manage and protect nature.

Convention on International Trade in Endangered Species of Wild Fauna and Flora (CITES): An international agreement by 143 nations to prohibit trade of endangered wildlife.

Critical habitat: A designated area considered necessary for the protection and preservation of a species that has been listed under the Endangered Species Act (ESA) in the United States. The area, either within the species' historical range or in an area similar to it, must provide an environment for normal behavior and reproduction so that the species may recover. The critical habitat designation does not prohibit human activity or create a refuge for the species. Once it has been established, though, any federal agencies planning to build or conduct activities within that area must seek the permission of the U.S. Fish and Wildlife Service (USFWS). The designation also serves to alert the public to the importance of the area in the species' survival.

Crustacean: A shellfish, such as a shrimp or crab, that has several pairs of legs and a segmented body with a hard outer shell.

Deciduous: Shedding seasonally; for example, a tree whose leaves fall off annually or a forest made up of trees that shed their leaves annually.

Deforestation: The loss of forests as they are rapidly cut down to produce timber or to make land available for agriculture.

Desertification: The gradual transformation of productive land into land with desertlike conditions.

Diurnal: Active during the day.

Domesticated: Animals trained to live with or be of use to humans.

Ecosystem: An ecological system, including all of its living things and their environment.

Ecotourism: Tourism, usually to a scenic natural place, that aims to raise awareness of threats and minimize environmental damage to the place.

Endangered: A classification indicating that a species is in danger of extinction in the foreseeable future.

Endangered Species Act (ESA): The legislation, passed by the U.S. Congress in 1973, which protects listed species.

Endangered Species List: The list of species protected under the U.S. Endangered Species Act.

Endemic species: A species native to, and found only in, a certain region.

Estivate: To hibernate (or sleep) through the summer.

Estuary: Coastal waters where a freshwater river empties into a saltwater sea or ocean.

Extinct: Refers to a species or subspecies that no longer exists because all of its living members have died.

Extirpated species: A species that no longer survives in the regions that were once part of its range.

Fauna: The animal life of a particular region, geological period, or environment.

Feral: An animal that has never been domesticated or has escaped from domestication and has become wild.

Fledge: When birds grow the feathers needed for flight.

Flora: The plants of a particular region, geological period, or environment.

Forage: To search for food.

Fragmentation: The breaking up of habitat into smaller areas that no longer border each other.

Gene: The basic biological unit of heredity that determines individual traits. Part of the DNA molecule, the gene is transmitted from parents to children during reproduction, and contains information for making particular proteins, which then make particular cells.

Genetic diversity: The variety of genes that exists among all the individuals of a particular species.

Gestation: Pregnancy.

Habitat: The environment in which specified organisms live.

Herbivore: An animal that eats mainly plants.

Hibernate: To spend the winter in an inactive state.

Historic range: The areas in which a species is believed to have lived in the past.

Hybrid: An animal or plant that is the offspring of two different species or varieties, resulting in a genetic mix.

Inbreeding: The mating or breeding of closely related individuals, usually within small communities. Inbreeding occurs when both parents have at least one common ancestor.

Indicator species: Plants or animals that, by their presence or chemical composition, give some distinctive indication of the health or quality of the environment.

International Union for the Conservation of Nature and Natural Resources (IUCN): An international conservation organization that publishes the IUCN Red List of Threatened Species.

Introduced species: Flora or fauna not native to an area, but introduced from a different ecosystem.

Invasive species: Species from a different ecosystem that cause harm when they are introduced into a new environment.

Invertebrate: An animal without a backbone.

Larval: The immature stage of certain insects and animals, usually of a species that develops by complete metamorphosis.

Lichen: A plantlike composite consisting of a fungus and an alga.

Marsupial: Mammals, such as the kangaroo and the opossum, whose young continue to develop after birth in a pouch on the outside of the mother's body.

Metamorphosis: A change in the form and habits of an animal during natural development.

Migration: The act of changing location (migrating) periodically, usually moving seasonally from one region to another.

Molting: The process of shedding an outer covering, such as skin or feathers, for replacement by a new growth.

Monogamous: Having just one mate for life.

Native species: The flora or fauna indigenous or native to an ecosystem, as opposed to introduced species.

Naturalist: A person who observes nature to find its laws.

Nocturnal: Most active at night.

Old-growth forest: A mature forest dominated by long-lived species (at least 200 years old), but also including younger trees; its complex physical structure includes multiple layers in the canopy, many large trees, and many large, dead, standing trees and dead logs.

Overhunting: Too much hunting of a particular species, resulting in a decline in the population of the species, which can lead to endangerment or extinction.

Perennial: A plant that lives, grows, flowers, and produces seeds for three or more continuous years.

Plumage: The covering of feathers on a bird.

Poaching: Illegally taking protected animals or plants.

Pollution: The contamination of air, water, or soil by the discharge of harmful substances.

Population: A group of organisms of one species occupying a defined area and usually isolated from similar groups of the same species.

Predator: An animal that preys on others.

Prehensile: Adapted for grasping or holding, especially by wrapping around something.

Pupal: An intermediate, inactive stage between the larva and adult stages in the life cycle of many insects.

Rain forest: A dense evergreen forest with an annual rainfall of at least 100 inches (254 centimeters); may be tropical (e.g., Amazon) or temperate (e.g., Pacific Northwest).

Range: The area naturally occupied by a species.

Recovery: The process of stopping or reversing the decline of an endangered or threatened species to ensure the species' long-term survival in the wild.

Reintroduction: The act of placing new members of a species into a habitat where that species had formerly disappeared.

Reserve: An area of land set aside for the use or protection of a species or group of species.

Rhizomatous plant: A plant having an underground horizontal stem that puts out shoots above ground and roots below.

Runoff: Water that drains away from the land's surface, such as after a heavy rain, bringing substances with it.

Savanna: A flat tropical or subtropical grassland.

Scavenger: An animal that feeds on carrion (dead animals) or scraps rather than hunting live prey.

Scrub: A tract of land covered with stunted or scraggly trees and shrubs.

Slash-and-burn agriculture: A farming practice in which forest is cut and burned to create new space for farmland.

Species: A group of individuals related by descent and able to breed among themselves but not with other organisms.

Steppe: Vast, semiarid grass-covered plains found in southeast Europe, Siberia, and central North America.

Subspecies: A population of a species distinguished from other such populations by certain characteristics.

Succulent: A plant that has thick, fleshy, water-storing leaves or stems.

Sustainable development: Methods of farming or building human communities that meet the needs of the current generation without depleting or damaging the natural resources in the area or compromising its ability to meet the needs of future generations.

Taproot: The main root of a plant growing straight downward from the stem.

Taxonomist: A biologist who classifies species on the basis of their genes, characteristics, and behavior.

Temperate: Characteristic of a region or climate that has mild temperatures.

Territoriality: The behavior displayed by an individual animal, a mating pair, or a group in vigorously defending its domain (territory) against intruders.

Trafficking: Dealing or trading in something illegal, such as protected animal and plant species.

Troglobite: A species that lives only in caves.

Tropical: Characteristic of a region or climate that is frost free, with temperatures high enough to support—with adequate precipitation—plant growth year round.

Tundra: A relatively flat, treeless plain in alpine, Arctic, and Antarctic regions.

Underbrush: Small trees, shrubs, or similar plants growing on the forest floor underneath taller trees.

Urban sprawl: The spreading of houses, shopping centers, and other city facilities through previously undeveloped land.

U.S. Fish and Wildlife Service (USFWS): A federal agency that oversees implementation of the Endangered Species Act.

Vegetation: Plants or the plant life of an area.

Vulnerable: A classification indicating that a species satisfies some of the risk criteria for endangerment, but not at a level that warrants its identification as endangered.

Wetland: A permanently moist lowland area such as a marsh or a swamp.

Wildlife biologist: A person who studies living organisms in the wild.

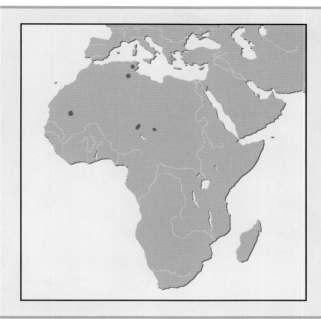

Addax
Addax nasomaculatus

PHYLUM: Chordata
CLASS: Mammalia
ORDER: Artiodactyla
FAMILY: Bovidae
STATUS: Critically endangered, IUCN
Endangered, ESA
RANGE: Chad, Mauritania, Niger,
Tunisia

Addax
Addax nasomaculatus

Description and biology

The addax is a large antelope whose coat is gray-brown in winter and almost white in summer. Black hair sprouts from its forehead and from the end of its 10- to 14-inch (25- to 36-centimeter) tail. Two long, thin, spiral horns (each twisting two or three times) extend up and back from the front of the animal's head. An average addax measures about 5 feet (1.5 meters) in length and about 3 feet (1 meter) in height at its shoulder. It weighs between 132 and 287 pounds (60 and 130 kilograms). A female addax usually gives birth to one infant after a gestation (pregnancy) period of eight to nine months.

The addax is at home in a desert environment. It receives all the water it needs from the plants it eats. With its long stride and splayed (spread-apart) hooves, the animal easily crosses vast sandy areas in search of sparse desert vegetation (plant life). Addaxes usually travel at night in groups of 5 to 20.

Hunting and drought have contributed to the decline of the addax population, which is native to the deserts of North Africa.
© CHAMELEONSEYE/SHUTTERSTOCK.COM.

Habitat and current distribution

It is estimated that fewer than 300 addaxes survive in their range. The majority of these are found in the Sahara Desert in eastern Niger, and small, fragmented (broken into smaller areas that no longer border each other) groups have been seen in remote areas of northern Chad. In 2007 addax tracks were found that indicated the presence of about 15 animals in central Mauritania, but there have been no sightings in that area since then.

History and conservation measures

The addax once ranged in Africa from Western Sahara and Mauritania to Egypt and Sudan. Ancient Egyptians domesticated the slow and tame animals. These very traits have led to the species' present-day decline, as hunters easily capture addaxes for their prized meat and hide. In 1900, tens of thousands of addaxes were distributed over most of the Sahara, from Mauritania in the west to Sudan in the east. The population of the species in the 1960s was estimated at slightly less than 10,000, with about 4,000 animals in Chad, about 5,000 in an area extending between Mauritania and Sudan, and 50 more in Algeria. By the early 1970s the population had been severely reduced to 2,000 animals distributed within a much smaller range in Mauritania, northern Mali, Libya, and northern Sudan. The International Union for Conservation of Nature and Natural Resources (IUCN) gave the addax an endangered status in 1996 and then uplisted the status to critically endangered in 1999 to more accurately reflect the huge dangers the species faces.

Despite laws protecting the animals, hunting remains a threat. Additional perils currently facing the addax include drought and tourists who destroy addax habitat with their vehicles while tracking and chasing the animals.

In Niger the Aïr and Ténéré National Nature Reserve includes a large protected habitat encompassing 4,945 square miles (12,810 square kilometers) for addaxes, but sightings there have been sporadic in recent years. The main population is located in the Termit and Tin Toumma region of Niger. In order to protect this and other endangered species in the area, the Termit and Tin Toumma National Nature and Cultural Reserve was established in 2012. At a size of 37,450 square miles (97,000 square kilometers), it is now the largest nature preserve in Africa of its kind. Efforts to protect the addax also include the reintroduction of the species into two national parks in Tunisia, which began in 2007 and have been successful. Aside from wild populations, about 1,700 addaxes are currently held in captivity in zoos around the world.

Anteater, giant
Myrmecophaga tridactyla

PHYLUM: Chordata
CLASS: Mammalia
ORDER: Pilosa
FAMILY: Myrmecophagidae
STATUS: Vulnerable, IUCN
RANGE: Argentina, Bolivia, Brazil, Colombia, Costa Rica, Ecuador, French Guiana, Guyana, Honduras, Nicaragua, Panama, Paraguay, Peru, Suriname, Venezuela

Anteater, giant
Myrmecophaga tridactyla

Description and biology

Coarse, shaggy gray hair covers the giant anteater's long, narrow body. A black and silver-white stripe extends across its shoulders and down its back. The giant anteater's neck and head taper to its distinctive long, cylindrical snout. The animal's eyes and ears are small. Its saliva-coated tongue, used to pluck prey from nests, can extend almost 24 inches (61 centimeters). Its powerful front legs and claws allow the animal to break into termite and ant colonies easily and also provide a means of defense against predators such as pumas and jaguars. An average giant anteater measures 40 to 50 inches (102 to 127 centimeters) from its head to the end of its body and weighs between 40 and 85 pounds (18 and 39 kilograms). Its shaggy tail can reach from 26 to 35 inches (66 to 89 centimeters) long.

A young giant anteater clings to his mother. Known for having low birthrates and specific dietary needs, the species is threatened by habitat loss in Central and South America. © BELIZAR/SHUTTERSTOCK.COM.

The giant anteater's home range may extend from 1 to 9.6 square miles (2.6 to 24.9 square kilometers). A single giant anteater exists by itself in the wild and comes in contact with other giant anteaters only to mate. A female giant anteater gives birth to a single infant after a 190-day gestation (pregnancy) period. The infant, which rides on the mother's back and nurses for the first six weeks, stays with the mother for more than a year.

Habitat and current distribution

Although the habitat of giant anteaters extends from Honduras in Central America to Argentina in South America, scientists believe these animals are almost extinct over much of this great range. The primary reason is habitat destruction, especially of tropical rain forests.

History and conservation measures

Giant anteaters are killed for their meat, for their claws and tails (which are highly prized), and because people wrongly believe they attack dogs, cattle, and humans. The greatest threat to these animals, however, is fire. During dry seasons, large fires sweep through much of central South America. Farmers also set forest fires in order to increase grazing land for their livestock—what is called slash-and-burn agriculture. Although almost all other animals escape these fires by running or flying, giant anteaters usually do not. They are slow moving, and their long hair burns easily.

Giant anteaters are protected from hunters in a number of national parks and nature reserves throughout their vast habitat. In Brazil alone, 10 parks and three reserves provide safe haven for the animals. Nonetheless, natural and human-made fires recognize no boundaries, so many giant anteaters have burned to death in protected areas.

Armadillo, giant
Priodontes maximus

PHYLUM: Chordata
CLASS: Mammalia
ORDER: Cingulata
FAMILY: Dasypodidae
STATUS: Vulnerable, IUCN
Endangered, ESA
RANGE: Argentina, Bolivia, Brazil, Colombia, Ecuador, French Guiana, Guyana, Paraguay, Peru, Suriname, Venezuela

Armadillo, giant
Priodontes maximus

Description and biology

The giant armadillo is the largest member of the armadillo family, which is composed of 21 species. Eleven to 13 movable bony plates cover a giant armadillo's back, and three to four flexible bands cover its neck. Its body is dark brown, whereas its head, tail, and a stripe around the bottom of its shell are whitish. A giant armadillo measures 30 to 39 inches (76 to 99 centimeters) from the tip of its nose to the end of its body. Its tail is about 20 inches (50 centimeters) long. It weighs between 44 and 88 pounds (20 and 40 kilograms).

Unlike certain members of the armadillo family, the giant armadillo cannot roll into a ball, protected by its body armor. To escape from danger, the giant armadillo quickly digs itself into the ground using the long claws on its front legs. The animal also uses these claws to dig for

The giant armadillo is threatened by demand for its meat and by loss of habitat in its native regions in South America. © STEFANO PATERNA/ALAMY.

ants, termites, worms, spiders, and other insects, which it feeds on at night.

The gestation (pregnancy) period of a female giant armadillo is about four months. She gives birth to one or two infants at a time, each weighing about 4 ounces (113 grams), and they nurse for four to six weeks. The life span of a giant armadillo is 12 to 15 years.

Habitat and current distribution

The giant armadillo is found in many South American countries, from Venezuela and Guyana south to Argentina. Its primary habitat is the Amazon rain forest, but it can also be found in savannas (flat, tropical or subtropical grasslands), floodplains, and woodlands in drier environments. It is typically found near large termite populations.

History and conservation measures

The International Union for Conservation of Nature and Natural Resources (IUCN) changed the status of the giant armadillo from endangered to vulnerable in 2006. However, giant armadillo numbers are decreasing, with a decline of 30 percent between the early 1990s and 2014.

Hunting, human settlement, and agricultural development have all contributed to the giant armadillo's decline. Although laws in Argentina, Brazil, Colombia, Paraguay, Peru, and Suriname protect the animal, it is still hunted for food in some areas. Of greater concern is the destruction of its habitat, as large areas of rain forest are cleared for homes and farms.

Less frequently, giant armadillos are captured and sold or traded illegally as pets. The species has been given Appendix I status in the Convention on International Trade in Endangered Species of Wild Fauna and Flora (CITES; an international treaty to protect wildlife). Appendix I status bans the trade of the armadillo between nations that have signed the treaty.

National parks and nature reserves in Brazil, Colombia, Peru, and Suriname provide safe habitats for giant armadillos, but rain forest destruction is a continuing problem. Current conservation efforts include plans to move giant armadillos to protected habitats and to breed them in captivity.

Did You Know?

Armadillos are carriers of the chronic bacterial disease leprosy, which has been infecting humans for thousands of years. Although armadillos did not carry leprosy until Europeans came to the Americas, many armadillos today have been infected and turned into long-term hosts for the disease. In humans, leprosy damages the upper respiratory tract (above the lungs) and can cause permanent damage to the skin, nerves, and eyes. Despite popular belief, human body parts do not fall off after infection. Armadillos carry the disease because their low body temperature (90°F/32°C) is perfect to grow the bacterium. Some people who handle or eat armadillos can and do get the disease.

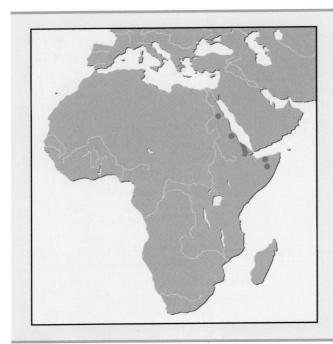

Ass, African wild
Equus africanus (also *Equus asinus*)

PHYLUM: Chordata
CLASS: Mammalia
ORDER: Perissodactyla
FAMILY: Equidae
STATUS: Critically endangered, IUCN Endangered, ESA
RANGE: Djibouti, Egypt, Eritrea, Ethiopia, Somalia, Sudan

Ass, African wild
Equus africanus (also *Equus asinus*)

Description and biology

The African wild ass is one of only seven surviving species of equids (horse family). Of these seven species, five are threatened or endangered. The smallest member of the horse family, the African wild ass stands about 4.5 feet (1.4 meters) tall at the shoulders and weighs about 550 to 600 pounds (250 to 275 kilograms). It has a gray coat with a white belly and a dark stripe up its back. With its long ears and short stubby mane, the African wild ass looks like its cousin, the American domestic donkey, and is in fact the donkey's ancestor. The African ass has strong teeth and sturdy narrow hooves. It eats the tough grasses and shrubs of the desert. Although its teeth wear down from grazing, they continue to grow throughout the life of the animal.

The African wild ass is most active in the cooler temperatures at dawn, dusk, and night and takes refuge from the heat during the daytime. Well adapted to the desert, the African ass can go longer without water than any other species of horse. It is also a very skilled runner and has been seen running at a rate of 31 miles (50 kilometers) per hour.

African wild asses sometimes live alone, but they often join temporary groups. Females generally live with their offspring in herds of about 50 animals. Some males live in their own territory and defend their water sources. They will allow other males and females into their territory, but they remain dominant in it. If a male does not have its own territory, it will usually travel with a small bachelor herd. African wild asses form small herds because the food in the regions in which they live is so scarce it could not support a large number. They communicate with each other through scent and by making vocal calls. The African wild ass mates during the rainy seasons. There is a one-year gestation (pregnancy) period, and females generally bear one offspring at a time. Female African wild asses usually give birth only every other year, although they are capable of breeding annually. In the wild, African wild asses can live up to about 30 or 40 years.

Habitat and current distribution

The African wild ass lives in desert regions, in hilly and stony areas where grasses and shrubs grow. It avoids sandy regions and needs to be near a water source. The surviving members of the species are found mainly in Ethiopia and Eritrea. They may also survive in isolated areas of Djibouti, Egypt, Sudan, and Somalia, although they have not been sighted in those countries in recent years. Biologists (people who study living organisms) estimate that there are no more than 600 individuals left in Ethiopia and Eritrea.

History and conservation measures

Humans have captured and domesticated, or tamed, the African wild ass to use for work and transportation in parts of Africa since 3000 BCE. The species was widespread throughout the Horn of Africa for many years. It has been estimated that in 1905 the African wild ass population in eastern Somalia alone was 10,000 animals. By the 1960s, however, there were only a few hundred survivors in the world.

The African wild ass, native to Ethiopia and Eritrea, is hunted for its meat and because its body parts are used in traditional medicines.
© SERGEI25/SHUTTERSTOCK
.COM.

There are several causes for the decline in the African wild ass population. In Ethiopia and Somalia, the wild ass has been captured for domestication and hunted for food and for traditional medicine (health practices used by specific cultures since before the time of modern medicine), as it is believed by some to cure hepatitis. The introduction of modern firearms in the area led to the slaughter of more animals. In the latter part of the 20th century, warfare and instability in the Horn of Africa led to more (and more deadly) weapons and ammunition being available, and this too led to a reduction in the wild ass population. Animal herders have at times killed wild asses in the belief that the animals were using up grasses and water resources that their domesticated animals needed to survive.

Efforts to breed the African wild ass in captivity have been successful. As of 2010 there were 183 of these animals in zoos around the world, as well as three in a nature reserve in Israel. The African wild ass is legally protected in Sudan, Somalia, and Ethiopia. Conservationists (people who work to manage and protect nature) are educating some of the people living in the species' range about methods of protecting their resources, including programs to save the African wild ass.

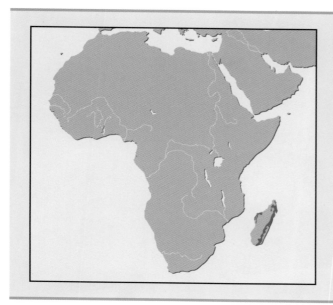

Aye-aye
Daubentonia madagascariensis

PHYLUM: Chordata
CLASS: Mammalia
ORDER: Primates
FAMILY: Daubentoniidae
STATUS: Endangered, IUCN
Endangered, ESA
RANGE: Madagascar

Aye-aye
Daubentonia madagascariensis

Description and biology

The unusual-looking aye-aye is covered with a coat of coarse blackish-brown hair, which overlays a denser coat of short white hair. This primate has very large, sensitive ears that stick out from its small, rounded head. It has sharp, rodent-like incisor (front) teeth and long, clawlike fingers and toes. An average aye-aye is 15 to 18 inches (38 to 46 centimeters) long from the top of its head to the end of its body. Its bushy tail measures 16 to 22 inches (41 to 56 centimeters) long. The animal weighs between 4.4 and 6.6 pounds (2 and 3 kilograms).

Although an aye-aye eats bamboo shoots, sugarcane, and some small animals, most of its diet consists of fruit (especially coconuts) and wood-boring insect larvae. Using its powerful incisors, the aye-aye breaks into coconuts and then scoops out the pulp with its very long, thin middle finger. The aye-aye's large ears allow it to hear insect larvae moving beneath the bark of trees. The animal strips off the bark

The aye-aye of Madagascar is often killed for food because it is considered a pest or because some believe it is a symbol of evil or bad luck. Other threats to the species include a loss of habitat and food supply due to deforestation. © IMAGEBRO-KER/ALAMY.

with its teeth and then crushes and eats the larvae using its middle finger.

The aye-aye is a nocturnal (active at night) creature. It builds a complex nest in the fork of a large tree for shelter during the day. When active, the animal spends most of its time in trees, often hanging by its hind legs. Biologists (people who study living organisms) know little about the aye-aye's social structure or mating habits. The animal's range is estimated to be 12 acres (5 hectares). A female aye-aye usually gives birth to a single infant every two to three years and nurses the young aye-aye for up to a year.

Habitat and current distribution

Aye-ayes are found in eastern, northern, and northwestern Madagascar, an island off the southeastern coast of Africa. The animals are able to survive in a variety of forest types: deciduous (made up of trees whose leaves fall off annually), secondary growth, and dry scrub (stunted trees and shrubs). They have also been found in coconut groves and mangrove swamps. Although aye-ayes are found over a large area of the island, their population numbers are low. Only a few thousand are believed to be alive in the mid-2010s.

History and conservation measures

Even though its only natural predator is the fossa, a slender mammal that resembles a cat, the aye-aye was once considered one of the most endangered mammals in Madagascar. The main threat to the aye-aye is habitat destruction. Because it needs large, old trees in which to build its nest, the aye-aye cannot exist in areas that have been cleared of trees. The animal is also at risk because of superstitious fear. Many people on Madagascar believe the aye-aye brings misfortune, even death, to those it meets. For this reason, many local people kill the animal on sight and sometimes eat it. The aye-aye is also killed by local farmers, who believe the animal is a threat to crops.

Even though a number of reserves have been set up for the aye-aye in Madagascar, the protection of these areas has not been enforced. Under a conservation program begun in 1966, however, nine aye-ayes were released on Nosy Mangabe, a 1,285-acre (520-hectare) island off the east coast of Madagascar. These animals have received special protection, and the reserve provides an area where the scientists can study the animals in their natural habitat. Important steps such as population studies and conservation action plans have not yet been taken to better protect the aye-aye in the rest of its range.

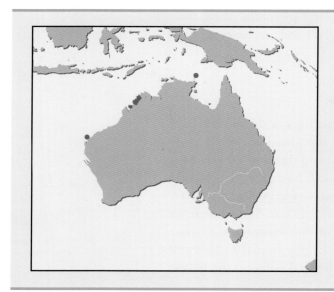

Bandicoot, golden
Isoodon auratus

PHYLUM: Chordata
CLASS: Mammalia
ORDER: Peramelemorphia
FAMILY: Peramelidae
STATUS: Vulnerable, IUCN
RANGE: Australia

Bandicoot, golden
Isoodon auratus

Description and biology

The golden bandicoot is part of a group of mammals known as marsupials, whose young continue to develop after birth in a pouch on the outside of the mother's body. The animal's coarse fur is a mixture of yellow-orange and dark brown hairs, giving it a golden appearance. It has a long, tapering snout and short, rounded ears. An average golden bandicoot measures 9 to 19 inches (23 to 48 centimeters) from the top of its head to the end of its body and weighs about 3 pounds (1.4 kilograms). Its tail is 3 to 8 inches (8 to 20 centimeters) long.

Golden bandicoots are nocturnal (active at night). During the day, they remain in their nests built on the ground, in a hollow, or in a rock pile. At night, the very quick, agile, and aggressive animals search for their diet of insects and worms. Golden bandicoots are solitary animals, so males and females come together only to mate. The female usually gives birth to a litter of four after a gestation (pregnancy) period of al-

The golden bandicoot once ranged across one-third of its native Australia. © ROLAND SEITRE/MINDEN PICTURES/CORBIS.

most two weeks. The young golden bandicoots remain in their mother's pouch for up to eight weeks.

Habitat and current distribution

Golden bandicoots once ranged across one-third of Australia, mainly in grassland habitats. They are now found in small parts of Western Australia and the Northern Territory, as well as on a few islands off Australia's coast. The most stable populations are found on Barrow Island and Middle Island.

History and conservation measures

Scientists and conservationists (people who work to manage and protect nature) are not quite sure why the number of golden bandicoots has decreased. They believe foxes and cats recently allowed into golden bandicoot territory have become predators of the animals. In addition, fires deliberately set by humans to manage grasslands may have destroyed the animals' natural habitat and made them easier prey. Nonnative black rats are also a threat because they compete with bandicoots in some areas. The bandicoot populations on Barrow and Middle Islands have been doing well because few nonnative species, such as cats or foxes, are present on these islands. To keep these populations protected, it is critical that such predators not be introduced to these islands in the future.

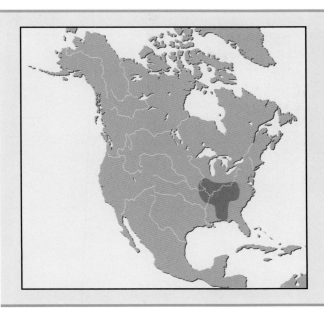

Bat, gray
Myotis grisescens

PHYLUM: Chordata
CLASS: Mammalia
ORDER: Chiroptera
FAMILY: Vespertilionidae
STATUS: Near threatened, IUCN
Endangered, ESA
RANGE: Central and southeastern
USA

Bat, gray
Myotis grisescens

Description and biology

The gray bat differs from other species of the *Myotis* genus (a group with similar characteristics) in that its wing membrane (a double membrane of skin) attaches to its ankle instead of the side of its foot. Its fur is uniformly gray from the base to the tip of each hair shaft, although the color can change to a chestnut brown after the breeding season (July or August). Its forearm measures 1.6 inches (4 centimeters) long, and it weighs about 0.35 ounces (10 grams). The gray bat feeds at night on insects, particularly insects found near lakes or rivers. It roosts in two different types of caves throughout the year: deep, vertical caves are preferred in the winter, while riverside caves are preferred in the summer.

Female gray bats begin hibernating immediately after mating in September, while adult males and juveniles continue to feed to replenish their stored fat; they then hibernate in early November. In late March the

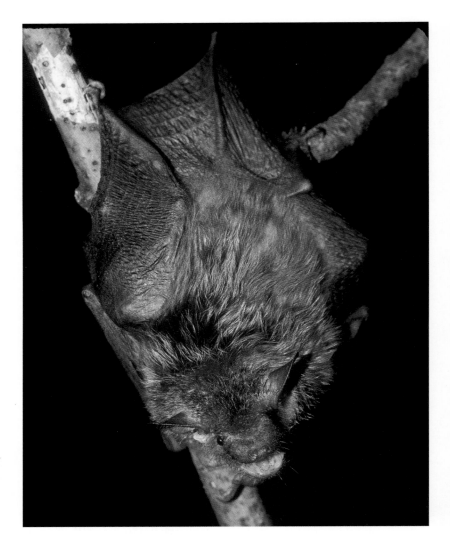

The gray bat has seen its numbers increase in the United States because of efforts to protect its cave habitats from being disturbed by humans.
© GAY BUMGARNER/ALAMY.

mature females emerge from hibernation, while the males and juveniles emerge about a month later. Using sperm they have stored all winter in their bodies, female gray bats fertilize a single egg, giving birth to a pup around late May.

Habitat and current distribution

In summer, while gray bats are raising their young, they roost in caves that have a temperature between 57°F and 77°F (14°C and 25°C). In winter, during hibernation, the bats roost in caves that have a temperature between 43°F and 52°F (6°C and 11°C). Gray bats are found concentrated in limestone caverns in Alabama, Arkansas, Kentucky, Missouri, and Tennessee. Their range extends from eastern Oklahoma and Kansas to southwestern Virginia and western North Carolina, and southward from southern Illinois and Indiana to northern Florida. In 1980 scientists estimated the gray bat population to be less than 1.6 million. By 2007, however, conservation efforts had increased that number to 3.4 million.

History and conservation measures

Before the American Civil War (1861–1865), millions of gray bats inhabited the southeastern United States. When the war began, soldiers needed large amounts of gunpowder to fire their weapons, and bat guano (feces) was a plentiful source of potassium nitrate, a component of gunpowder. When humans entered roosting and hibernation caves to collect the guano, however, the bats were disturbed, which is particularly harmful during their hibernation. When awakened during this period, a gray bat is forced to use its stored fat to maintain body warmth and may starve to death before emerging in spring, or it may not have enough energy for the spring migration.

In modern times, spelunking (cave exploring), tourism, and flooding caused by the construction of dams have all led to the destruction of gray bat habitat. Between 1960 and 1980 the gray bat population decreased by almost 80 percent. Water pollution and pesticides that the bats ingested by eating contaminated insects also contributed to this decline. In 2012 the fungus responsible for the bat-killing disease known as white-nose syndrome was discovered on individual gray bats, although large-scale die-offs have not been recorded for this species.

Since the early 1980s, many bat caves have been protected from human disturbance with gates placed in front of openings. In addition, programs to reduce pesticides have been implemented at all U.S. military installations where gray bats live, and activity around major bat hibernation sites has been reduced as much as possible. In the years since the bat protection plan was put in place, populations of gray bats have stopped declining and have even increased enough for the International Union for Conservation of Nature and Natural Resources (IUCN) to upgrade the species' status from endangered to near threatened. Although a delisting (removal from the U.S. Endangered Species List) was not anticipated, the U.S. Fish and Wildlife Service in 2014 began a five-year review regarding the gray bat's status.

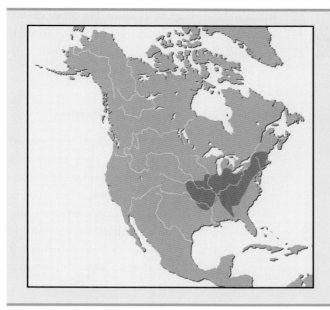

Bat, Indiana
Myotis sodalis

PHYLUM: Chordata
CLASS: Mammalia
ORDER: Chiroptera
FAMILY: Vespertilionidae
STATUS: Endangered, IUCN
Endangered, ESA
RANGE: Eastern USA

Bat, Indiana
Myotis sodalis

Description and biology

The Indiana bat has dark brown, gray, or black fur. It is a midsized bat, weighing only about a quarter of an ounce (7 grams), with a body that is only 1.5 to 2 inches (3.8 to 5 centimeters) long. Its wingspan, however, can reach from 9 to 11 inches (23 to 28 centimeters).

Indiana bats usually live from 5 to 10 years in the wild. During the summer, the bats keep cool during the day by roosting in tree cavities of species like shagbark hickory, elm, and beech, and inside the loose bark of dead or dying trees. Female bats have only one baby a year in midsummer; the baby bats can fly after a month. In the winter, the bats move to caves, where they hibernate in tight clusters on the walls and ceiling.

Like many bats, Indiana bats locate food by using echolocation, which is a kind of sonar. The bats emit high-pitched squeaks and then

Did You Know?

White-nose syndrome was first discovered on bats in New York in 2006. The fungus that causes the disease is thought to be a species introduced from Europe. It thrives in caves and on animals. Bat immune systems weaken during hibernation. As the fungus grows, it increases carbon dioxide levels in bats' blood. This forces them to wake up from their hibernation and move around in order to lower the level of gases in their bloodstream. Waking up uses a lot of energy, and the bats can run out of fat reserves and starve to death during the winter. White-nose syndrome has spread across the East Coast since 2006, and millions of bats have died.

listen to hear the echoes bouncing off of objects around them. Echolocation allows bats in flight to locate the beetles, flies, moths, and other flying insects that make up their diet.

Habitat and current distribution

Indiana bats are found through the eastern United States as far north as New Hampshire and as far south as northern Florida; the western edge of their range reaches Iowa, Missouri, and Oklahoma. A 2009 population estimate found around 387,000 Indiana bats in the United States. About half of these bats hibernate in caves in southern Indiana. Some hibernation caves can include as many as 50,000 bats.

History and conservation measures

Indiana bats were first discovered in the Wyandotte Caves in southern Indiana. In 1899, tens of thousands of bats were reported there. Since that time, however, numbers of Indiana bats have steadily diminished. In 1967, when the species was placed on the U.S. list of endangered species, there were estimated to be about 900,000 in the United States. By 2005, that number had dropped by half—and has fallen even further since.

Several challenges face Indiana bats. Because they hibernate in large numbers in only a relatively few caves, a single disturbance can cause the death of many bats. If a spelunker—a cave explorer—stumbles upon a group of bats and wakes them up, the bats will use up energy getting away. They will then have fewer reserves to make it through the winter, and some will die.

People sometimes also deliberately disturb bats or shoot them. Because many caves are now open to tourists, it is harder for the Indiana bat to find suitable places to hibernate. Bats also have been harmed by the clearing of their summer forest habitats to make way for new homes and development, and by the use of pesticides, which poison the insects they eat.

The Indiana bat has seen its numbers decline because of human disturbance of the caves in which it hibernates, as well as loss of its summer habitats.
© JOHN MACGREGOR/GETTY IMAGES.

Another serious danger to Indiana bats is white nose syndrome (WNS). WNS is a disease in which a white ring of fungus forms on the faces and wings of the bats. First identified in 2006, WNS is believed to have killed more than a million bats of various species. Biologists (people who study living organisms) have experimented with a treatment for WNS, but it is still not clear how effective it will be when used on a larger scale.

Indiana bats are officially endangered and are protected by law in the United States. Bat-friendly gates, which keep humans out, have been installed in some caves. Humans sometimes destroy bats out of fear or hatred. Teaching people that bats eat insect pests and are harmless to humans is therefore an important part of conservation efforts.

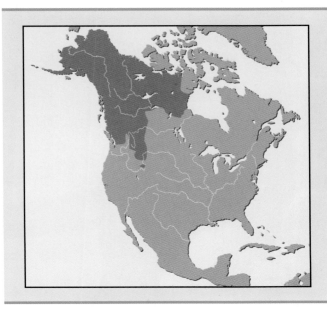

Bear, grizzly
Ursus arctos horribilis

PHYLUM: Chordata
CLASS: Mammalia
ORDER: Carnivora
FAMILY: Ursidae
STATUS: Threatened, ESA
RANGE: Canada, USA (Alaska, Idaho, Montana, Washington, Wyoming)

Bear, grizzly
Ursus arctos horribilis

Description and biology

The grizzly bear, a subspecies of the brown bear (*Ursus arctos*), is one of the largest land mammals in North America. An average male grizzly has a head and body length of 6 to 8 feet (1.8 to 2.4 meters), stands 3.5 to 4 feet (1 to 1.2 meters) at its shoulder, and may weigh up to 800 pounds (360 kilograms). Female grizzly bears are smaller and weigh between 200 and 400 pounds (90 and 180 kilograms). The grizzly bear is so named because its thick, light brown to black fur is streaked with gray, giving it a "grizzled" look. Grizzly bears have short, rounded ears, humped shoulders, and long, curved claws.

Although grizzly bears are omnivores (they eat both plants and animals), most of their diet consists of vegetation (plant life): fruits, berries, nuts, and the bulbs and roots of plants. They also eat ants and other insects. The meat in a grizzly bear's diet comes from deer or smaller

A grizzly bear feasts on salmon, one of the main foods in its diet. The grizzly's habitat, which once included much of the western half of North America, is now limited to Canada and the U.S. states of Alaska, Idaho, Montana, Washington, and Wyoming.
© ANTONI MURCIA/SHUTTERSTOCK.COM.

mammals, such as elk or moose calves. Salmon make up a large part of the diet of the grizzly bears that inhabit Alaska and the west coast of Canada.

Grizzly bears store large amounts of fat, which their bodies rely on during their long winter hibernation. Grizzlies build their dens in early fall, often on high, remote mountain slopes underneath the roots of large trees. Once they enter their dens in October or November, they do not emerge for five or six months (females usually emerge one month after the males in the spring).

Male and female grizzly bears usually mate in June or July. After a gestation (pregnancy) period of about six months, a female grizzly gives birth during hibernation to one to three cubs. The infant bears usually weigh 1 pound (0.45 kilograms) at birth, but they gain as much as 20 pounds (9 kilograms) by the time spring arrives. Female grizzlies nurse their cubs for up to one year, and the cubs remain with their mother for two to three additional years. The average life span of a grizzly bear is 15 to 20 years.

Habitat and current distribution

The grizzly bear's home range is quite large: up to 500 square miles (1,300 square kilometers) for males and 300 square miles (780 square kilometers) for females. That range may extend over a variety of forests, meadows, and grasslands in or near mountains. Grizzlies are active at lower elevations during most of the year. For hibernation, they move to higher altitudes.

Wildlife biologists (people who study living organisms in the wild) estimate that there are more than 20,000 grizzly bears in western Canada. Most of these are in British Columbia, though Yukon has a population of at least 6,000 and the Northwest Territories has at least 3,500. There are more than 30,000 brown bears in Alaska, most of which are grizzlies. In the contiguous United States (the connected 48 states) the largest grizzly population is in Yellowstone National Park (Idaho, Montana, and Wyoming), with more than 700 bears. Smaller grizzly bear populations are found in Glacier National Park (Montana) and North Cascades National Park (Washington).

History and conservation measures

Grizzly bears used to range over the entire western half of North America, from Mexico up to the Arctic Circle. In 1800 the grizzly bear population in the contiguous United States exceeded 50,000. By 1975 that number had been reduced to fewer than 1,000. Habitat destruction and hunting are the two main reasons for this drastic decline. As pioneers moved west during the 19th century and settled mountainous regions, grizzly bears were forced out of their natural habitat. These pioneers also shot and trapped grizzlies, believing the animals posed a threat.

As the wild areas of the American West continue to be developed (such as the building of recreation areas), the survival of grizzly bears will continue to be jeopardized. Even though they are protected by laws, grizzlies are still shot by hunters who mistake the animals for black bears.

During the last decades of the 20th century, the U.S. government worked with state agencies and Native American tribes in an effort to manage and protect grizzly bear habitat. These efforts were highly successful in areas such as the Yellowstone National Park ecosystem (an ecological system including all of its living things and their environment), where the grizzly bear population exceeded target levels. Conservation efforts have included building underpasses for them so that their large ranges can remain interconnected and their interactions with humans can be minimized. These and other actions have been so successful in increasing the number of grizzly bears that, in late 2014, advisers to the U.S. Fish and Wildlife Service recommended that the grizzly be removed from the threatened species list.

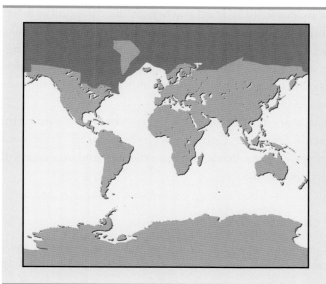

Bear, polar
Ursus maritimus

PHYLUM: Chordata
CLASS: Mammalia
ORDER: Carnivora
FAMILY: Ursidae
STATUS: Vulnerable, IUCN
Threatened, ESA
RANGE: Canada, Greenland, Norway, Russia, USA (Alaska)

Bear, polar
Ursus maritimus

Description and biology

Polar bears are large white bears that live mostly on the sea ice of the Arctic Ocean. They are adapted to thrive in very cold climates. Their fur is thick and insulating and covers a layer of fat. Under their fur, their skin is black so as to better absorb the sun's warmth. Even their paws have fur to protect their feet from freezing when they walk on ice.

Polar bears are 7.25 to 8 feet (2.2 to 2.4 meters) long and weigh from 900 to 1,600 pounds (410 to 725 kilograms). Their diet consists mostly of seals, which they eat for their high fat content. Polar bears spend 50 percent of their time hunting, but only about 2 percent of their hunts are successful. Polar bears hunt in places where seals may surface for air, such as cracks or holes in the ice or the edges of the ice. Polar bears will also eat carrion (decaying flesh of dead animals), such as whale carcasses. These bears are at the top of the food chain in the Arctic; other than humans, they have no natural predators.

Polar bears are powerful swimmers; they paddle through the water with their slightly webbed front paws while using their back legs like a rudder to steer. Studies have found that polar bears can make long-distance swims of as much as 200 miles (322 kilometers) over a period of about 10 days. Such long swims are sometimes necessary in summer months when sea ice retreats.

Female polar bears dig dens in snow drifts, where they give birth, usually to twin cubs, in winter. Cubs stay with their mothers for around 28 months. Male polar bears do not help raise the cubs and may even kill them if they encounter them.

Habitat and current distribution

Polar bears live in the Arctic, mostly on the sea ice. Some live in the pack ice of the central Arctic, but they are more common on the surrounding

The melting of sea ice in the Arctic regions caused by global climate change, as well as other environmental threats caused by human activity, has resulted in a significant decline in the polar bear population. © LARRY B. KING/SHUTTERSTOCK.COM.

U•X•L Endangered Species, 3rd Edition

Did You Know?

Global warming is reducing the range of the polar bear as its Arctic sea ice habitat disappears, but it may be increasing the range of the polar bear's close relative: the brown bear, or grizzly bear. As temperatures rise, grizzlies move farther north, where they sometimes encounter polar bears and occasionally mate with them. The resulting "grolar" bears are half polar bear and half grizzly bear, often with brown fur that has patches of white. The bears are also called "pizzly" bears.

Grolar bears are quite rare, and the idea of finding one in the wild is exciting. But hybridization (when two different species mate and have offspring) ultimately poses an additional risk to polar bears as a species. When an endangered species, such as polar bears, starts to hybridize with a more populous one, such as grizzly bears, the endangered species may experience a reduction in the numbers of its young. In this case, polar bears may eventually breed away altogether, resulting in the species' extinction.

seasonal ice. When sea ice lasts all year long, bears will hunt throughout the year as well. In areas where sea ice melts in the summer, bears spend several months on land eating little and living on their fat reserves.

About two-thirds of the world's polar bears live in Canada. The rest are found in Arctic areas of Alaska, Greenland, Norway, and Russia. Only about 20,000 to 25,000 polar bears are estimated to exist in the wild.

History and conservation measures

Polar bear origins are uncertain, but scientists believe they diverged from brown bears between 130,000 and 650,000 years ago. The native Inuit people, who live in the Arctic regions of Canada, Alaska, and Greenland, have revered and hunted polar bears for thousands of years, using their meat for food and their pelts for warmth.

The main threat to polar bears is global warming. The Arctic is very sensitive to climate change. Bears rely on sea ice to hunt seals. If more ice melts in summer months, bears will not be able to hunt seals during this time and may be forced onto land. There, they may be more vulnerable to human hunting.

Polar bears are also threatened by pollution. Seals store pollutants from fish in their fat, and then the pollutants are passed on to bears when they eat seals. These pollutants may affect bear growth rates and reproduction. Oil spills may also affect bears as more drilling occurs in the Arctic.

The polar bear has become a symbol of the dangers of climate change. Research is being done on how to manage polar bear populations. Arctic nations are working together to create conservation goals and policies, such as reducing polar bear hunting and banning the export and import of polar bear products. The Inuit people, however, are concerned that these policies will prevent them from pursuing their traditional hunting practices. They argue that their practices help sustain polar bear populations.

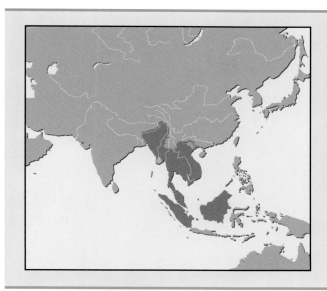

Bear, sun
Helarctos malayanus

PHYLUM: Chordata
CLASS: Mammalia
ORDER: Carnivora
FAMILY: Ursidae
STATUS: Vulnerable, IUCN
RANGE: Bangladesh, Brunei, Cambodia, China, India, Indonesia, Laos, Malaysia, Myanmar, Thailand, Vietnam

Bear, sun
Helarctos malayanus

Description and biology

The smallest member of the bear family, the sun bear has an average head and body length of 3.5 to 4.5 feet (1 to 1.4 meters). Its shoulder height is about 26.5 inches (67 centimeters) and its weight is between 60 and 140 pounds (27 and 64 kilograms). The animal's short tail extends only 1 to 3 inches (2.5 to 7.5 centimeters). The fur on the sun bear's body is very short and black; the fur on its muzzle is almost white. Most individuals of this species have a white to yellow-orange horseshoe-shaped marking on their chests.

The sun bear's curved and pointed claws make it an excellent climber. It spends most of its day sleeping or sunning on a platform it builds in trees 7 to 20 feet (2 to 6 meters) above the ground. It uses its strong claws to open bees' nests or to pull back the bark of trees to locate the larvae of wood-boring insects. The sun bear's diet also includes termites and other insects, fruits, birds, and small mammals.

Logging, fires, and drought threaten the habitat of the sun bear, which is found in the tropical forests of Southeast Asia as well as parts of India and China. © MOLLY MARSHALL/SHUTTERSTOCK.COM.

Because it is so fond of honey, the sun bear is sometimes called the honey bear.

Sun bears do not hibernate, and they can mate at any time during the year. After a gestation (pregnancy) period of 95 to 240 days, a female sun bear gives birth to one or two cubs.

Habitat and current distribution

Sun bears are found scattered throughout tropical and subtropical forests in Southeast Asia.

History and conservation measures

Although biologists (people who study living organisms) are unsure of the total number of existing sun bears, they believe the population of these animals is declining. Throughout their range, the animals are killed and used for food and medicinal purposes. Sun bear cubs are often captured and kept as pets after their mothers have been killed. Countries in the habitat area have laws that prohibit the hunting of sun bears. Nevertheless, poaching (illegal hunting) continues.

Another critical threat to sun bears is the destruction of their forest habitat from logging and for the creation of agricultural land. A number of reserves have been set up for the animals throughout their range, but biologists do not know if these reserves provide the habitat necessary for sun bear survival. The International Union for Conservation of Nature and Natural Resources (IUCN) changed the status of the sun bear from data deficient to vulnerable in 2008 because of the rate at which its forests were being cleared. Despite this change, there is still a lack of data on the current range and population of the sun bear.

Bison, American
Bison bison

PHYLUM: Chordata
CLASS: Mammalia
ORDER: Artiodactyla
FAMILY: Bovidae
STATUS: Near threatened, IUCN
Threatened, ESA (subspecies
athabascae only)
RANGE: Canada, USA

Bison, American
Bison bison

Description and biology

The American bison (commonly known as the buffalo) has a massive body, humped shoulders, and pointed horns that curve up and in. In winter its coat is dark brown and shaggy. In the spring this coat is shed and replaced by one that is short and light brown. Hair on the head, neck, shoulders, and forelegs remains long and shaggy throughout the year. A beard also hangs from the chin of the animal's huge, low-slung head. An average American bison has a head and body length of 7 to 12.5 feet (2.1 to 3.8 meters) and a shoulder height of 5 to 6.5 feet (1.5 to 2 meters). It weighs between 700 and 2,200 pounds (320 and 1,000 kilograms). The animal's relatively short tail is 12 to 35 inches (31 to 89 centimeters) long and ends in a tuft of hair.

The American bison species is divided biologically into two subspecies: the plains bison (*Bison bison bison*) and the wood bison (*Bison*

bison athabascae). The main physical difference between the two is the color of the hair on the shoulders. On the plains bison, this hair is lighter in color than the hair on the rest of its body. The difference in hair color on the wood bison is not as pronounced. In addition, the plains bison is smaller than the wood bison.

The bison is a fast runner and good swimmer and has a keen sense of smell. It is active during both day and night, feeding on prairie grasses and sedges (grasslike plants). Bison usually travel in herds, although some males (bulls) tend to be solitary. Mating season lasts from June to September. The gestation (pregnancy) period of the female American bison is about nine months, and she gives birth to a single calf. The calf, which is reddish brown in color when born, is cared for by its mother for up to a year.

Habitat and current distribution

About 54 herds of plains bison live in parks and wildlife reserves, numbering about 19,000 animals. The largest herd of plains bison on public land is found in Yellowstone National Park in northwestern Wyoming, southern Montana, and eastern Idaho. This herd numbers about 4,900 individuals. There are also an estimated 500,000 plains bison living on private ranches in the United States. There are 11 herds of wood bison, totaling about 11,000 animals. These herds exist in a number of sanctuaries in Canada, including Wood Buffalo National Park in northern Alberta and southern Northwest Territories.

History and conservation measures

American bison once ranged from Alaska and western Canada into the United States and northern Mexico. Scientists have estimated that in the early 19th century more bison—60 million total—than humans

Did You Know?

Many people make the mistake of thinking that bison and buffalo are docile (easily controlled) animals like their relative, the domestic cow. In fact, these species are powerful and wild creatures, and the animals can be dangerous to humans that try to joke around with them. The Cape buffalo in Africa, in particular, is thought to be one of the most dangerous animals on the continent and is even known to attack lions. In Yellowstone National Park, many people walk up to solitary American bison to touch them and take selfies with them. The bison consider this to be a threat, and sometimes they attack. People have been gored, trampled, or thrown. However, despite many notices and signs warning visitors to keep away from the animals, people continue to approach bison without regard to the danger. The National Park Service warns that bison can run up to 35 miles (56 kilometers) per hour—much faster than the average human.

The American bison was nearly extinct in North America in the 19th century, but conservation efforts have increased its popula-tion in both captive and wild herds. © SCHALKE FOTOGRAFIE|MELISSA SCHALKE/SHUTTERSTOCK.COM.

existed in North America. These large animals were an essential part of the culture and livelihoods of many Native American peoples, who depended on them for food and hides. As American and European settlers moved west during that century, the number of bison began to decline. The animals were hunted for their hides, meat, and tongues, which were considered a delicacy. When railroads were built to cross the country, passengers began shooting bison from the train for sport, leaving the carcasses to rot. Furthermore, bison were slaughtered by the millions as part of the U.S. government's strategy to subdue Native Americans. By the late 19th century, only about 300 American bison remained in the wild.

In 1902 the U.S. government placed a herd of some two dozen captive and wild plains bison under protection in Yellowstone National Park. This herd grew into the one that exists in the park today. In 1922 the Canadian government established Wood Buffalo National Park to protect the last surviving wood bison. However, plains bison were shortly afterward released into the park, where they mated with the wood bison. The resulting offspring were a hybrid, or genetic mixture, of the two subspecies. In the late 1950s a small herd of genetically similar wood bison were located in the park. Two herds of wood bison were established from this relatively pure genetic group.

Beginning in 1990, Montana Department of Livestock workers shot plains bison that wandered outside the boundaries of Yellowstone National Park. Even though the animals are protected within the park, an agreement between Montana and the U.S. government gives Montana officials the right to kill bison if they cross onto private land. Both Montana officials and private ranchers feared the bison would infect cattle grazing near the park with brucellosis (pronounced brew-suh-LOW-sus). The disease causes pregnant cows to miscarry (lose the unborn baby because they are physically unable to continue the pregnancy). This miscarriage is what carries the brucellosis bacteria, and the most likely method of transmission is consumption of the shed birthing material. Even so, relatively few susceptible cattle graze with bison, and most cattle are not present when transmission of brucellosis can occur—making it highly unlikely for the bacteria to spread between species.

In the early 21st century, legislation was written and passed in Montana allowing "sport hunting" of the bison that left the park and crossed into Montana as a method of controlling brucellosis transmission. This means that private citizens with a permit can shoot bison for sport. Conservationists (people who work to manage and protect nature) have called for better means of controlling the population in the park and for more research into the transmission of the disease, although today Montana is classified as brucellosis free.

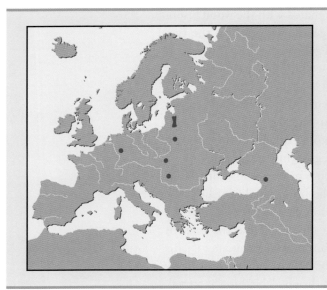

Bison, European
Bison bonasus

PHYLUM: Chordata
CLASS: Mammalia
ORDER: Artiodactyla
FAMILY: Bovidae
STATUS: Vulnerable, IUCN
RANGE: Belarus, Germany, Latvia, Lithuania, Poland, Romania, Russia, Slovakia, Ukraine

Bison, European
Bison bonasus

Description and biology

European bison (often called wisent, from the German word for "bison") are the largest land mammals in Europe but are slightly smaller than their close relative, the American bison. The adult male European bison weighs in the range of 880 to 2,030 pounds (400 to 920 kilograms); the female weighs from 650 to 1,200 pounds (300 to 540 kilograms). A good-sized male has a shoulder height of about 6 to 6.5 feet (1.8 to 2 meters), and his body is about 10 feet (3 meters) long. Females are slightly smaller, measuring about 5.5 feet (1.7 meters) tall at the shoulder and 9 feet (2.7 meters) long. The head is very big, and both males and females have horns. European bison are varying shades of brown, and they have long hair growing from their necks and foreheads and a short beard on their chins. They have a shoulder hump and carry their heads high. In winter, they grow an extra coat of fur to protect themselves from the cold.

Unlike American bison, which live on the plains, European bison live in forests where they can browse (eat) on the tender shoots, twigs, and leaves of trees and bushes. They generally live close to moist clearings where they graze on grass, moss, herbs, and other greens. During the spring, autumn, and summer, they spend most of their time browsing and grazing. In the primary home of bison in the Bialowieza Forest, which straddles the border between Poland and Belarus, there is a centuries-old tradition of humans providing hay for the bison to eat in

The European bison faced extinction because of agriculture, logging, and hunting in the 19th and early 20th centuries, but captive breeding and conservation efforts allowed the animal to be reintroduced in various areas of central Europe. © MILOUSSK/SHUTTER-STOCK.COM.

winter. Thus it has become part of the seasonal habit of the species to gather in large groups in winter around the places where the humans have laid out food for them. In the 21st century, park wardens continue to provide European bison with hay, oats, and sugar beets in the winter.

Female bison, with their calves and sexually immature young, live in herds of about 20 to 30 animals. Bulls (males) live alone most of the year. When the mating season begins in August of each year, the bulls join up with the herds and fight each other for females. Each mating bull may take up to about a dozen females to mate. When the mating season is over, the bulls go back to living alone. For the females, the gestation (pregnancy) period is about nine months. During calving season, from May to July, the female leaves the herd. Female European bison generally bear one offspring in a season, and occasionally two. In winter, European bison gather into larger groups near their feeding stations. Their life span is about 25 years or longer.

Habitat and current distribution

In the 2010s the largest concentration of European bison live in Poland's Bialowieza National Park. The park, which covers an area of about 40 square miles (105 square kilometers), lies within the 548-square-mile (1,419-square-kilometer) Bialowieza Forest, which is Europe's last remaining primeval forest (one that has been there since ancient times). Early in the 20th century, hunters killed off the last of the wild European bison, and since then, captured bison raised in zoos have been successfully reintroduced into their natural habitat, particularly in Bialowieza, where they are protected. Beginning in the 1950s, European bison have also been either reintroduced or introduced to the wild from captivity in other areas, including Russia, Belarus, Lithuania, Ukraine, Germany, and Romania.

History and conservation measures

The restoration of the European bison to its natural habitat during the second half of the 20th century is one of the major success stories in the history of animal species protection. Since ancient times, European bison ranged through the deciduous (made up of trees whose leaves fall off annually) forests extending from Great Britain across Europe into Russia. The Bialowieza Forest in what is now Poland and Belarus was protected for royal hunting from the 15th to the 18th centuries; during that time the game in the forest was fed by humans. In the 19th century, Russia took control of the forests. Overhunting caused a significant reduction in bison, as well as other animals. During World War I (1914–1918), a tremendous number of bison were killed by hunters and soldiers, and in the early 1920s the last bison in the wild was killed by a poacher (illegal hunter).

In 1923 the 54 European bison living in zoos represented the entire population of the species. These were placed in breeding programs for several decades. In the 1950s the animals bred in captivity were released into the wild in Bialowieza, which had been declared a national park in the 1930s. These animals have been carefully protected and have prospered. There are approximately 5,000 animals in existence today. About 3,200 of them live in the wild, while the rest are in captivity. They are all the descendants of 12 European bison from the breeding-in-captivity programs started in the 1920s. This is potentially a problem for the species in terms of introducing enough genetic diversity (variety of biological units that pass on inherited traits) within the herds in the wild.

The reintroduction of bison into the Bialowieza Forest has been so successful that some carefully managed culling (eliminating some of the bison so that the habitat is preserved for the rest) is necessary. Programs expanding the bison's range are also ongoing in Belarus, Ukraine, Russia, Germany, Romania, and elsewhere. One of the biggest concerns for the preservation of the European bison is to foster genetic variation among thousands of animals with only 12 ancestors.

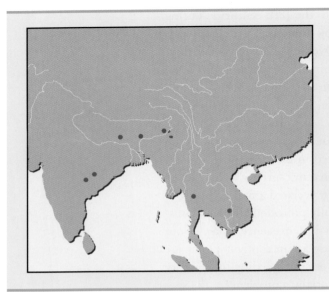

Buffalo, wild water
Bubalus arnee

PHYLUM: Chordata
CLASS: Mammalia
ORDER: Artiodactyla
FAMILY: Bovidae
STATUS: Endangered, IUCN
RANGE: Bhutan, Cambodia, India,
Myanmar, Nepal, Thailand

Buffalo, wild water
Bubalus arnee

Description and biology

The wild water buffalo, also known as the Asian or Indian buffalo, is a large animal, averaging 7.75 to 10 feet (2.4 to 3 meters) long. It stands 5 to 6.25 feet (1.5 to 1.9 meters) tall at its shoulder and weighs between 1,550 and 2,650 pounds (700 and 1,200 kilograms). Long, coarse hair covers the buffalo's ash gray to black body. Both male and female water buffalo have small ears, thin faces, and widely spread horns. The horns, thick where they emerge from the animal's head, form a semicircle by curving out and back. Ending in a point, these horns may reach a length of 6.5 feet (2 meters).

The wild water buffalo's diet consists of grasses and other vegetation (plant life) that grow along the shores of lakes and rivers. Although the animal is fast and aggressive, it can fall prey to tigers. Leopards also often prey on young water buffalo. A female water buffalo gives birth to a single infant after a gestation (pregnancy) period of 310 to 340 days. The

The wild water buffalo population is at risk because of interbreeding with other species, hunting, loss of habitat, and disease from domesticated animals. © MARC ANDERSON/ALAMY.

infant is then nursed for up to nine months. The wild water buffalo is able to breed with the domestic water buffalo (*Bubalus bubalis*), which is considered the same species despite having a different Latin name.

Habitat and current distribution

Wild water buffalo inhabit swampy or wet grassland, or river valleys with dense vegetation. The animals like to wallow in mud, which helps protect them against biting insects. To further escape insects, they will often submerge themselves in water so that only their nostrils are exposed.

The International Union for Conservation of Nature and Natural Resources (IUCN) estimates that although there are fewer than 4,000 wild water buffalo left in the world, the true figure may actually be closer to 200 surviving animals. In contrast, the worldwide population of domestic water buffalo, which are used to pull carts and plows, is about 172 million. Because of interbreeding between domestic and the larger wild water buffalo, biologists (people who study living organisms) believe that no purebred wild water buffalo remain.

History and conservation measures

Several factors have contributed to the disappearance of wild water buffalo: excessive hunting, the destruction of buffalo habitat to create agricultural land, and diseases transmitted by cattle and other domestic livestock. Although the remaining known populations of wild water buffalo live primarily in a small number of protected areas throughout its habitat area, the greatest threat to the wild water buffalo's survival is interbreeding with other species, such as the domestic water buffalo.

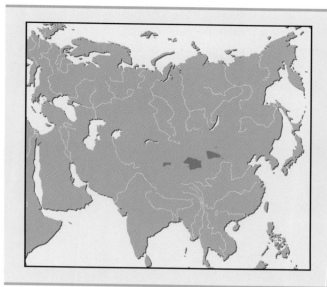

Camel, Bactrian
Camelus bactrianus ferus (also
Camelus ferus)

PHYLUM: Chordata
CLASS: Mammalia
ORDER: Artiodactyla
FAMILY: Camelidae
STATUS: Critically endangered, IUCN
Endangered, ESA
RANGE: China, Mongolia

Camel, Bactrian
Camelus bactrianus ferus (also *Camelus ferus*)

Description and biology

The Bactrian camel and the better-known Arabian camel (*Camelus dromedarius*) are the only two living species of true camel. Whereas the Arabian camel has only one hump, the Bactrian camel has two. An average Bactrian camel stands 6 to 7.5 feet (1.8 to 2.3 meters) in height and weighs between 1,000 and 1,575 pounds (455 and 715 kilograms). The coat of a wild Bactrian camel is short and gray-brown in color; that of a domestic or tame version of the animal is long and dark brown.

The Bactrian camel is well adapted to its desert habitat. Its special eyelids help wipe sand from the surface of the animal's eye. Its nostrils close to slits to keep out blowing sand. Its broad, thick-soled feet allow it to move steadily and quickly over shifting sand, achieving speeds up to 40 miles (64 kilometers) per hour. The humps of the Bactrian camel store fat like those of other camels. When full, the humps are plump and erect. If the animal has not eaten for a period of time, the humps begin

The Bactrian camel faces threats from hunters, industrial development, and shrinking access to water and grazing lands. © MELBA PHOTO AGENCY/ALAMY.

to shrink and sag to one side. Bactrian camels eat mostly low-lying desert shrubs; they also may eat grasses and the leaves of trees growing near water. The camels may go without drinking water for long periods of time only if they receive enough moisture from the plants they eat.

Male Bactrian camels fight for the opportunity to mate with female Bactrian camels. The competitions between males are quite fierce, and some end in death. A dominant male will gather a group of 10 to 20 females with which to mate. After a gestation (pregnancy) period of almost 13 months, a female Bactrian camel gives birth to a single infant, usually in March or April. The infant camel, weighing about 80 pounds (36 kilograms) at birth, nurses for at least its first year.

Habitat and current distribution

Wild Bactrian camels live in remote deserts of central Asia. In China they can be found in the Taklimakan and Lop Nur Deserts. In Mongolia the population is restricted to a protected area of the Gobi Desert, where their numbers have declined about 70 percent since the mid-20th century. Biologists (people who study living organisms) estimate that about 600 Bactrian camels remain in China and about 350 Bactrian camels remain in Mongolia.

History and conservation measures

Humans in China and Mongolia probably began to use Bactrian camels as pack animals to carry supplies as far back as 2500 BCE. Up until the beginning of the 20th century, the range of wild Bactrian camels extended from Asia Minor to northern China. As human populations grew in this large area, the camels were confined to a smaller and smaller range.

Habitat loss continues to be a major threat to the Bactrian camel. Both the Chinese and Mongolian governments have declared the camel a protected species. Several reserves have been established to safeguard the animals, including the Great Gobi National Park in Mongolia, the Annanba Nature Reserve in Gansu (China), and the Altun Mountain National Nature Reserve in Xinjiang (China). However, wolves continually prey on Bactrian camels in the Gobi park, and those camels that stray outside the park are often killed for food by humans. In 2000 China established a new park, the Arjin Shan Lop Nur Nature Reserve. The population is still in decline, and interbreeding with domestic camels has further reduced the population of genetically pure wild Bactrian camels.

In 2002 the International Union for Conservation of Nature and Natural Resources (IUCN) downgraded the status of the wild Bactrian camel from endangered to critically endangered. A series of five expeditions into China and Mongolia in the late 1990s produced data showing that the species was facing a population size reduction of at least 80 percent within the following three generations. Bactrian camels are hunted for food and for sport, are killed by wolves, and must compete with other camels and goats in their habitat area for food and water. In China illegal mining, natural-gas pipeline installations, and industrial development are destroying more of the Bactrian camel's habitat. Only 15 wild (undomesticated) Bactrian camels live in captivity in China and Mongolia. The species breeds slowly, so programs to breed the animals in captivity are essential to save the species from possible extinction.

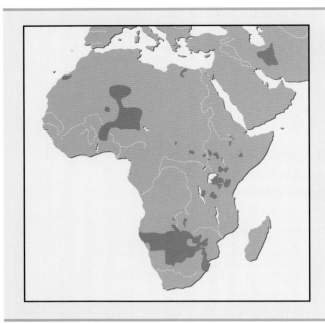

Cheetah
Acinonyx jubatus

PHYLUM: Chordata
CLASS: Mammalia
ORDER: Carnivora
FAMILY: Felidae
STATUS: Vulnerable, IUCN
Endangered, ESA
RANGE: Algeria, Angola, Benin,
Botswana, Burkina Faso, Central African
Republic, Chad, Democratic Republic
of the Congo, Ethiopia, Iran, Kenya,
Mozambique, Namibia, Niger, Soma-
lia, South Africa, South Sudan, Sudan,
Swaziland, Tanzania, Togo, Uganda,
Zambia, Zimbabwe

Cheetah
Acinonyx jubatus

Description and biology

The name *cheetah* comes from the Hindi (a language of India) word
chita, meaning "spotted one." Round black spots cover the cheetah's
tawny fur, and a black streak runs down each cheek. An average cheetah
measures 4.5 to 5 feet (1.4 to 1.5 meters) long and stands between 27
and 34 inches (69 and 86 centimeters) high at its shoulder. Its tail extends 24 to 32 inches (61 to 81 centimeters). It weighs between 80 and
145 pounds (36 and 66 kilograms).

Cheetahs are the world's fastest land animal. They are capable of
bursts of speed up to 70 miles (110 kilometers) per hour, but they usually
cannot keep up this top speed for more than 1,500 feet (460 meters). It
was once believed that cheetahs could not run farther than this because
of the possibility of fatal overheating; evidence has been found, however,

A cheetah is seen at a national reserve in Kenya, which is one of several African countries to establish protected areas in an effort to conserve cheetah populations. © BRYAN BUSOVICKI/SHUTTERSTOCK.COM.

suggesting that this is not true. They do not just rely on raw speed; instead, they use rapid acceleration, deceleration, and agility to catch prey. Cheetahs can use their tails like a rotor in the middle of a chase to balance their weight, allowing them to quickly change directions.

Unlike other cats, a cheetah cannot retract its claws. This physical feature allows the animal to dig into the ground as it runs, giving it more speed. Whereas leopards and tigers ambush their prey, cheetahs chase their prey down. Because they exert themselves so much when catching prey, cheetahs often have to rest for up to half an hour before they can eat their kill; but they cannot wait too long after successfully hunting an animal because other carnivores (animals that eat mainly meat) and scavengers, such as lions and hyenas, often try to steal their kills. Typical cheetah prey includes gazelles, wildebeests, antelope, warthogs, hares, and ground birds.

Did You Know?

When large numbers of animals die at the same time, it can create a *bottleneck effect*, meaning that the number of different genes in the species has been massively reduced. When genetic diversity becomes low enough, animals have to mate with relatives, which is referred to as *inbreeding*. This is dangerous and can even lead to extinction, as mating with relatives increases the chance that offspring will suffer from genetic diseases. It is thought that cheetahs went through a bottleneck 12,000 years ago, resulting in inbreeding among cheetahs today. Although some scientists think that cheetah genetic diversity still has variety, it is entirely possible that a further loss of genetic diversity could drive the cheetah to extinction.

Male cheetahs often live with their male littermates (brothers) in groups called coalitions. Much more solitary, female cheetahs join their male counterparts only to mate. After a gestation (pregnancy) period of 90 to 95 days, a female cheetah gives birth to a litter of one to five cubs, which she nurses for two months. Once the cubs are about six months old, a mother will frequently bring small, live prey to help them develop hunting skills.

Habitat and current distribution

Cheetahs prefer to inhabit savannas (flat, tropical or subtropical grasslands). The animals are now restricted to the continent of Africa, except for a small population of the Asiatic cheetah subspecies (*Acinonyx jubatus venaticus*) still present in Iran. The largest number of cheetahs is found in southern Africa, and cheetahs are considered extinct in much of their previous range. Wildlife biologists (people who study living organisms in the wild) estimate that the total population ranges from 7,000 to 10,000. The Iranian cheetah population numbers between 60 and 100.

History and conservation measures

Cheetahs once ranged over Africa, Arabia, the Middle East, and northern India. Because they can be tamed, cheetahs have been kept for centuries by kings and nobles as pets and hunting animals. In the mid-1950s the world cheetah population was estimated to be 28,000. Within 20 years, however, that number had been cut in half.

Hunting and habitat destruction are the main causes for this drastic decline. Although cheetahs are legally protected in most countries, poachers (illegal hunters) still hunt them for their fur, which remains popular in Asia and Europe. Farmers also kill cheetahs, believing the animals might harm their livestock. As grassland is converted into pasture and agricultural land, cheetahs are confined to smaller and smaller areas, limiting their hunting ability.

Reserves have been set up in Africa, but in these protected areas cheetahs face fierce competition from other predators, such as lions and hyenas. Some African countries, such as Namibia, have tried to introduce cheetahs into areas where they would face few animal or human predators.

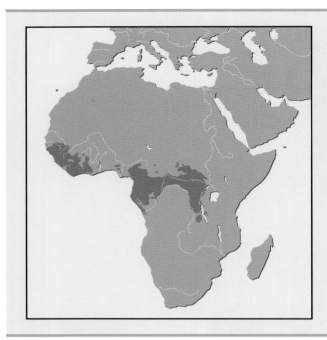

Chimpanzee
Pan troglodytes

PHYLUM: Chordata
CLASS: Mammalia
ORDER: Primates
FAMILY: Hominidae
STATUS: Endangered, IUCN
Endangered, ESA
RANGE: Angola, Burundi, Cameroon, Central African Republic, Côte d'Ivoire, Democratic Republic of the Congo, Equatorial Guinea, Gabon, Ghana, Guinea, Guinea-Bissau, Liberia, Mali, Nigeria, Republic of the Congo, Rwanda, Senegal, Sierra Leone, South Sudan, Tanzania, Uganda

Chimpanzee
Pan troglodytes

Description and biology

Chimpanzees, gorillas, and orangutans are all considered great apes. Of the three, chimpanzees are the most closely related to humans. Chimpanzees and humans share 98 percent of the same genetic makeup. In addition, the two groups share many social and psychological traits. Researchers have documented chimpanzees making and using tools, expressing complex emotions, forming bonds and friendships, and communicating using sign language.

An average chimpanzee stands 5 feet (1.5 meters) tall and weighs about 150 pounds (68 kilograms). Because its arms are longer than its legs, a chimpanzee walks on the ground using the soles of its feet and the knuckles of its hands. Most of its body is covered with long, black hair. A chimpanzee's hairless face can range in color from almost white to almost black. The hair around a chimpanzee's face grays with age, and older chimpanzees often become bald.

Highly social mammals, chimpanzees live in communities made up of 30 to 60 members. During the day, the animals often travel on the ground. At night, they stay in nests they build in treetops. A chimpanzee's diet consists mainly of fruit, but they also eat insects, leaves, flowers, bark, seeds, tree resin, eggs, and meat. At times, chimpanzees band together to hunt animals, such as antelope and monkeys.

A chimpanzee perches in a tree in its African forest habitat, which is threatened by agriculture and industrial development. © KJERSTI JOER-GENSEN/SHUTTERSTOCK.COM.

Mating between male and female chimpanzees takes place anytime during the year. Unlike many other animal species, female chimpanzees do not have to mate with the dominant male in their group. Instead, females often mate with males of their choosing. After a gestation (pregnancy) period of 230 to 240 days, a female chimpanzee gives birth to a single infant. During the course of her life, an average female chimpanzee will give birth to fewer than five infants. Bonds between mothers and infants are very strong, and some last a lifetime.

Habitat and current distribution

A few centuries ago, several million chimpanzees existed in the equatorial regions of Africa. They inhabited a range of ecosystems (ecological systems including all of their living things and their environment), from dense forests to open savannas (flat, tropical or subtropical grasslands). Present-day estimates vary, but it is thought that there are fewer than 300,000 chimpanzees in the wild. They can be found across a wide area of central Africa near the equator that extends over 25 countries. They are most likely extinct, however, in four of the countries in that range.

Thousands of chimpanzees exist in captivity worldwide, 2,000 in the United States alone. Many are used as subjects in medical research; others are zoo exhibits, entertainment props, or pets. In 2015 the U.S. government designated all chimpanzees as endangered, ending a long-standing legal distinction between wild and captive chimpanzees. This means that all captive chimpanzees in the United States are covered by the same protections that limit the selling and buying of wild chimpanzees under the Endangered Species Act. But the endangered designation does not affect the use of chimpanzees as pets or in the entertainment industry.

History and conservation measures

Habitat destruction, disease, and expanding human populations have led to the decline in the number of chimpanzees. Mining has destroyed the chimpanzee habitat in the diamond districts of Sierra Leone and the iron districts of Liberia. The cutting of forests for timber has destroyed the animals' habitat in Uganda. And the conversion of forests into agricultural land has threatened chimpanzees in Rwanda and Burundi.

Certain laws prohibit the hunting and sale of chimpanzees, but these laws are not always enforced. Many chimpanzees are killed for their meat; others are caught and traded illegally. For each chimpanzee successfully shipped overseas, 10 die during transport as a result of mistreatment and malnutrition. Two sanctuaries exist in Gambia and Zambia for orphaned chimpanzees and those seized from illegal traders. Most African nations have passed laws and have set aside areas to protect chimpanzees. As human populations in Africa continue to grow, however, many of these reserves may be used to fill human needs.

In 2003 a group of scientists and conservationists (people who work to manage and protect nature) called for a downgrade in the status of chimpanzees from endangered to critically endangered. Data coming from Gabon and the Democratic Republic of the Congo, where most of the world's chimpanzees live, revealed that the ape population there had decreased by half between 1983 and 2000. The reasons for the decline were continued hunting and outbreaks among chimpanzees and gorillas of the Ebola virus, a very deadly and contagious virus that was discovered in Africa during the 1970s and afflicts humans as well. The group of scientists warned that chimpanzees and gorillas are in greater jeopardy of extinction than had been formerly realized. They called for greater enforcement of laws against hunting and capturing chimpanzees and an increased focus on research of the Ebola virus in primates. In 2015 scientists at Plymouth University in the United Kingdom announced that they had successfully created an Ebola vaccine for chimpanzees and other primates, which is good news for wild chimpanzee populations.

Did You Know?

Jane Goodall (1934–) is one of the most famous primatologists (scientists who study primates) working in the world today. In 1961 she reported seeing chimpanzees using tools to obtain food. The chimpanzees would fashion long probes out of twigs, insert them into termite mounds, and pull out termites to snack on. As patterns of tool use were unique in various chimpanzee communities, Goodall further reasoned that the tools could be the signs of different animal cultures. Other scientists did not believe her work at first, but over time more evidence was collected demonstrating chimpanzee tool use. This was a revolutionary finding because it showed that animals were able to use foresight and their intelligence to create things. Prior to this discovery, scientists believed this was something only humans could do.

Chinchilla, short-tailed
Chinchilla chinchilla

PHYLUM: Chordata
CLASS: Mammalia
ORDER: Rodentia
FAMILY: Chinchillidae
STATUS: Critically endangered, IUCN
Endangered, ESA
RANGE: Argentina, Bolivia, Chile

Chinchilla, short-tailed
Chinchilla chinchilla

Description and biology

The short-tailed chinchilla is a nocturnal (active at night) rodent with soft fur, large ears, and a bushy tail. It is one of two species of chinchilla—the other is the long-tailed chinchilla (*Chinchilla lanigera*). An average chinchilla has a head and body length between 9 and 15 inches (23 and 38 centimeters) and a tail length between 3 and 6 inches (7.5 and 15 centimeters). Female chinchillas weigh up to 28 ounces (79 grams), whereas the smaller males weigh up to 18 ounces (510 grams). A short-tailed chinchilla's silky fur is mostly gray in color. The animal's hind legs are much larger than its front legs, making it an agile jumper.

The short-tailed chinchilla's diet includes leaves, seeds, fruits, and other vegetation (plant life). While eating, it often stands erect and holds the food with its forepaws. A female chinchilla may give birth to up to

The short-tailed chinchilla, native to the Andes Mountains in South America, was once a target for hunters, but successful captive breeding has helped to lessen the threat to the animal in the wild. © TONY CAMACHO/SCIENCE SOURCE.

six infants at a time. The gestation (pregnancy) period lasts between 105 and 128 days.

Habitat and current distribution

Short-tailed chinchillas prefer to live in the cold, mountainous regions of Argentina, Bolivia, and Chile at elevations over 6,560 feet (2,000 meters). They live among crevices and rocks in barren areas covered with dense shrubs and grasses. The number of short-tailed chinchillas in the wild is unknown, but centuries of hunting has severely reduced their population.

History and conservation measures

Humans have prized chinchilla fur since the days of the Incas, the native Quechuan people of Peru who established an empire in South America in the 15th century. Commercial hunting of the chinchilla for its fur began in 1828. By the early 20th century, more than half a million chinchilla skins were being exported from Chile every year. Coats made from the animal's soft fur have sold for over $100,000.

Before laws were passed protecting wild chinchillas, hunters almost made the animals extinct. Reserves have been established to provide wild short-tailed chinchillas with a protected habitat. Although millions of chinchillas have been raised on farms for use in the fur industry since the start of legal protections in the 1920s, illegal hunting still threatens the animals in the wild. The destruction of their habitat is another reason the number of short-tailed chinchillas continues to decline.

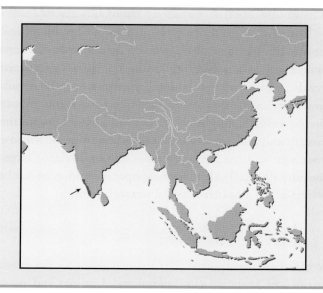

Civet, Malabar large-spotted
Viverra civettina

PHYLUM: Chordata
CLASS: Mammalia
ORDER: Carnivora
FAMILY: Viverridae
STATUS: Critically endangered, IUCN
Endangered, ESA
RANGE: India

Civet, Malabar large-spotted
Viverra civettina

Description and biology

The Malabar large-spotted civet is nearly identical to, or is in fact the same species as, the large-spotted civet (*Viverra megaspila*). Adults of this species usually weigh about 18 to 20 pounds (8 to 9 kilograms). Their long gray coats are mottled with large black spots. They have long tails banded in black and a black crest of long fur down their backs. Although most civets look like cats, the Malabar large-spotted civet more closely resembles a dog with its long legs and doglike head.

Malabar civets stay hidden in the thickets during the day and forage for food at night. They have never been seen in trees and probably obtain their food on the ground. They are thought to eat eggs, small mammals, and some vegetation (plant life). Solitary animals, they can become aggressive when they encounter members of their own species. Female Malabar large-spotted civets usually have from one to four offspring at a time, and they raise their young in the cover of thickets in the woods.

Habitat and current distribution

The original home of the Malabar large-spotted civet was in the Western Ghats, a mountain range in southwestern India. The species is believed to live in the wooded plains and natural forests surrounding the mountains. In 1999 it was estimated that there were fewer than 250 surviving adult animals in the wild, making it one of the rarest mammals in the world. A more recent and precise estimate has not been possible because scientists have not seen or been able to photograph the Malabar large-spotted civet since the 1990s. Small, scattered populations may still exist in certain areas of the South Malabar region of southern India.

History and conservation measures

At one time the Malabar large-spotted civet roamed about southwestern India in the districts of Malabar and Travancore. As more and more humans moved into the area, clearing it for residential, industrial, and agricultural purposes, the forests nearly disappeared. With the elimination of its habitat, the Malabar large-spotted civet population declined drastically. By the 1960s, the species was thought to be extinct. Members of the species were found in the late 1980s, however, and some isolated groups may still exist.

The Malabar large-spotted civet is native to India. © NVK ASHRAF/ARKIVE.ORG.

One of the reasons for the disappearance of the Malabar civet was that they were once hunted as a source of "civet musk," a product used in perfumes. Many have also been killed by dogs. The largest threat to the species, however, is the deforestation (large-scale removal of trees) of its original habitat in the Western Ghats, which forces the population into tiny isolated areas. The refuge of the last remaining Malabar civets during the last decades of the 20th century was the area's cashew plantations, which are not weeded and therefore provided the dense thickets the animals could use as their homes. These plantations are increasingly being cleared for rubber plantations.

The Malabar civet is protected under Indian wildlife laws. The area where the civets live is not protected, however, and is unlikely to be preserved as a natural habitat. Additional research is needed to determine if the Malabar large-spotted civet still exists or if it has already gone extinct.

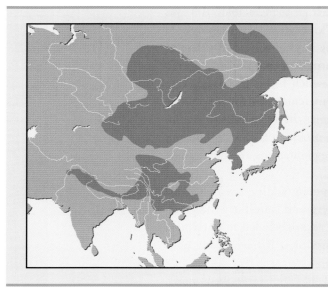

Deer, musk
Moschus spp. (all species)

PHYLUM: Chordata
CLASS: Mammalia
ORDER: Artiodactyla
FAMILY: Moschidae
STATUS: Endangered, IUCN (most
species)
Endangered, ESA (all species)
RANGE: Afghanistan, Bhutan, China,
India, Kazakhstan, Mongolia, Myanmar,
Nepal, North Korea, Pakistan, Russia,
South Korea, Vietnam

Deer, musk
Moschus spp. (all species)

Description and biology

Musk deer are so named because the males of the species have a gland, called a pod, that develops in the skin of their abdomen. This gland produces a waxy substance called musk, which may be used by males to attract females. An average musk deer has a head and body length of 28 to 39 inches (71 to 99 centimeters), stands 20 to 24 inches (51 to 61 centimeters) at its shoulder, and weighs between 15 and 40 pounds (7 and 18 kilograms). The musk deer's hair is long and coarse. It varies in color from dark to golden brown, depending on the species.

The hind legs of a musk deer are almost one-third larger than its front legs. This helps to make the animal a quick and agile jumper. Unlike most other deer, musk deer have no antlers. The upper canine teeth of male musk deer grow into narrow, pointed tusks that curve down and backward from the animal's mouth. Males use these 2.5- to 3-inch (6.4- to 7.6-centimeter) teeth when fighting each other over the right to mate with females.

A male musk deer is targeted by hunters for its musk pod, a gland that secretes a substance used in perfumes and traditional medicines. As shown here, the upper canine teeth of male musk deer grow into narrow, pointed tusks that curve down and backward from the animal's mouth. © REDMOND O. DURRELL/ALAMY.

Mating takes place in November and December. A male musk deer pursues a female until she is too exhausted to run anymore. After a gestation (pregnancy) period of 150 to 198 days, a female musk deer gives birth to one or two infants, which are born with spotted coats.

Musk deer feed on leaves, flowers, twigs, mosses, grasses, and lichens (organisms composed of an alga and a fungus growing together) during morning and evening hours.

Habitat and current distribution

Musk deer species live in wet forests and brush of central, northeastern, and eastern Asia. During summer the animals can be found in mountain forests ranging over 8,500 feet (2,590 meters) in elevation. They prefer dense vegetation (plant life) and brush so they can easily find shelter during the day.

Wildlife biologists (people who study living organisms in the wild) are unsure of the total number of all species of musk deer alive today because reliable estimates are not available from the various countries in their habitats. Population estimates range from 30,000 to 100,000 and show that the total number of each species is declining. Species of musk deer include the alpine musk deer, black musk deer, forest musk deer, Himalayan musk deer, and Siberian musk deer.

History and conservation measures

Humans have hunted musk deer not for their meat or hide but solely for their musk. Deer musk has been used in traditional East Asian medicine for hundreds of years and was also widely used in Europe as a perfume ingredient. A large international demand for raw musk results in over-hunting and poaching (illegal hunting). The musk is produced only by adult males, but hunting also results in the unnecessary killing of female and young musk deer.

Deer musk farming is used as an alternative in Russia and China. Musk can be extracted from farmed deer without killing the animal. Conservationists (people who work to manage and protect nature) recommend that efforts be undertaken to make this method easier and more cost effective than killing wild musk deer. Poor regulations and oversight and habitat destruction also endanger the present-day survival of all musk deer species.

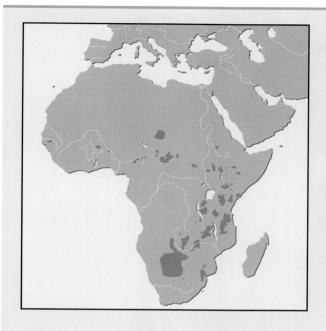

Dog, African wild
Lycaon pictus

PHYLUM: Chordata
CLASS: Mammalia
ORDER: Carnivora
FAMILY: Canidae
STATUS: Endangered, IUCN
Endangered, ESA
RANGE: Angola, Benin, Botswana, Burkina Faso, Central African Republic, Chad, Côte d'Ivoire, Democratic Republic of the Congo, Ethiopia, Guinea-Bissau, Kenya, Malawi, Mali, Mozambique, Namibia, Niger, Nigeria, Republic of the Congo, Senegal, South Africa, South Sudan, Sudan, Tanzania, Togo, Uganda, Zambia, Zimbabwe

Dog, African wild
Lycaon pictus

Description and biology

The African wild dog, also called the African painted wolf, has a streaked, multicolored coat. The tan, black, and white pattern varies between individual dogs, but each animal's head is usually dark. An African wild dog has large rounded ears, which it uses to signal other dogs and to control body temperature by radiating (giving off) heat. Its 12- to 16-inch (30- to 41-centimeter) tail ends in a plume that is white tipped. The dog's legs are long and thin. An average African wild dog has a head and body length of 30 to 44 inches (76 to 112 centimeters) and a shoulder height of 24 to 31 inches (61 to 79 centimeters). It weighs between 37 and 79 pounds (17 and 36 kilograms).

African wild dogs have a tightly knit social structure. They form packs of 2 to 45 members that hunt cooperatively. Prey includes impalas,

An African wild dog roams at a national park in Botswana. Animals in the wild are threatened by loss of habitat, hunters, and disease. © SAM DCRUZ/SHUTTERSTOCK.COM.

antelope, gazelles, zebras, wildebeests, and warthogs. The dogs are swift runners and can reach speeds up to 40 miles (64 kilometers) per hour. Their hunting range varies widely from 600 to 1,500 square miles (1,555 to 3,885 square kilometers).

In a pack, all males are related to each other and all females are related to each other, but males and females are not related. Male and female groups often travel from packs to join new ones. In most cases, mating takes place between the dominant male and dominant female in a pack. After a gestation (pregnancy) period of 69 to 72 days, a female African wild dog gives birth to up to 16 pups. About half of these pups do not survive infancy. All members of the pack care for the pups, which are allowed to eat first after the pack makes a kill.

Habitat and current distribution

African wild dogs are found throughout Africa south of the Sahara Desert. The animals prefer to inhabit savannas (flat, tropical or subtropical grasslands), open woodlands, forests, and brush. Groups of African wild dogs survive better in areas where they have no contact with humans or human activity and where prey is available.

African wild dogs were once common throughout the African continent. At the beginning of the 20th century, packs of 100 or more dogs roamed the Serengeti Plain in northern Tanzania. In 2012 biologists (people who study living organisms) estimated the world population of African wild dogs at 6,600.

History and conservation measures

As the human population in Africa has grown, wild dog habitat has decreased. The animals have also suffered because of the widespread—but unfounded—belief that they are pests. In many areas in Africa, people have shot, poisoned, and trapped them. The greatest threat to African wild dogs, however, is increased contact with domestic dogs. Canine diseases such as distemper and rabies run rampant when introduced into an African wild dog pack, and that can result in the death of most or all of the pack in a short amount of time.

The breeding of African wild dogs in zoos has been moderately successful. Strategies to expand and protect African wild dog populations vary from region to region.

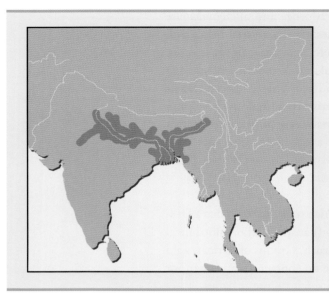

Dolphin, Ganges River
Platanista gangetica gangetica

PHYLUM: Chordata
CLASS: Mammalia
ORDER: Cetacea
FAMILY: Platanistidae
STATUS: Endangered, IUCN
RANGE: Bangladesh, India, Nepal

Dolphin, Ganges River
Platanista gangetica gangetica

Description and biology

The Ganges River dolphin is a freshwater species with gray-brown, smooth, hairless skin. It has a long beak with large, visible teeth. Although Ganges River dolphins spend their lives in the water, they breathe air. They generally surface every 4 to 5 minutes, but they can hold their breath for up to 10 minutes.

Adult dolphins are 7 to 9 feet (2.1 to 2.7 meters) long and weigh 330 to 375 pounds (150 to 170 kilograms). Females are larger than males and give birth every two to three years to one calf. The calves are chocolate brown at birth and are weaned (given solid food instead of the mother's milk) at about 1 year of age. They reach sexual maturity at about 10. Dolphins can live to be about 30 years old in the wild.

Because it lives in muddy waters, the Ganges River dolphin has little need for vision, and its eyes are nonfunctional. Rather than relying on sight, the dolphins navigate and hunt by using echolocation—a kind of sonar. The dolphins make ultrasonic sounds, which bounce off their surroundings. They hear the echoes and use that "picture" of their surroundings to navigate around obstacles and to target prey. They eat mostly small fish and invertebrates, feeding in shallow areas at the bottom of the river by poking into the silt and mud with their beaks or flippers.

Ganges River dolphins migrate seasonally. During the dry season they stay in deep pools or the main river channels. Following the monsoons (heavy rainfalls accompanying high winds), they move upstream to tributaries.

Habitat and current distribution

The Ganges River dolphin is native to the Ganges-Brahmaputra-Meghna and Karanphuli-Sangu river systems of Bangladesh, Nepal, and India. It is nearly extinct in much of its range, however. It is believed that there are fewer than 2,000 dolphins remaining, although this is only a guess, and the number could be considerably lower or higher. The greatest known number of remaining dolphins are within India, in the Ganges River between Manihari Ghat and Buxar and in the Vikramshila Gangetic Dolphin Sanctuary.

The Ganges River dolphin is threatened by dams and canals built in the waters of its habitat in south Asia, pollution, hunting, and fishing nets. © ROLAND SEITRE/MINDEN PICTURES/CORBIS.

Did You Know?

The Ganges River dolphin is closely related to the Indus River dolphin. Until the late 1990s the two dolphins were classified as different species, but they are now considered subspecies of the South Asian river dolphin. The Ganges River dolphin is designated *Platanista gangetica gangetica*, and the Indus River dolphin is classified as *Platanista gangetica minor*.

Indus River dolphins are slightly smaller than Ganges River dolphins. They are mostly found in the Indus River in south-central Pakistan. They face many of the same threats as their Ganges River cousins, including dams, pollution, drought, and killing by humans. However, they are even more threatened; a 2001 survey put the number of Indus River dolphins in the wild at only about 1,000. Pakistan has declared part of the Indus River a reserve for the dolphins, and bans on killing them seem to have helped the population recover to some degree.

History and conservation measures

The Ganges River dolphin was first scientifically identified in 1801. Its population has seriously declined since that time. This population decline is directly related to the dolphin living in one of the most heavily populated areas in the world.

The main threat to the Ganges River dolphin is the use of dams for irrigation and electricity. Damming their rivers prevents dolphins from migrating and isolates dolphin populations. Dolphins can often swim downstream during the wet season, but the strong downstream currents prevent them from returning upstream during the dry season. This puts them at risk because they have less access to food sources. At least 50 dams have been built in the dolphins' habitat, and more dams are planned, so the population of the Ganges River dolphin is therefore expected to continue to decline.

Dolphins are also threatened by fertilizer, pesticides, and industrial pollution, which kill the fish they feed on. Humans hunt dolphins for meat or oil. Dolphins often look for fish in the same places that humans do, and many become entangled in fishing nets, which can result in their deaths. Boat traffic on the Ganges River is also a threat to dolphins. The motor noise interferes with their echolocation, and the boats themselves often strike dolphins, killing or injuring them.

Ganges River dolphins are officially protected from hunting, although the protection is not always enforced or effective. Dolphin populations have increased in the upper Ganges because of conservation efforts. Dolphins in parts of national parks or sanctuaries, such as the Kaziranga National Park in Assam, India, receive some additional protection.

Ganges River dolphin oil is often used in the preparation of bait for other fish. Recent discoveries of possible oil substitutes may help reduce the hunting of the river dolphins.

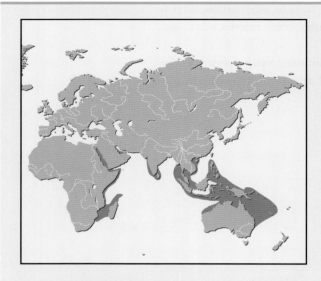

Dugong
Dugong dugon

PHYLUM: Chordata
CLASS: Mammalia
ORDER: Sirenia
FAMILY: Dugongidae
STATUS: Vulnerable, IUCN
Endangered, ESA
RANGE: Indian and Pacific Oceans: Australia, Bahrain, Brunei, Cambodia, China, Cocos (Keeling) Islands, Comoros, Djibouti, Egypt, Eritrea, India, Indonesia, Japan, Jordan, Kenya, Madagascar, Malaysia, Mayotte, Mozambique, New Caledonia, Palau, Papua New Guinea, Philippines, Qatar, Saudi Arabia, Seychelles, Singapore, Solomon Islands, Somalia, Sri Lanka, Sudan, Tanzania, Thailand, Timor-Leste, United Arab Emirates, Vanuatu, Vietnam, Yemen

Dugong
Dugong dugon

Description and biology

Dugongs are large sea mammals, sometimes called "sea cows." They have been familiar to humans for centuries and even gave rise to the mermaid myths of the past. Adult dugongs, both male and female, range in size from 8 to 13 feet (2.4 to 4 meters). They weigh between 500 and 1,100 pounds (225 to 500 kilograms) and have a big roll of fat around their bodies. Dugongs are gray or rusty brown in color; their young, called calves, are born a creamy beige and then darken as they grow.

Although dugongs breathe air into their lungs like land mammals, they live in the ocean and never come onto land. They are able to stay underwater for up to about six minutes at a time, but their dives usually last only one to three minutes before they come up for air. They have nostrils near the top of their long snouts on a large lip that can reach up to the water's surface to make breathing easier. Dugongs have a broad flat tail with a notch at its center and paddle-shaped flippers. They flap their tails in an up-and-down motion to propel them through the water, steering and balancing with their flippers.

Dugongs are herbivores (animals that eat mainly plants) who graze on sea grasses on the ocean floors in warm shallow waters. Although their eyesight is poor, they have bristles on the lips of their snouts that help them find the grasses they eat. They spend a good deal of their time grazing.

Dugongs are social animals. At one time they were known to travel in large herds of several hundred or even thousands of animals. Since their numbers have declined, they usually travel in herds of about six animals. Not much is known about this shy species, but evidence suggests that lasting bonds form between mated dugongs and also that there are distinct family groups within the larger herd. Aggressive behavior is not normal. Dugongs make whistling sounds among themselves that communicate fear; calves make a bleating sound.

Mating takes place throughout the year. Females give birth to one offspring at a time, and they generally give birth only once every three to seven years. A newborn calf is delivered in shallow water and is able to swim immediately to the surface for air. The offspring will stay with the mother for about a year. Sexual maturity occurs at about 10 years of age or later. Dugongs in the wild can live to be up to 70 years old. Because they breed at a slow rate, they cannot recover quickly from population declines, and they are thus more threatened by them.

Habitat and current distribution

Biologists (people who study living organisms) are not able to accurately estimate the number of dugongs alive today. Although some believe the number of dugongs is underestimated, their numbers appear to be declining sharply. Dugongs prefer to live in undisturbed, isolated areas in shallow waters of tropical seas with abundant sea grass beds. They are found in the Pacific and Indian Oceans within a very wide range, but the populations within this range are scattered. There are known populations of dugongs in waters around Australia, New Guinea, Sri Lanka, Indonesia, and the Pacific Islands, as well as in the waters of the Persian Gulf and the Red Sea and those off the coast of eastern Africa. The

The dugong lives in the coastal waters of the Indian and Pacific Oceans. © KRISTINA VACKOVA/SHUTTERSTOCK.COM.

number of dugongs worldwide was estimated at the end of the 1990s at approximately 100,000; no more recent figure was available in 2015. Australia has the largest population. Many areas report significant declines in the population.

History and conservation measures

The dugong is reported in the literature of the ancient world: it was seen in Greece, in Egypt, and in the Mediterranean, but there have not been dugongs in those areas for centuries. Dugong populations have disappeared from their former habitats off several island groups in the Indian Ocean. They are declining along the mainland coast of eastern Asia. A very serious decline has occurred along the coasts of India, southwestern Asia, Africa, and Madagascar. The Torres Strait off Australia, where the dugong has always been abundant, has also lost significant numbers as a result of overhunting. Aboriginal and Torres Strait Islanders, indigenous (native) people of Australia for whom the animal is a traditional food, are allowed by law to hunt dugongs using only spears thrown by hand. As of 2005, nearly 1,000 dugongs were being killed each year in the Torres Strait.

Dugongs have natural enemies, but their biggest threat comes from humans and is largely due to hunting. Dugong meat is said to taste like tender veal. Dugong hide has been used to make good-quality leather. There is also a strong market for dugong oil, bones, and teeth. Dugongs are still legally hunted in some parts of their range. Humans also kill the dugong by accident. Coastal areas in which the dugong have lived are increasingly being used for residential, recreational, and agricultural purposes. Shark nets set up around beaches to protect swimmers from predators trap and kill dugongs regularly. Gill nets used by fishers also trap the dugong. Increasing boat traffic has taken a toll. Pollution has resulted in the loss of sea grass beds essential to their survival. Other enemies to the dugong are sharks and some other sea predators. Hurricanes at sea sometimes strand dugongs.

In Australia dugongs are protected, and there are a number of programs in progress to restore the sea grass beds and protect the natural habitat of the dugong. Net fishing has been banned in dugong areas, and fishers have been required to take a course on endangered species in order to reduce the number of accidents. Many of Australia's indigenous communities have agreed to stop hunting the animal and are educating their populations about dugong management. At beaches, alternatives to shark nets are being used to protect swimmers without endangering dugongs. Further research about the species, its population numbers, and the true range of its habitat is underway. Worldwide, protection of the dugong and its habitat is inconsistent.

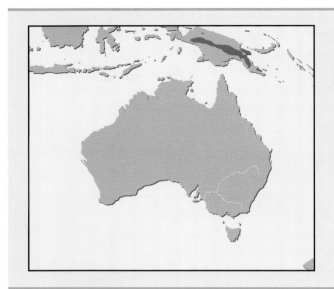

Echidna, eastern long-beaked
Zaglossus bartoni

PHYLUM:	Chordata
CLASS:	Mammalia
ORDER:	Monotremata
FAMILY:	Tachyglossidae
STATUS:	Critically endangered, IUCN
RANGE:	Indonesia, Papua New Guinea

Echidna, eastern long-beaked
Zaglossus bartoni

Description and biology

The eastern long-beaked echidna is a small animal that looks something like a hedgehog with a long, curved, tubular snout. The echidna's spines are light colored and stick out of a thick fur coat, which spreads beyond the spines to cover the head, neck, and undersides. Its claws, tail, and beak are blackish brown. The adult echidna is 24 to 39 inches (60 to 100 centimeters) long and weighs 11 to 22 pounds (5 to 10 kilograms). When threatened, echidnas will try to wedge themselves into a protected area with their spines out. If no other protection is available, the echidna can curl into a spiky ball.

Eastern long-beaked echidnas are nocturnal (active at night), sleeping during the day in underground dens or hollow logs and coming out at night to feed. They root on the forest floor for food, digging with their claws and using their long tongues to scoop up earthworms, which are their primary food. They sometimes also eat ants and termites and will

Did You Know?

Electroreception refers to the ability of some animals to detect the weak electrical fields generated by all living things. Electroreception is a useful sense in cases where darkness or murky environments make it difficult to see. Because water is a better conductor of electricity than air, electroreception is most common among marine animals. For example, sharks, rays, and electric eels all make use of electroreception. Some species, such as the electric eel, have developed this talent further and can actually generate an electrical field, which they use for communication and to shock prey.

Monotremes (egg-laying mammals) such as the platypus and echidna are some of the only mammals that have electroreception. The platypus, which is aquatic, uses electroreceptors in its beak to find prey in muddy river bottoms. The echidna has a much less developed electrical sense in its snout. Regardless, electroreception does help the echidna find earthworms in damp earth. Scientists believe echidnas may have evolved from a platypus-like ancestor, which is why they retain electrical abilities usually reserved for aquatic creatures.

open logs to get at insect larvae. The echidna's snout has electroreceptors (sensory cells) that allow it to detect weak electrical fields; this sense allows it to find its invertebrate (animals without backbones) prey at night. The echidna can range over large areas searching for food. In captivity, echidnas have lived for as long as 30 years.

The eastern long-beaked echidna is one of the few species of monotremes (pronounced MAH-nuh-treemz), or egg-laying mammals. Little is known specifically about the eastern long-beaked echidna's reproduction, but researchers believe it is similar to that of other echidnas. The solitary echidnas come together seasonally to mate. Females develop a pouch on the abdomen during breeding season; one egg is laid inside, and it hatches about 10 days later. The young stays in the pouch for six to seven weeks feeding on its mother's milk. After that the mother places them outside in a protected area such as a burrow, visiting them frequently and giving them milk until they are ready to go out on their own, about five to seven months later.

Habitat and current distribution

The eastern long-beaked echidna lives mostly in tropical and subalpine forests and grasslands. The species has lived throughout the mountains of central New Guinea, as well as on that island's Foja Mountains and

The eastern long-beaked echidna, native to Papua New Guinea and Indonesia, is at risk because of hunting and loss of habitat.
© TRAVELSCAPE IMAGES/ALAMY.

Huon Peninsula. Its numbers are declining, however, and conservationists (people who work to manage and protect nature) believe it has probably vanished from most of this territory. It has been largely wiped out in areas of dense human habitation but may be more common in remote areas. Its population seems most stable in the eastern part of its range on New Guinea.

History and conservation measures

Monotremes such as the eastern long-beaked echidna have changed little over the past 100 million years, according to fossil remains. Exactly how monotremes are related to marsupials (mammals whose young continue to develop after birth in a pouch on the outside of the mother's body) and placental mammals is uncertain, although monotremes are thought to be some of the earliest mammal species.

The eastern long-beaked echidna population is declining. The echidnas are endangered by humans in multiple ways. People frequently hunt them for food, and farmers destroy their habitat to create new agricultural land. A nickel mine proposed in the Wowo Gap area of Papua New Guinea could threaten one of the most substantial remaining populations.

To protect this species, conservationists have urged local governments to regulate the hunting of it. They also propose that additional surveys of the animal's range be undertaken to find centers of population that need to be protected.

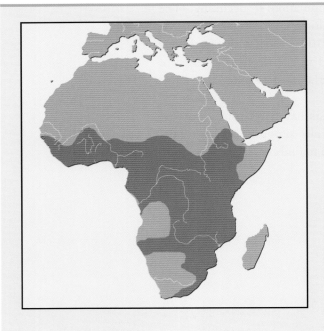

Elephant, African
Loxodonta africana

PHYLUM: Chordata
CLASS: Mammalia
ORDER: Proboscidea
FAMILY: Elephantidae
STATUS: Vulnerable, IUCN
Threatened, ESA
RANGE: Angola, Benin, Botswana, Burkina Faso, Cameroon, Central African Republic, Chad, Côte d'Ivoire, Democratic Republic of the Congo, Equatorial Guinea, Eritrea, Ethiopia, Gabon, Ghana, Guinea, Guinea-Bissau, Kenya, Liberia, Malawi, Mali, Mozambique, Namibia, Niger, Nigeria, Republic of the Congo, Rwanda, Senegal, Sierra Leone, Somalia, South Africa, South Sudan, Swaziland, Tanzania, Togo, Uganda, Zambia, Zimbabwe

Elephant, African
Loxodonta africana

Description and biology

The world's largest living land mammal, the African elephant is larger than its relative, the Asian elephant, and has much larger ears. An average adult male stands 10 feet (3 meters) tall at its shoulder and weighs between 11,000 and 14,000 pounds (5,000 and 6,350 kilograms). Females are a little shorter in height and weigh between 8,000 and 10,000 pounds (3,625 and 4,550 kilograms). The animal's thick, loose skin is dark muddy gray in color. Its large ears hold many prominent veins, and the African elephant flaps its ears vigorously to cool its blood during the heat of the day. Its long white tusks are actually elongated incisor teeth. It has only four other teeth—all molars—that it uses to grind food. These teeth are replaced up to six times, as they wear away periodically during an elephant's lifetime, which can be up to 70 years.

Other than its tusks, the elephant has another unique feature—its trunk, which is an extension of its nose and upper lip. The animal uses its trunk for drinking, bathing, smelling, breathing, feeling, greeting, communicating, and grasping. The African elephant has two fingerlike tips at the end of its trunk that are sensitive enough to pick up very small objects.

African elephants are prized by poachers for their ivory and meat, but laws and conservation programs help to protect the animal from this threat. © PICTURESWILD/SHUTTERSTOCK.COM.

African elephants are herbivores (animals that eat mainly plants), consuming tree bark, fruits, grasses, and the leaves of trees and shrubs. They require approximately 300 to 400 pounds (135 to 180 kilograms) of food and 50 gallons (190 liters) of water a day. The animals never stray far from a source of water, which they use for drinking, bathing, and cooling. After bathing each day, the elephants coat themselves in dust and dirt for protection against insects.

Elephants are social animals that form strong family ties. Family units, or herds, are made up of females (called cows) and their young (calves). The entire herd is led by an older cow called the matriarch, to which all other members of the herd are related. When a member of the herd dies, other members "grieve" over the loss, covering the dead elephant with leaves and twigs and staying by the grave for hours.

Older male elephants (bulls) live by themselves or with other males in small groups called bachelor herds. They associate with females only to breed. After a gestation (pregnancy) period of about 22 months, a female elephant gives birth to a single calf, which weighs between 150 and 300 pounds (70 and 140 kilograms). Other females are often present during the birth and help keep predators away. The calf nurses for 6 to 18 months and remains dependent on the mother for four to five years.

Habitat and current distribution

African elephants are found in most areas of Africa south of the Sahara Desert. Those elephants living in central or western Africa inhabit forest areas, whereas the elephants in the eastern and southern regions of the continent live in savanna (flat, tropical or subtropical grasslands) and bush habitats. There are thought to be around 500,000 elephants roaming Africa, a significant decrease from the 3 million to 5 million that lived there in the early 20th century. The animals once ranged in northern Africa up to the Mediterranean coast, but they became extinct there during the European Middle Ages (c. 500–c. 1500; the period of European history between ancient times and the Renaissance).

History and conservation measures

As the human population in Africa grows, the elephant's habitat continues to shrink. Habitat loss is one of the biggest threats to the species. The other threat to the future of African elephants continues to be poaching, or illegal hunting. African elephants have been hunted for centuries for their tusks, which are composed of ivory. This substance has been used to make a variety of items, ranging from jewelry to piano keys.

In 1989, through the international treaty to protect wildlife known as the Convention on International Trade in Endangered Species of Wild Fauna and Flora (CITES), a worldwide ban on the sale of elephant ivory was adopted. However, the demand for ivory is high in the United States and in China, and people smuggle it out of Africa in large amounts. Organized crime syndicates and terrorists also hunt elephants for their tusks, selling the ivory for money to buy weapons and ammunition. In 2015 the United States and China began working together to try to stop the illegal trade of ivory.

Several African countries have also taken steps to protect the animals from poachers and have established elephant conservation programs. They have set aside national parks and reserves to try to safeguard the animals and allow tourists to see them in their natural habitat. The African elephant was downlisted from endangered to vulnerable by the International Union for Conservation of Nature and Natural Resources (IUCN) in 2004. Up to 70 percent of the species' range is outside protected land, however, and poachers continue to sneak into protected areas and kill elephants for their tusks. Poaching activity has increased in recent years.

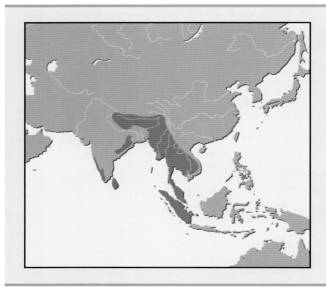

Elephant, Asian
Elephas maximus

PHYLUM: Chordata
CLASS: Mammalia
ORDER: Proboscidea
FAMILY: Elephantidae
STATUS: Endangered, IUCN
Endangered, ESA
RANGE: Bangladesh, Bhutan, Cambodia, China, India, Indonesia, Laos, Malaysia, Myanmar, Nepal, Sri Lanka, Thailand, Vietnam

Elephant, Asian
Elephas maximus

Description and biology

The Asian elephant, also known as the Indian elephant, is smaller than its relative, the African elephant. An average male Asian elephant weighs up to 11,500 pounds (5,220 kilograms) and stands 8.5 feet (2.6 meters) tall at its shoulder. Females of the species are slightly shorter in height and weigh up to 6,000 pounds (2,720 kilograms). The elephant has an arched back and a flat forehead. Its ears are smaller and its trunk shorter and smoother than those of the African elephant.

The Asian elephant's trunk, which is an extension of its nose and upper lip, has one fingerlike tip at the end that is used to grasp food and other items. Elephants also use their trunks for drinking, bathing, smelling, breathing, feeling, greeting, and communicating. All elephants can create a variety of sounds with their trunks, from rumbling noises to the well-known trumpeting sound.

The Asian elephant's habitat, which once stretched from China to Iran, is now limited to nations in the southern and eastern reaches of the Asian continent. © ADITYA SINGH/SHUTTERSTOCK.COM.

Unlike African elephants, only some male Asian elephants (and no females) have tusks, which are enlarged incisor teeth. Like its relative, the Asian elephant has four molar teeth, which are replaced up to six times during its lifetime. When the final set of teeth is worn out, the elephant can no longer chew its food, and it dies of starvation.

Asian elephants feed on more than 100 species of plants, including grasses, leaves, twigs, roots, and bark. The animals spend 17 to 18 hours foraging for the 330 pounds (150 kilograms) of food they require each day. They need large areas of forest habitat to supply this food, but they never travel far from a source of water, which they use daily for drinking and bathing.

Elephants have a close and complex social structure. Related females (mothers, daughters, and sisters) and their young form herds headed by an older related female, called the matriarch. Older males live singly or together in a small group known as a bachelor herd. The relationships elephants form with each other last a lifetime, which is up to 70 years. When a member of a herd dies, the other members cover the dead body with leaves and twigs and then remain at the site for hours.

Males and females associate with each other only for mating and sometimes for feeding. After a gestation (pregnancy) period of 18 to 22 months, a female Asian elephant gives birth to a single calf. The calf nurses and remains dependent on its mother for three to four years.

Habitat and current distribution

Asian elephants once ranged from coastal Iran to southern China. They are extinct in West Asia, Java (Indonesia), and most of China and are now found only in the forests and jungles of South and Southeast Asia. Biologists (people who study living organisms) estimate that about 50,000 Asian elephants remain in the wild. Whereas they once lived across an area encompassing more than 3.5 million square miles (9 million square kilometers), they now occupy a habitat of only about 190,000 square miles (492,000 square kilometers) and in highly fragmented (broken into smaller areas that no longer border each other) populations. The largest population is found in India.

History and conservation measures

Humans have domesticated Asian elephants for centuries, using them to carry people and goods. The elephants have been used extensively in the timber industry, carrying items such as logs with their trunks. Because many Asian elephants do not have tusks, they have not been hunted to supply the ivory trade as much as African elephants have. (Tusks are composed of ivory, a substance that has been used to make items ranging from jewelry to piano keys.) Nevertheless, the Asian elephant faces greater threats to its existence than its African relative.

Deforestation, the loss of forests as they are cut down to produce timber or to make land available for farming, has had a devastating impact on Asian elephants. The animals need large forest areas to supply their daily food needs. Growing human populations in the region have converted vast areas of forested land into farmland. (In India alone, the human population more than tripled in the 20th century.) As a result, much of the elephant's habitat has been reduced, and they are forced to live in pockets of forest surrounded by cultivated land. Seeking food, they often eat crops planted on farms that were once their feeding grounds. This brings them into greater conflict with humans. Conservationists (people who work to manage and protect nature) believe that improved management of human-elephant conflicts would result in the local recognition of elephants as an asset instead of a threat. Unless protected areas are established for the animals and human populations stabilize in the region, the continued survival of the Asian elephant is in jeopardy.

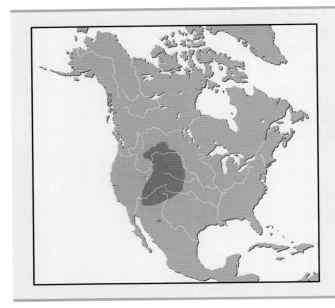

Ferret, black-footed
Mustela nigripes

PHYLUM: Chordata
CLASS: Mammalia
ORDER: Carnivora
FAMILY: Mustelidae
STATUS: Endangered, IUCN
Endangered, ESA
RANGE: Canada, Mexico, USA
(Arizona, Colorado, Kansas, Montana,
Nebraska, New Mexico, North Dakota,
South Dakota, Utah, Wyoming)

Ferret, black-footed
Mustela nigripes

Description and biology

The black-footed ferret is a member of the weasel family (which also includes weasels, badgers, martens, fishers, otters, minks, and wolverines). Similar in size to a mink, the black-footed ferret has a long, slender body covered in short, pale yellowish-brown fur. On its throat and belly, the fur is nearly white. The animal has a brownish head, a brownish-black mask across its eyes, black feet and legs, and a black tip on its tail. An average black-footed ferret is 18 to 24 inches (46 to 61 centimeters) long, which includes a tail length of 5 to 6 inches (13 to 15 centimeters). It weighs 18 to 36 ounces (510 to 1,020 grams). Females are generally slightly smaller than males.

Black-footed ferrets prey on prairie dogs and live in prairie dog burrows. They hunt at night and are rarely active aboveground during the day. Ferrets also eat mice, voles, ground squirrels, gophers, birds, and insects. They are preyed on by great horned owls, golden eagles, coyotes, and badgers.

Ferrets are solitary animals. They each have a territory that they mark with musk from scent glands. Males often have a larger range than that of females. The two sexes come together only to mate in March and April. After a gestation (pregnancy) period of 41 to 45 days, a female black-footed ferret gives birth in a burrow to three to five kits. The kits do not come out of the burrow until they are two months old. Then the mother separates the kits into different burrows, where they learn to take care of themselves. By early fall, they are on their own. Most kits do not survive their first year, and most adult ferrets live more than three years in the wild.

Habitat and current distribution

Black-footed ferrets once ranged throughout the Great Plains—from Texas to southern Saskatchewan, Canada, and from the Rocky Mountains to the Dakotas, Nebraska, and Kansas. Considered one of the most endangered mammals in the United States, the black-footed ferret did not exist in the wild between 1987 and 1991.

History and conservation measures

When American pioneers moved west across the plains in the 19th and early 20th centuries, they destroyed prairie dog habitat in order to create land for livestock and agriculture. Hunting, habitat destruction, and poisoning (as pests) reduced the prairie dog population by 90 percent. As prairie dogs and their habitat disappeared, so did the primary food source and habitat for black-footed ferrets. A severe outbreak of canine distemper (a viral disease) in the 1950s further reduced the small number of remaining black-footed ferrets, as did the appearance of sylvatic plague (caused by the same bacterium responsible for the European Black Death in the 1300s).

Because no black-footed ferrets were found in the wild between 1972 and 1981, the animal was thought to be extinct. In 1981, however, a small population of ferrets was discovered near Meeteetse, Wyoming. The population increased over the next few years, but an outbreak of canine distemper in 1985 severely threatened the survival of the species.

In 1987 the U.S. Fish and Wildlife Service placed the last 18 known wild black-footed ferrets in a captive-breeding facility. The goal of this program was to maintain a breeding population of black-footed ferrets

The black-footed ferret declined in the wild in the 20th century when farmers in the plains and grasslands of North America targeted its main prey, the prairie dog, as an agricultural pest. © ALL CANADA PHOTOS/ALAMY.

in captivity and to return their offspring to the wild. In 1991, 49 captive-bred young ferrets were released into the Shirley Basin in Wyoming. Several of these animals survived the winter and bred successfully.

The captive-breeding programs that followed have been highly successful. By 1998 the captive-breeding programs were producing record-breaking numbers of kits, many of which were reintroduced to the wilderness. All the reintroduced ferret populations have produced healthy numbers of litters in the wild. As of 2013, there were approximately 500 ferrets in the wild and 300 living in captive-breeding facilities, with over 4,500 ferrets released into the wild over the preceding 20 years. Black-footed ferret reintroduction sites, totaling 22, are spread over Wyoming, Montana, South Dakota, Utah, Arizona, Colorado,

New Mexico, and Kansas, with one each in Chihuahua, Mexico, and in Saskatchewan, Canada.

The black-footed ferret is still threatened by the poisoning of its most important food source, the prairie dog. Farmers find the prairie dog to be a pest and use poison to manage its populations. This can be a problem in areas where ferret reintroduction and the poisoning of prairie dogs are taking place at the same time. For instance, in 2002 ferrets were released at a new managed prairie dog/black-footed ferret site on the Rosebud Sioux reservation in South Dakota. The tribe was expected to take a leading role in ferret recovery on their lands, but they also used poison to control prairie dogs. The U.S. government began investigations into these actions in 2008, leading the Rosebud Sioux to request that the ferrets be removed from reservation lands.

The U.S. Fish and Wildlife Service reports that there are limited sites in North America with suitable prairie dog populations to support the ferret populations currently being released in the wild. Further work on managing prairie dog populations and their habitat is needed to maintain the progress made on the recovery of the black-footed ferret in the wild. The U.S. Geological Survey is also conducting research on treatments for sylvatic plague and canine distemper.

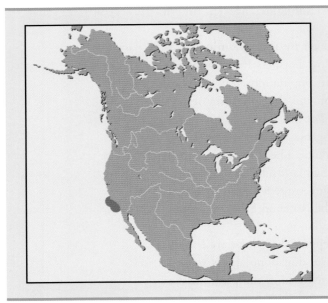

Fox, island gray
Urocyon littoralis

PHYLUM: Chordata
CLASS: Mammalia
ORDER: Carnivora
FAMILY: Canidae
STATUS: Near threatened, IUCN
Endangered, ESA (certain
subspecies)
RANGE: USA (California)

Fox, island gray
Urocyon littoralis

Description and biology

Although the island gray fox is mostly gray, its belly and throat are white, and the sides of its neck and the underside of its tail are rust colored. Black markings often accent its face and limbs. An average island gray fox has a head and body length of about 20 inches (51 centimeters) and stands roughly 12 inches (30 centimeters) tall, which makes it about the size of a house cat. Its tail is noticeably short, and the fox weighs between 3 and 6 pounds (1.4 and 2.8 kilograms).

The island gray fox hunts for food primarily in the early morning and late evening. It is an omnivore, which means it will eat both plants and animals. Insects, such as grasshoppers and crickets, and fruits constitute the main portion of its diet, with small mammals, birds, reptiles, and eggs making up the remainder.

Male island gray foxes are larger than females. Male and female foxes come together to mate between late January and early March. A female island gray fox usually gives birth to a litter of one to five pups after a gestation (pregnancy) period of 50 to 53 days. The mother nurses her pups for six weeks, while the father hunts for food. The island gray fox is not generally afraid of humans.

Habitat and current distribution

The island gray fox thrives in all the natural habitats found on its islands, including grasslands, coastal scrub, sand dunes, and forested

The island gray fox is found only on the Channel Islands off the coast of Southern California. © KEVIN SCHAFER/ALAMY.

areas. It is found only on the six largest Channel Islands, which extend along the southern coast of California. It was originally thought that the island gray fox was separated from its mainland ancestor when the Channel Islands split off from mainland California some 11,500 years ago and that the islands then broke apart from each other over the next 2,000 years. However, the oldest fossil remains of the island gray fox are only 6,000 years old, suggesting that humans transported the foxes onto the islands *after* the land's formation. The separation of the species by water resulted in the island gray foxes evolving independently from mainland foxes and from those on the other islands, forming unique subspecies on each island. Four of the six subspecies are listed as endangered on the U.S. Endangered Species List.

History and conservation measures

There are several factors leading to the decline of the island gray fox. When bald eagles became endangered in the 1970s because of poisoning from the pesticide DDT, the golden eagle took over the bald eagle's position as apex (top) predator in the Channel Islands. Whereas bald eagles usually do not eat island gray foxes, golden eagles do, and they hunted the fox to near extinction. Since then, canine distemper (a viral disease) has also caused a large decline in some island subspecies. The fox is also in danger of being struck by vehicles, and many are killed in this way.

The species has been successfully reintroduced on some of the Channel Islands. Many subspecies were taken into captivity and used to establish breeding programs at the beginning of the 21st century. Over time, many were released into the wild. By 2011 the number of island gray foxes in the wild had increased to more than 5,000.

Long-term recovery plans for the island gray fox involve the relocation of golden eagles from some of the Channel Islands and the reintroduction of bald eagles. Even one pair of golden eagles can put pressure on the fox population, making the eagles' removal a top priority. In addition, a number of foxes are vaccinated against canine distemper and rabies every year. The captive breeding that has been performed for the islands is helping to offset the damage done by golden eagle predation (killing and eating of other animals). In addition, more research is being done to give wildlife managers the best information possible on the recovery of the species.

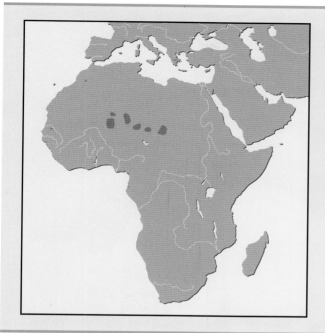

Gazelle, dama
Nanger dama (also *Gazella dama*)

PHYLUM: Chordata
CLASS: Mammalia
ORDER: Artiodactyla
FAMILY: Bovidae
STATUS: Critically endangered, IUCN
Endangered, ESA
RANGE: Algeria, Chad, Mali, Morocco, Niger, Senegal, Sudan

Gazelle, dama
Nanger dama (also *Gazella dama*)

Description and biology

The dama gazelle (also known as the addra gazelle) is a graceful antelope found in the Sahara Desert region of Africa. It has long legs, a long neck, and ringed horns curved back in the shape of a lyre (an ancient harp-like instrument). Its neck and a portion of its back are reddish brown in color, while the rest of its body is white (including one spot on the inside of its neck). The actual color patterns vary by region; gazelles in the western part of their range have more reddish-brown coloring than those in the east. This species is the largest of the gazelles, and an average dama gazelle has a head and body length of 40 to 67 inches (102 to 170 centimeters) and measures 35 to 42 inches (89 and 107 centimeters) high at its shoulder. Its tail, white with a black tip, extends 9 to 12 inches (23 to 30 centimeters). The animal weighs between 90 and 165 pounds (41 and 75 kilograms).

Widespread hunting has been a major factor in the dramatic decline of the dama gazelle population. © JEFFREY B. BANKE/SHUTTERSTOCK.COM.

Like most species of gazelle, the dama gazelle has keen senses of hearing and smell. It grazes on shrubs and trees, such as acacia and desert date. This gazelle travels alone or in small groups in search of food. A female dama gazelle gives birth usually to one fawn after a gestation (pregnancy) period of about six and a half months.

Habitat and current distribution

Once populous in the countries of Libya and Morocco, the dama gazelle is now virtually extinct in northern Africa. The animal currently ranges across several countries in central and western Africa, mostly in Mali, Chad, and Niger. Only very small and scattered populations survive in other African countries. They are thought to be extinct in Mauritania, Nigeria, and Burkina Faso. Although they may still be in Sudan, the last sightings were reported by local people in 1999 and were not confirmed by biologists (people who study living organisms). Fewer than 300 individuals of this species are believed to be left in the wild.

In its range, the dama gazelle inhabits the arid (dry) grassy zone between the Sahara and the Sahel (a semiarid area south of the Sahara). It prefers to live on rocky terrain, especially around the edges of hills.

History and conservation measures

Like many other gazelle species, the dama gazelle is vanishing from its traditional range because of illegal hunting, habitat destruction, and competition for food from domestic livestock.

Nature reserves in Chad and Niger harbor some of the last remaining wild herds of dama gazelle, but these protected areas afford the animal little security. Illegal hunting, especially from motor vehicles, occurs inside and outside the reserves. In addition, dama gazelle habitat is disappearing as irrigation and other agricultural methods have turned North African deserts and grasslands into farmland. Facing competition from grazing livestock, dama gazelles have been forced to move south of their usual range in search of food. Such movement has brought the animals into even greater contact with humans, leading to increased hunting of the species. Hunting and habitat loss caused an estimated decline of more than 80 percent of its population over a 10-year period from the mid-1990s to the middle of the first decade of the 21st century. This steep decline led the International Union for Conservation of Nature and Natural Resources (IUCN) to downgrade the species' status from endangered to critically endangered in 2006.

Some recovery programs are under way to reverse the dama gazelle's decline. About 1,500 individuals exist in captivity in zoos and ranches around the world, and efforts are under way to introduce captive-bred animals back into the wild. The species was extinct in Senegal but has been reintroduced there. There are two nature preserves in Senegal protecting herds of dama gazelles. Furthermore, there are a number of semi-captive gazelles that are intended to be part of a reintroduction program in Morocco. The species has also been listed on Appendix I of the Convention on International Trade in Endangered Species of Wild Fauna and Flora (CITES; an international treaty to protect wildlife), meaning that international trade of the species is prohibited (except for scientific research).

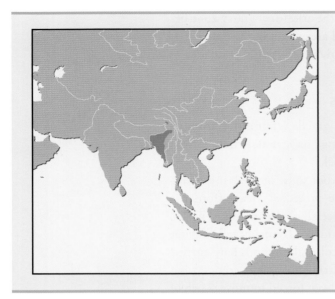

Gibbon, hoolock
Hoolock spp. (both species)

PHYLUM: Chordata
CLASS: Mammalia
ORDER: Primates
FAMILY: Hylobatidae
STATUS: Endangered, IUCN (*Hoolock hoolock*)
Vulnerable, IUCN (*Hoolock leuconedys*)
RANGE: Bangladesh, China, India, Myanmar

Gibbon, hoolock
Hoolock spp. (both species)

Description and biology

Gibbons are apes, related to gorillas and chimpanzees, but they are known as "lesser apes" because of their small size. There are 13 or more kinds of gibbons. Hoolock gibbons are the second-largest kind, generally growing to about 13 pounds (6 kilograms). Adults are about 24 to 35 inches (60 to 90 centimeters) long and have no tail. Male hoolocks have black fur with white eyebrows, whereas females have beige or red-brown fur with dark brown eyebrows and cheek areas.

Gibbons are amazing acrobats when it comes to brachiating, or swinging by their arms along the treetops. Hoolocks' bodies are built for this movement. They have very long arms and long, hook-shaped hands. They swing by their arms from one branch to another, with their hand forming a hook on the limb. They are capable of leaping long distances through the air from branch to branch or running atop the leaves in the treetops. Their diet is made up mainly of fruit and leaves, along with

A male hoolock gibbon perches in a tree in its forest habitat in northeast India. The animal is also native to Bangladesh, China, and Myanmar. © ADITYA SINGH/IMAGEBROKER/CORBIS.

some insects and flowers. Figs are a favorite food. Hoolocks are diurnal, meaning they roam the forests during the day and sleep at night. A family of hoolocks generally sleeps sitting up in one or two favored treetops. On the ground, hoolocks walk on two feet in an upright position.

Most gibbons live in family units consisting of two parents with several immature offspring. They are monogamous (have just one mate for life). Gibbons generally give birth to one offspring at a time. Baby hoolock gibbons are born with no hair and depend on their mothers for warmth. The offspring usually stay with their parents until they are six to nine years old and have reached sexual maturity. Each gibbon family group lives within its own specific territory, usually about 30 to 50 acres (12 to 20 hectares) in size, which they defend from the intrusion of other gibbons. The life span of a gibbon in the wild is not known but is probably about 30 to 40 years.

Hoolocks, like other gibbons, are very musical mammals, with a distinctive form of vocal communication displayed in half-hour-long morning songs performed by the family each day. The male and female partners sing a kind of duet together, and then other members of the family may join in to sing solos. These morning songs communicate to other gibbons that the hoolock family's area is claimed and will be defended, and the songs may also serve as mating calls from the younger family members. The folklore of the indigenous (native) people of Southeast Asia includes many stories about this magical music of the rain forests. Unfortunately, these morning songs also inform hunters of the location of the gibbon families.

The only known enemy to hoolock gibbons is the human being.

Habitat and current distribution

Gibbons have lived in the forests of Southeast Asia for millions of years. The hoolock is found in tropical (a climate warm enough year-round to sustain plant life) and subtropical evergreen forests, as well as in mountain forests produced by seasonal monsoons (heavy rainfalls accompanying high winds). Currently hoolocks live in eastern Bangladesh, northeastern India, and northwestern Myanmar. They are also believed to still be found in the Yunnan Province of China. They are no longer seen in the most northeastern part of India because the habitat there has been destroyed for agriculture and tea cultivation. There are two species of hoolock gibbons, the eastern (*Hoolock leuconedys*) and western (*Hoolock hoolock*). They are divided by the Chindwin River in Myanmar. Hoolocks range from the Brahmaputra River (in Bangladesh, India, and China) in the north and west to the Salween River (in China and Myanmar) in the east.

History and conservation measures

The habitat in which hoolock gibbons live is shrinking rapidly. The tropical and subtropical forests are being cut down and burned in order to make way for tea plantations and other crops, for logging and taking out other fuel, and for human settlement.

As their habitat is fragmented (broken into smaller areas that no longer border each other) by the clearing of forests, hoolock gibbons become more vulnerable to humans because they must come down from the treetops to cross from one food source to the next. Humans hunt hoolocks for food and to sell as pets, and gibbon bones and meat are valued in some traditional Asian medicines. Among some groups in Myanmar, for example, it is believed that eating the dried hands and legs of hoolocks will promote fertility (the ability to have children) in women.

As of 2005, biologists (people who study living organisms) estimated the western hoolock gibbon population in India at about 2,600 animals and in Bangladesh at 200 to 280 animals. There is no current data about western hoolock gibbons in Myanmar, where little attention has been paid to its habitat range and population, but it is possible that their largest population lives there. Biologists estimate that the total number of western hoolocks worldwide decreased 50 percent between the late 1960s and the early 21st century. Because of this decrease, the International Union for Conservation of Nature and Natural Resources (IUCN) has given the western hoolock gibbon a status of endangered. Eastern hoolock gibbons have not decreased as rapidly but are expected to decrease by 30 percent by 2050, so they are listed as vulnerable. Eastern hoolocks are known to live mostly in Myanmar, with at least 10,000 but possibly up to 50,000 still present in that country. Between 50 and 300 eastern hoolock gibbons reside in China, and a population of 170 may reside in India.

Preserving the remaining rain forest habitat and eliminating hunting of hoolock gibbons are key factors in the effort to save the species from extinction in the wild. Since the 1990s some sanctuaries and reserves have been created within hoolock gibbon habitats. China and India have laws protecting gibbons, but the enforcement is not strict and poachers (illegal hunters) continue to profit from killing hoolocks in the wild.

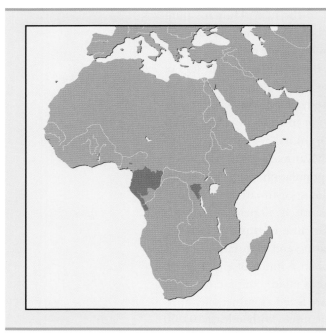

Gorilla
Gorilla spp. (all species)

PHYLUM: Chordata
CLASS: Mammalia
ORDER: Primates
FAMILY: Hominidae
STATUS: Critically endangered, IUCN (*Gorilla gorilla*)
Endangered, IUCN (*Gorilla beringei*)
Endangered, ESA (*Gorilla gorilla*)
RANGE: Angola, Cameroon, Central African Republic, Democratic Republic of the Congo, Equatorial Guinea, Gabon, Nigeria, Republic of the Congo, Rwanda, Uganda

Gorilla
Gorilla spp. (all species)

Description and biology

The gorilla is considered to be one of the most intelligent land animals. It is the largest of the living primates, an order of mammals that also includes lemurs, monkeys, chimpanzees, orangutans, and humans. When standing on its hind legs, an average male gorilla measures 5 to 5.75 feet (1.5 to 1.75 meters) high. It can weigh between 300 and 500 pounds (136 and 227 kilograms). Females are smaller, measuring about 5 feet (1.5 meters) in height and weighing between 200 and 250 pounds (91 and 114 kilograms). The color of a gorilla's coat varies from brown-gray to black. In males the hair on the back begins to turn silver after 10 years of age. Males also have a large bone on top of their skull (called the sagittal crest) that supports their massive jaw muscles and gives them their distinctive high forehead. Both sexes have small ears, broad nostrils, and a black, hairless face.

Gorillas are active during the day, foraging for a variety of vines, herbs, leaves, fruits, roots, and bark. During the wet season they tend to consume more fruit, while during the dry season their diet is composed primarily of fibrous vegetables and herbs. At night, gorillas build individual nests from branches and leaves in trees or on the ground.

Highly social animals, gorillas form groups of 5 to 10 members, although larger groups have been documented. An average group is composed of a dominant mature male (called a silverback) and several females and their young. When young males in the group become mature (at about age 11), they leave to form their own groups. Young females also leave upon reaching maturity (at about age 8), joining lone males or other groups.

Breeding between males and females can take place anytime during the year. After a gestation (pregnancy) period of 250 to 270 days, a

The gorilla faces threats to its population in the tropical forests of central Africa from hunters and disease, including the Ebola virus. © ERNI/SHUTTERSTOCK.COM.

female gorilla gives birth to a single infant. She will carry her infant for the first few months of its life, after which time it will begin to crawl and then walk. The young gorilla will remain dependent on its mother for up to three years. Almost half of all infant gorillas die before reaching maturity, being more vulnerable to predators, disease, and many other dangers that adults can withstand. Female gorillas successfully raise only two to three young during their lives, which in the wild can be more than 40 years.

Scientists have recognized two species of gorilla, each with two subspecies: (1) the western gorilla (*Gorilla gorilla*), which includes the western lowland gorilla (*Gorilla gorilla gorilla*) and the Cross River gorilla (*Gorilla gorilla diehli*); and (2) the eastern gorilla (*Gorilla beringei*), which includes the eastern lowland gorilla (*Gorilla beringei graueri*) and the mountain gorilla (*Gorilla beringei beringei*).

Habitat and current distribution

All four gorilla subspecies prefer forest habitats. The eastern lowland gorilla, having a population between 3,000 and 5,000, is found primarily in eastern Democratic Republic of the Congo. The mountain gorilla is found in the Virunga Mountains, a range of volcanic mountains stretching across eastern Democratic Republic of the Congo, southwestern Uganda, and northwestern Rwanda. With a population of about 880, the mountain gorilla is one of the more endangered of the gorilla subspecies.

The western lowland gorilla is found in Nigeria, Cameroon, the Central African Republic, Mbini (the mainland portion of Equatorial Guinea; also known as Río Muni), Gabon, the Republic of the Congo, and Angola. Its population has been estimated to be about 95,000, although it is most likely much lower than that. The Cross River gorilla is the rarest gorilla of all. It is restricted to a small area of highland forest along the Cross River, which crosses the border of Cameroon into Nigeria. This subspecies numbers only 250 to 300 individuals.

History and conservation measures

For years, hunting has been the leading threat to gorillas. The animals are killed for food or trapped to become pets. Although current international agreements ban the selling or trading of gorillas as pets, illegal capture of the animals continues.

The destruction of African forests is another serious threat to gorillas. More and more of their habitat has been cleared to create farms and to supply European and Asian timber companies. Logging roads, built deep into the forests, also allow hunters easy access to poach (illegally hunt) remaining gorillas.

In 2007 the International Union for Conservation of Nature and Natural Resources (IUCN) downgraded the status of the western gorilla from endangered to critically endangered. In some areas, more than 90 percent of the western gorilla population had been killed, contributing to an overall decline in the species' population of about 60 percent between the mid-1980s and the middle of the first decade of the 21st century. The reasons for the decline were continued hunting and outbreaks among gorillas of the Ebola virus, a deadly and contagious virus discovered in Africa in the 1970s. The eastern gorilla's population is declining at a slower rate than the western gorilla, and it is listed as endangered.

African countries within the gorilla's range are trying to establish conservation programs for the animal. These efforts, though, are often thwarted by limited finances and social and political unrest. One successful program has been the Mountain Gorilla Veterinary Project, which provides health care for injured and sick mountain gorillas in Rwanda, the Democratic Republic of the Congo, and Uganda. It is one of the few programs in the world to provide treatment to an endangered species in its natural habitat.

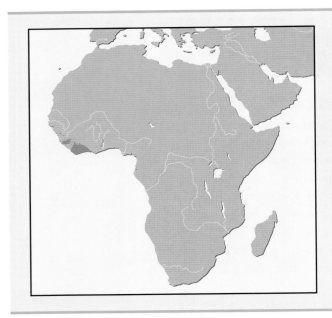

Hippopotamus, pygmy
Hexaprotodon liberiensis (also
Choeropsis liberiensis)

PHYLUM: Chordata
CLASS: Mammalia
ORDER: Artiodactyla
FAMILY: Hippopotamidae
STATUS: Endangered, IUCN
RANGE: Côte d'Ivoire, Guinea, Liberia, Sierra Leone

Hippopotamus, pygmy
Hexaprotodon liberiensis (also *Choeropsis liberiensis*)

Description and biology

The pygmy hippopotamus is smaller and more piglike in appearance than its larger relative, the common hippopotamus. Its skin color is generally black, with a greenish tinge on the top of its back. Its belly is cream or yellow-gray. Its eyes are on the side of its round head instead of on top as in the common hippo. An average pygmy hippo has a head and body length of 5 to 5.5 feet (1.5 to 1.7 meters) and a shoulder height of 30 to 39 inches (76 to 99 centimeters). It weighs between 355 and 600 pounds (161 and 272 kilograms). By contrast, an average common hippo weighs between 2,425 and 5,720 pounds (1,100 and 2,595 kilograms).

The pygmy hippo is a solitary animal, spending much of its time on the shore near swamps and rivers. Like the common hippo, the pygmy hippo has glands beneath its skin that secrete a pink, sweat-like sub-

The pygmy hippopotamus has found its habitat in the forests, swamps, and streams of western Africa diminished and fragmented by deforestation and hunting in the region.
© KLETR/SHUTTERSTOCK.COM.

stance. This biological fact has inspired the myth that hippos "sweat blood." This pink substance helps to regulate the hippo's skin temperature. The pygmy hippo feeds at night on leaves, shoots, grasses, roots, and fruits.

Male and female pygmy hippos usually mate in the water at any time during the year. After a gestation (pregnancy) period of about 188 days, a female pygmy hippo gives birth to one calf. She then nurses that calf for six to eight months.

Habitat and current distribution

Pygmy hippos inhabit lowland forests. They are found in the tropical region of western Africa, primarily in the country of Liberia. Although estimates of population are difficult to make, evidence from cameras placed in pygmy hippopotamus habitats suggest that population densities are low. Scientists estimate that the number of mature individuals in the population is fewer than 2,500.

History and conservation measures

Deforestation (large-scale removal of trees) and hunting are the major threats to pygmy hippopotamuses. Forests within the species' range are cut down for timber, converted to crop plantations, or settled by humans. The remaining forests are fragmented (broken into smaller areas that no longer border each other), isolating the hippo and increasing the likelihood of local extinction. Forest fragmentation has made it easier for humans to track and kill the animal. Hunters sell hippo meat for food and the bones for use in traditional medicine (health practices used by specific cultures since before the time of modern medicine).

Pygmy hippos are now found primarily in protected areas, and international trade of the animals is regulated by the Convention on International Trade in Endangered Species of Wild Fauna and Flora (CITES; an international treaty to protect wildlife). Conservation plans and research programs targeting the pygmy hippo have been established in all the countries in its range, and institutions worldwide have begun captive-breeding programs. Most captive hippos are older, however, and include many more females than males. This makes it more difficult for breeding programs to succeed.

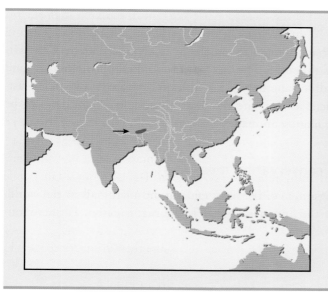

Hog, pygmy
Sus salvanius (also *Porcula salvania*)

PHYLUM: Chordata
CLASS: Mammalia
ORDER: Artiodactyla
FAMILY: Suidae
STATUS: Critically endangered, IUCN
Endangered, ESA
RANGE: India

Hog, pygmy
Sus salvanius (also *Porcula salvania*)

Description and biology

The pygmy hog is the smallest of all pig species. An average adult pygmy hog is 25 inches (63.5 centimeters) long, stands 10 inches (25 centimeters) tall at its shoulder, and weighs 19 pounds (8.6 kilograms). Its short tail measures only 1 inch (2.5 centimeters). Its hide is covered with coarse dark brown or black bristles. Because of its small, bullet-like shape, the animal is extremely agile.

Male pygmy hogs are larger than their female counterparts and have exposed tusks. The normally solitary males interact with the females only during mating season. A female pygmy hog gives birth to a litter of two to six infants, usually in late April or May, after a gestation (pregnancy) period of about 100 days. Both males and females build and use their nests throughout the year.

Habitat and current distribution

Pygmy hogs inhabit dense, tall grasslands in areas just south of the Himalayan mountain range. They are currently found only in and around the Manas Wildlife Sanctuary in northwestern Assam (a state in far eastern India). Scientists estimate the total number of pygmy hogs to be fewer than 250 mature animals.

History and conservation measures

The pygmy hog is one of the most endangered mammals in the world. Destruction of the animal's habitat is the main reason. Farmers rou-

The pygmy hog's habitat has been reduced to a small area of India as human settlement, agriculture, and forestry have eliminated much of the grasslands where it once lived. © ZUMA PRESS, INC./ALAMY.

tinely set fire to grassland forests to clear them for agricultural use. Many pygmy hogs are killed because they cannot escape the extensive fires. Those that do escape are forced onto very small grassland areas, where they are sometimes killed by unexpected fires, or onto tea plantations, where they are often killed by hunters.

The international wildlife community and the Indian government have focused much attention on the pygmy hog's plight. In 1985 the International Union for Conservation of Nature and Natural Resources (IUCN) placed the pygmy hog on its first list of the 12 most threatened species in the world. The Indian government has given the animal the maximum legal protection allowed under its Wildlife Protection Act. In 1986 the United Nations Educational, Scientific, and Cultural Organization (UNESCO) designated the Manas Wildlife Sanctuary as a World Heritage site.

All these measures have done little to stop the destruction of pygmy hog habitat. If grassland fires in their habitat are allowed to continue unchecked, pygmy hogs will face extinction. A special conservation program in India established in 1995 is actively working to prevent the extinction of pygmy hogs and other endangered species of the tall grasslands of the region. It conducts field research and breeds pygmy hogs in captivity for reintroduction to restored habitats. Awareness campaigns are also carried out in the villages near the protected area to engage the cooperation of local residents.

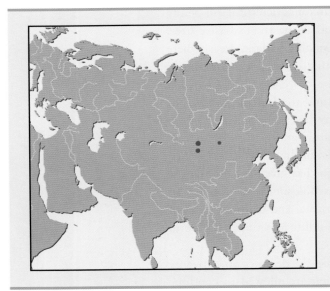

Horse, Przewalski's
Equus przewalskii

PHYLUM: Chordata
CLASS: Mammalia
ORDER: Perissodactyla
FAMILY: Equidae
STATUS: Endangered, IUCN
Endangered, ESA
RANGE: China, Mongolia

Horse, Przewalski's
Equus przewalskii

Description and biology

Przewalski's horse is the last truly wild horse. Slightly smaller than most domestic horses, it has a compact body with a thick neck and large head. The color of its upper body is dun (a dull grayish brown), while its belly and muzzle are much lighter. The horse has a dark stripe along its backbone and a dark, plumed tail. The dark hair on its head and along its neck (the mane) is short and stands erect. Unlike the domestic horse, Przewalski's horse sheds its mane and the short hairs at the base of its tail annually.

An average Przewalski's horse may reach 8 feet (2.4 meters) in length and stand 4 to 4.5 feet (1.2 to 1.4 meters) high at its shoulders. It may vary in weight between 440 and 750 pounds (200 and 340 kilograms). The horse feeds primarily on grass and other low vegetation (plant life).

Groups of Przewalski's horses are headed by a dominant stallion (male), which is responsible for breeding with most of the group's females. The females usually give birth to a single foal (infant) between April and June, after a gestation (pregnancy) period of 330 to 340 days. The foals may nurse for up to two years.

Habitat and current distribution

Przewalski's horses prefer open grassland, steppe (vast, semiarid grass-covered plain), and semi-desert areas. Przewalski's horse was extinct in the wild as of 1968. A number of programs for breeding horses in captivity have been extremely successful and eventually produced more than 1,500 animals. Almost 400 Przewalski's horses now live in the wild at three sites in Mongolia: Takhin Tal Nature Reserve, Hustai National Park, and Khomin Tal. They have been reintroduced in China in the Kalamaili Nature Reserve and the Dunhuang Xihu National Nature Reserve, although they are not yet completely wild at these locations because they are fed in the winter. There are also reintroduced animals living in very large reserve enclosures in France, Ukraine, Hungary, and Uzbekistan.

History and conservation measures

Przewalski's horse was discovered in 1878 by Russian geographer and explorer Nikolai Mikhailovich Przhevalsky (1839–1888). Scientists believe the horse once ranged from western Mongolia to northern Xinjiang (a province in northwestern China) and western Kazakhstan.

By 1900 hunting and competition with domestic horses for food and water had greatly reduced the Przewalski's horse population. By the 1950s the remaining animals were seen in a small area between southwestern Mongolia and northwestern China called the Takhin-Shara-Nuru (meaning "mountain of the yellow horses" in Mongolian). After a last sighting of the animal in the wild in 1968, Przewalski's horses in two European zoos were the only ones known to remain in the world.

Did You Know?

The 1986 Chernobyl nuclear power plant disaster in Ukraine—an explosion resulting in radioactive contamination in Ukraine and Europe—was the worst nuclear accident in human history to date. Human access is restricted within an exclusion zone of about 1,000 square miles (2,600 square kilometers) around the former power plant. Despite the high levels of radioactivity, the absence of humans has turned the zone into an unintentional habitat sanctuary. Many animal species have returned to the zone and thrived, including deer, foxes, moose, bears, pigs, lynx, wolves, and birds.

In the late 1990s some 31 Przewalski's horses born in captivity were released in the exclusion zone, and they reproduced in large numbers. As many as 200 Przewalski's horses lived in the zone before poaching (illegal hunting) for meat reduced the number to about 40 by 2011.

Przewalski's horse, which once ranged from eastern Russia through northern China, has benefited from programs to reintroduce the species into the wild, particularly in Mongolia. ©ANITA HUSZTI/SHUTTERSTOCK.COM.

The International Union for Conservation of Nature and Natural Resources (IUCN) listed the species as extinct in the wild in 1996. Subsequently, however, the Przewalski's horse became a great success story in the ongoing efforts to preserve species through reintroduction to the wild. In 1992, 16 horses bred in captivity and chosen for their genetic (inherited) traits were slowly and carefully reintroduced to the wilderness at Hustai National Park in Mongolia. By 2000 a total of 84 horses had been reintroduced and 114 foals had been born in the wild. By 2014 there were 387 horses in the wild in Mongolian sites, and the animals appeared to be doing better each year. They are being very carefully watched and protected as they continue to adapt to the original habitat of the species in central Asia and to the habitats at other free-range conservation sites around the world.

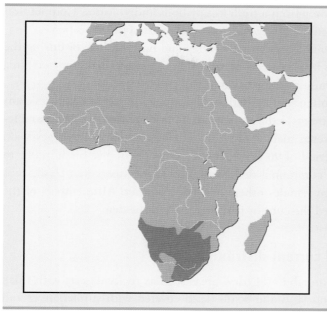

Hyena, brown
Parahyaena brunnea (also *Hyaena brunnea*)

PHYLUM: Chordata
CLASS: Mammalia
ORDER: Carnivora
FAMILY: Hyaenidae
STATUS: Near threatened, IUCN
Endangered, ESA
RANGE: Angola, Botswana, Lesotho,
Mozambique, Namibia, South Africa,
Swaziland, Zimbabwe

Hyena, brown
Parahyaena brunnea (also *Hyaena brunnea*)

Description and biology

The brown hyena, also known as the strand wolf, has a long, brown, shaggy coat with lighter underparts. Its face and legs are gray to black, although its neck and shoulders are lighter. An average brown hyena measures 43 to 53 inches (109 to 135 centimeters) long and stands 25 to 35 inches (64 to 89 centimeters) high at its shoulder. It weighs between 82 and 104 pounds (37 and 47 kilograms). Males are larger than females.

The brown hyena feeds primarily on the remains of prey killed by other predators. With its strong teeth and jaws, the animal can crush and eat bones. It also feeds on insects, eggs, fruits, and an occasional small animal or bird that it kills. Although it has acute vision and hearing, the brown hyena locates its prey by scent. It hunts alone. Lions and spotted hyenas are the animal's main predators. In addition, the brown hyena can be forced away from a fresh kill by lions and vultures. Competition for food between brown hyenas and black-backed jackals is fierce.

Brown hyenas sleep during the day and hunt at dusk or during the night. A brown hyena can cover more than 20 miles (32 kilometers) in a single nightly hunting expedition.

Although often solitary in their habits, brown hyenas will form clans of up to 13 members, led by a matriarch (an older female). Male and female brown hyenas mate at any time during the year. After a gestation (pregnancy) period of 90 to 100 days, a female will give birth to one to five cubs. In a communal den (shared by all members in a clan), cubs may nurse from females other than their mother. All members of the clan help to feed the cubs by carrying food to the den.

Habitat and current distribution

Brown hyenas inhabit arid (dry) areas such as rocky deserts with thick brush, open grassland and scrub (land covered with stunted trees and

The brown hyena, native to southern Africa, is often hunted as a pest or predator or killed for its bones, which are used in traditional medicine and rituals. © ECOPRINT/SHUT-TERSTOCK.COM.

shrubs), and semideserts. They sleep in dense vegetation (plant life), under sheltering rocks, or in burrows dug by other animals.

The species lives in southern Africa, but its range has shrunk significantly since the end of the 18th century. Of the eight African countries where brown hyenas can be found, Botswana hosts the largest population. There are thought to be between 5,000 and 8,000 hyenas left in the wild.

History and conservation measures

Brown hyenas are regarded as a threat to livestock in many areas, despite the finding that they rarely prey on domestic animals. The hyena has no reason to hunt livestock, as it is a scavenger that feeds mostly on carrion (decaying flesh of dead animals). Despite these facts, brown hyenas are often hunted with guns and dogs or simply poisoned. Such persecution has led to the hyena's local extinction in some areas of Namibia.

Brown hyenas are protected in several conservation areas in the Kalahari, an arid plateau stretching about 100,000 square miles (259,000 square kilometers) across southern Africa. However, a significant portion of the global brown hyena population is found in non-protected areas.

Did You Know?

Water is crucial to life because it helps balance salt concentrations in the body, delivers important nutrients to cells, regulates body temperature, and flushes out toxins. However, the brown hyena can survive for extended periods without drinking water, and it is not the only animal that can do so. In dry and hot deserts, some animals have adapted to life without water. One of the animal record holders is the desert kangaroo rat, which almost never has to drink water. Instead, it can survive for long periods on water obtained from metabolic processes (the breaking down of food).

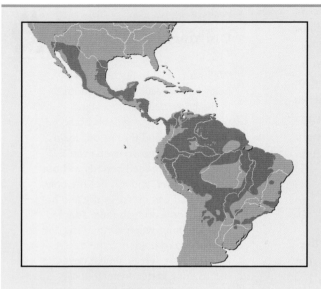

Jaguar
Panthera onca

PHYLUM: Chordata
CLASS: Mammalia
ORDER: Carnivora
FAMILY: Felidae
STATUS: Near threatened, IUCN Endangered, ESA
RANGE: Argentina, Belize, Bolivia, Brazil, Colombia, Costa Rica, Ecuador, French Guiana, Guatemala, Guyana, Honduras, Mexico, Nicaragua, Panama, Paraguay, Peru, Suriname, USA (Arizona, California, New Mexico, Texas), Venezuela

Jaguar
Panthera onca

Description and biology

The jaguar is the largest living member of the cat family in North and South America and the third largest in the world. Its coat ranges from yellow-brown to auburn and is covered with black spots and rosettes, or rings, encircling spots. An average adult jaguar has a head and body length of 4 to 6 feet (1.2 to 1.8 meters) and a tail length of 18 to 30 inches (46 to 76 centimeters). It stands about 2.5 feet (0.8 meters) high at its shoulder and weighs between 100 and 250 pounds (45 and 115 kilograms). Of the big cats, only the jaguar and the snow leopard do not seem to roar.

Jaguars are good swimmers, runners, and tree climbers. Their diet includes fish, frogs, turtles, small alligators, iguanas, peccaries (mammals related to the pig), monkeys, birds, deer, dogs, and cattle. Jaguars are solitary mammals and are quick to defend their chosen hunting ter-

The jaguar, native to tropical areas of North, Central, and South America, has benefited from laws protecting it from hunters but remains threatened by loss of habitat. © MATT GIBSON/SHUTTERSTOCK.COM.

ritory. For male jaguars, this territory ranges between 8 and 80 square miles (21 and 210 square kilometers); for females, it ranges between 4 and 27 square miles (10 and 70 square kilometers).

Male and female jaguars come together only to mate. In tropical areas, mating takes place at any time during the year. In areas with cooler climates, jaguars mate in the spring. After a gestation (pregnancy) period of 90 to 110 days, a female jaguar gives birth to a litter of one to four cubs. She raises the cubs on her own, and they may stay with her for up to two years.

Habitat and current distribution

Jaguars are found in parts of North, Central, and South America, from the southwestern United States to northern Argentina. Because the animals are secretive and rare, biologists (people who study living organisms) have not been able to determine the exact number remaining in the wild. One estimate, however, has put the number at 15,000 animals remaining in the wild.

Jaguars live in a variety of habitats, including tropical (a climate warm enough year-round to sustain plant life) and subtropical forests, open woodlands, mangroves, swamps, scrub thickets, and savannas (flat, tropical or subtropical grasslands).

History and conservation measures

Jaguars are extinct in more than 40 percent of their historic habitat, and the largest remaining population of jaguars is believed to live in the Amazon rain forest. The primary reasons for the animal's decline are deforestation (large-scale removal of trees) and other human activities in their natural habitat, as well as ruthless hunting for sport and for the jaguar's prized coat. In the early to mid-1960s, spotted cat skins were in great demand. International treaties have all but eliminated the commercial trade of cat pelts.

Jaguars continue to face the threat of habitat destruction. The clearing of forests to build ranches and farms has rapidly eliminated the animals' original habitat. Forced to live next to farmland, jaguars are often killed by farmers because they prey on domestic animals and cattle.

Small populations of jaguars are protected in large national parks in Bolivia, Brazil, Colombia, Peru, and Venezuela. Smaller reserves and private ranches in these areas provide protection to isolated pairs or families. In the United States, where jaguars once roamed throughout the Southwest as far north as the Grand Canyon, only a small number of males have been spotted since 1982, all near the border with Mexico. In 2014 the U.S. Fish and Wildlife Service designated 1,194 square miles (3,092 square kilometers) of critical habitat in southern Arizona and New Mexico for jaguar conservation.

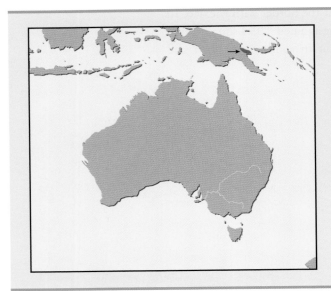

Kangaroo, Matschie's tree
Dendrolagus matschiei

PHYLUM: Chordata
CLASS: Mammalia
ORDER: Diprotodontia
FAMILY: Macropodidae
STATUS: Endangered, IUCN
RANGE: Papua New Guinea

Kangaroo, Matschie's tree
Dendrolagus matschiei

Description and biology

Matschie's tree kangaroo, also known as the Huon tree kangaroo, is a marsupial. Marsupial young are born undeveloped and are initially carried in a pouch on the outside of their mother's body. The Matschie's tree kangaroo is one of 10 kinds of tree kangaroos, all living in Australia and nearby islands. A Matschie's tree kangaroo is usually about 20 to 35 inches (51 to 89 centimeters) long in its head and body; its large tail is 16 to 37 inches (41 to 94 centimeters) long. Females are slightly larger than males, with females weighing about 17 pounds (8 kilograms) and males about 15 pounds (7 kilograms). The animals' coats are usually reddish brown or dark brown, but their belly, face, part of their tail, and feet are yellow. Fur on their necks and backs grows in an opposite direction to the rest of their fur, allowing the kangaroo to shed rain when it gets into the right position.

Matschie's tree kangaroos are arboreal (they live in trees) and nocturnal (active at night). Their bodies are similar to those of other

Did You Know?

How can scientists know so much about animals that are difficult or impossible to observe in the wild? Conservationists (people who work to manage and protect nature) studying the Matschie's tree kangaroo use a variety of scientific and research methods to obtain data.

One of the methods used to understand the population—how many, where, how dense—is called distance sampling. First, the researchers locate Matschie's tree kangaroo dung (excrement) and record the distances between specimens and measure how much they find. They can then determine an estimated population density (how many animals exist within a measured area) by using statistics, a form of math in which numbers are collected, analyzed, and interpreted. Animal dung is also used in the lab in genetic studies (biological studies dealing with heredity and the variation among living things). Through modern procedures the dung samples can be used to identify individual animals in a region and to learn about the size of their home ranges.

Another method of studying the animals is to use a camera trap—a camera set up in an animal's habitat and left there for a period of time. These "traps" are harmless to animals; in fact, they allow researchers to capture images of hard-to-find species, such as the Matschie's tree kangaroo, with very little disturbance. Infrared sensors on the camera detect movement when an animal passes nearby, triggering the camera to snap a photo. The result can be a close-range image of a wild animal but only if the camera has been placed in a suitable location, such as near an animal trail or a watering hole.

In addition, scientists interview local people about their experiences with Matschie's tree kangaroos to learn about such things as their history in the area and their eating habits. Further studies have included a survey of the biodiversity (the variety of life-forms) in the Huon Peninsula. Finally, habitat mapping can provide geographical information on the best spots for conservation.

kinds of kangaroos, except they are designed for getting around in trees. In contrast with ground kangaroos, the hind limbs of Matschie's tree kangaroos are the same length as their front limbs, and their front limbs are big and strong for tree climbing. They have large feet with pads that keep them from slipping on wet branches, along with a long, heavy tail that helps them balance their weight. They have long claws, and their feet can turn sideways in order to grasp branches. Matschie's tree kangaroos are capable of jumping long distances—up to 30 to 40 feet (9 to 12 meters)—but they generally climb up and down trees slowly and carefully. Their large eyes aid in judging distances when they leap from branch to branch. Their diet consists of leaves and fruit.

Matschie's tree kangaroo is at risk of its numbers declining because of hunting and loss of habitat as the region of Papua New Guinea in which it lives experiences increased development. © IMAGEBROKER/ALAMY.

Matschie's tree kangaroos are solitary animals. Each individual lives within its own home range, but a male's home range may overlap several females' home ranges. They mate throughout the year. The female gives birth to one offspring after a 35- to 45-day gestation (pregnancy) period. The "joey," or newborn infant, unformed and only about an inch long, nurses in the pouch for about 350 days as it develops and then stays with its mother until it is about a year and a half old. The life span of a Matschie's tree kangaroo is thought to be about 14 years.

Habitat and current distribution

Matschie's tree kangaroos live in high elevations of mountainous tropical rain forests of Papua New Guinea, specifically in the Huon Peninsula and on the island of Umboi. Because Matschie's tree kangaroos live in inaccessible places, biologists (people who study living organisms) are not able to accurately estimate how many are currently alive.

History and conservation measures

Matschie's tree kangaroos are hunted by the people of Papua New Guinea for their meat and fur. Hunters in the past used dingoes (Australian wild dogs) to locate tree kangaroos by their scent and then to pull them out of the trees. After guns were introduced in Papua New Guinea, hunters became much more efficient, and the Matschie's tree kangaroo population began to decline. At the same time, the species is threatened by the destruction of its habitat in the Huon Peninsula as a result of logging, mineral and oil exploration, and farming. Because the Matschie's tree kangaroo lives only in this one unique area, its chances of survival are very slim unless this habitat is preserved. Papua New Guinea's traditional communities control the use and management of the nation's natural resources.

In 1996 the Tree Kangaroo Conservation Program (TKCP) was established to promote the management and protection of tree kangaroos and their habitat while at the same time working to meet the needs of the local people. Because conservation (protection of the natural world) depends on educating the traditional landowners about the value of biodiversity (the variety of life-forms) and the need to use sustainable development practices (methods of farming or building communities that do not deplete or damage the natural resources of an area), the program has focused on education. The TKCP works with villagers from 35 communities in the Yopno, Uruwa, and Som River areas; together, they helped establish the Yopno-Uruwa-Som Conservation Area in the Huon Peninsula in 2009. The protected area covers 293 square miles (760 square kilometers), which the neighboring peoples protect against hunting, logging, mining, and other human activities that harm tree kangaroo habitats.

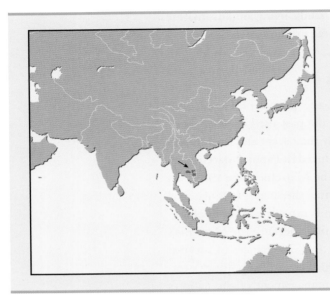

Kouprey
Bos sauveli

PHYLUM: Chordata
CLASS: Mammalia
ORDER: Artiodactyla
FAMILY: Bovidae
STATUS: Critically endangered, IUCN
Endangered, ESA
RANGE: Cambodia, Laos, Thailand,
Vietnam

Kouprey

Bos sauveli

Description and biology

The kouprey, also called the Cambodian forest ox, the gray ox, or the wild forest ox of Indochina, is one of the rarest species of wild cattle and may be the most endangered large mammal in the world. Koupreys were not known to humans until 1937, and there has been no close observation of a kouprey since 1969. Most of the information that exists on the species today comes from a zoologist who studied and filmed the animal in the wild for two months in 1957.

Koupreys are massive animals, weighing from 1,500 to 2,000 pounds (680 to 910 kilograms). They stand between 5.5 and 6.5 feet (1.7 and 2 meters) tall at the shoulder, and their bodies are about 7 feet (2.1 meters) long. They have long legs and humped backs. Koupreys are born brown but turn gray as they mature, and males then turn black or very dark brown as they get older. Both males and females have white patches on their shoulders, legs, and hindquarters. Males have horns that are wide-spreading and arch forward and upward with a distinctive splintered fringe, growing to about 32 inches (81 centimeters) long. Female horns are about 16 inches (41 centimeters) long. Adult male koupreys have a very large dewlap, a sack of skin that hangs about 16 inches (41 centimeters) from the base of the neck, sometimes reaching down to the ground.

Koupreys live and travel in herds. Females and their young form separate herds from the male herds. The animals graze (eat grass in the meadows and fields) and browse (feed on the tender shoots and leaves of bushes and trees) during the early part of the day. During the night they travel, sometimes great distances. The whole herd forms a tight circle in the early afternoon to sleep. April is the mating season, and females give birth to one offspring sometime between December and February. The kouprey's life span in the wild is thought to be about 20 years.

The kouprey was so extensively targeted by hunters for its meat and body parts that it was pushed to extinction in Southeast Asia.
© BLICKWINKEL/ALAMY.

Habitat and current distribution

The kouprey's habitat is composed of low, rolling hills covered in a mixture of open forest and dense monsoon (heavy rain) forest. The range of the kouprey is believed to be Cambodia, Laos, Thailand, and Vietnam, but many wildlife biologists (people who study living organisms in the wild) believe that the species is extinct in all its former habitats.

History and conservation measures

As far as is known to humans, koupreys have always had a low population. The animals were most likely hunted throughout their habitat area for both food and their horns. When first discovered in 1937, there were an estimated 800 koupreys. From a high of 1,000 animals in 1940, the population went into a decline. By 1970 there were only 30 to 70 koupreys left in the world.

There are many reasons for the population decline, but war was a major factor. The war in Vietnam (1954–1975) is thought to have decimated the koupreys in that country. During the war koupreys were hunted without restriction by locals and by the military. They were killed by land mines, and their habitat was destroyed. In Thailand, poaching (illegal hunting) was responsible for a major population decline. In all areas, loss of habitat caused by illegal logging and slash-and-burn farming (a farming practice in which forest is cut and burned to create space for farmland) and disease transmitted from domestic stock took a heavy toll. Laos and Cambodia have experienced periods of violent political upheaval, making it difficult to initiate conservation programs or send out expeditions to study the species in the wild. Koupreys are now legally protected in all of the countries in their range.

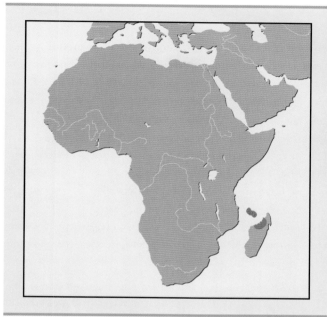

Lemur, mongoose
Eulemur mongoz

PHYLUM: Chordata
CLASS: Mammalia
ORDER: Primates
FAMILY: Lemuridae
STATUS: Critically endangered, IUCN
RANGE: Comoros, Madagascar

Lemur, mongoose
Eulemur mongoz

Description and biology

Lemurs are mammals with monkey-like bodies and limbs. They are found only on Madagascar (the large island lying in the Indian Ocean off the eastern coast of the African country of Mozambique) and adjacent islands. The mongoose lemur is one of only two lemur species found both on Madagascar and in the Comoros (a group of islands between northeastern Mozambique and northwestern Madagascar). It is covered with long, soft fur and has a ruff (projecting growth of fur) around its neck and ears. The upper bodies of male mongoose lemurs are dark gray. The male mongoose lemur has a pale gray face with bushy, reddish-brown cheeks. The upper bodies of females are gray-brown. They have a dark face with bushy, white cheeks. Both sexes are light gray underneath.

An average mongoose lemur has a head and body length of 12 to 17 inches (30 to 43 centimeters) and weighs 3 to 4 pounds (1.4 to

The mongoose lemur mainly eats flowers, fruit, and leaves.
© BGSMITH/SHUTTERSTOCK
.COM.

1.8 kilograms). The tail of the mongoose lemur is longer than its body, extending 16 to 25 inches (41 to 64 centimeters).

Mongoose lemurs are active either at night or during the day, depending on the season and area. Their diet is mainly composed of flowers, fruit, and leaves. Family groups are made up of a male, a female, and their infants. Female mongoose lemurs normally give birth to one infant in mid-October after a gestation (pregnancy) period of 128 to 135 days.

Habitat and current distribution

The mongoose lemur inhabits dry deciduous (made up of trees whose leaves fall off annually) forests on northwestern Madagascar and humid forests on the Comoros islands of Anjouan, Mohéli, and Grande Comore. The lemurs in the Comoros are probably descendants of lemurs brought to the islands by fishers from Madagascar.

History and conservation measures

Biologists (people who study living organisms) believe the number of mongoose lemurs in existence has decreased by 80 percent or more since around 1990 and that this loss is continuing. Therefore, in 2014 the International Union for Conservation of Nature and Natural Resources (IUCN) changed this species' listing from vulnerable to critically endangered. It is illegal to buy or sell mongoose lemurs internationally.

In Madagascar, mongoose lemurs are found in two protected areas—the Ankarafantsika National Park and the Mahavavy-Kinkony Wetland Complex—as well as in several unprotected areas. The densest population of mongoose lemurs lives in the Mahavavy-Kinkony Wetland Complex. Although this area is protected, human residents clear forested land near or within it to gather wood and to create areas for crops and grazing. This destroys large areas of forest and breaks up the remaining forest into smaller areas, called fragments. Lemurs do not seem to like to travel between different forest fragments, so fragmentation causes their range to shrink. Mongoose lemurs are also hunted for food. In the Comoros Islands, residents have traditionally protected the species, but people from Madagascar who move to these islands view the animal as a nuisance and do not protect it.

Conservationists (people who work to manage and protect nature) insist that the laws protecting the mongoose lemur's habitat be enforced. Nonprofit organizations are educating communities about the importance of the species. These groups are also training forest rangers to survey and monitor the mongoose lemur population.

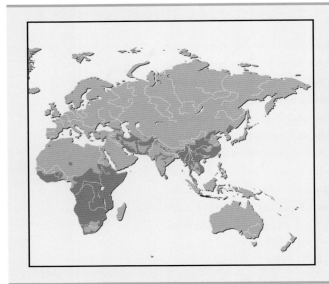

Leopard
Panthera pardus

PHYLUM: Chordata
CLASS: Mammalia
ORDER: Carnivora
FAMILY: Felidae
STATUS: Near threatened, IUCN
Threatened, ESA (parts of Africa)
Endangered, ESA (elsewhere)
RANGE: Africa, southern and south-eastern Asia, and the Middle East

Leopard
Panthera pardus

Description and biology

A large member of the cat family, the leopard is known for its light to tawny brown coat patterned with black spots and rosettes, or rings. Unlike those of the jaguar, the rosettes of the leopard never have spots inside them. Some leopards are born with a black coat that still has the characteristic spotting, and are commonly called black panthers. The term *black panther* is also used to describe other species of big cats with black coats, however, so not all black panthers are necessarily leopards. An average leopard has a head and body length of 38 to 75 inches (97 to 191 centimeters) and weighs 65 to 155 pounds (30 to 70 kilograms). Its tail can reach a length of up to 3 feet (1 meter).

Leopards are solitary mammals that hunt primarily at night. Their diet includes small mammals, such as monkeys and rodents; birds; and insects. Good climbers, leopards often store their dead prey in trees. They cover a home range of about 4 to 20 square miles (10 to 51 square kilometers) in search of food.

The leopard, which ranges from Africa into the Middle East and across Asia, is at risk due to habitat loss, poaching by hunters seeking its skin and body parts, and killing by fearful humans protecting their livestock or themselves. © BILDAGENTUR ZOONAR GMBH/SHUTTERSTOCK.COM.

Male and female leopards come together only to mate, which can occur at any time during the year. After a gestation (pregnancy) period of 90 to 105 days, a female leopard gives birth to a litter of three to five cubs. She alone cares for the cubs, hiding them until they are six to eight weeks old. The young leopards nurse for several months and may stay with the mother for 18 to 20 months.

Habitat and current distribution

Leopards have the ability to adapt to almost any environment. As long as prey is available, these cats inhabit areas ranging from semidesert to dense rain forest. They are found in Africa, the Middle East, and parts of Asia. Even though they have the largest distribution of the large cats, their population is declining and may soon be vulnerable to extinction.

Estimates commonly place the leopard population in Africa at about 700,000 and in India at about 10,000, but some scientists believe that these estimates are flawed and inaccurate. The leopard is also not currently found in almost 40 percent of its historic habitat in Africa and more than half of its historic habitat in Asia.

History and conservation measures

Threats to the leopard's survival include the continued loss of habitat and fragmentation (breaking up of habitat into smaller areas that no longer border each other), competition for prey with humans, and being killed by humans. Like most spotted cats, the leopard has been a victim of the fur trade. Although global treaties protect the leopard, poachers (illegal hunters) still hunt the animal to sell on the international market. In Africa, it is legal to hunt leopards for sport and they have protection only in national parks, where they are considered a tourist attraction.

Contact between humans and leopards has not favored the animals. As more and more of their habitat has been converted to farmland and ranch land, leopards have been forced to prey on domestic livestock. In response, farmers and ranchers have actively sought to poison the animals.

Various plans to prevent the endangerment of leopards as a species include: integrate the needs of leopards and local peoples and livestock; expand and enforce protected zones to provide areas large enough to support a healthy leopard population; and increase legal protections, with stronger laws on the illegal trade of leopard skins or other hunting "trophies."

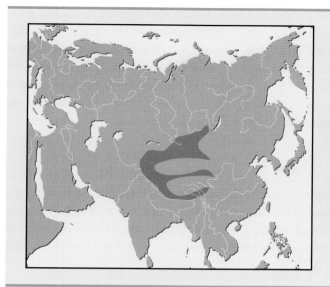

Leopard, snow
Panthera uncia (also *Uncia uncia*)

PHYLUM: Chordata
CLASS: Mammalia
ORDER: Carnivora
FAMILY: Felidae
STATUS: Endangered, IUCN
Endangered, ESA
RANGE: Afghanistan, Bhutan, China, India, Kazakhstan, Kyrgyzstan, Mongolia, Nepal, Pakistan, Russia, Tajikistan, Uzbekistan

Leopard, snow
Panthera uncia (also *Uncia uncia*)

Description and biology

The snow leopard, or ounce, has a beautiful coat of long, pale gray fur with white underneath. Its coat is patterned with solid black spots on its head and legs and dark gray rosettes (rings) on the rest of its body. Although it is called a leopard, it is most closely related to the tiger (*Panthera tigris*). An average snow leopard has a head and body length of 48 to 56 inches (122 to 142 centimeters) and weighs 132 to 165 pounds (60 to 75 kilograms). Its heavy, thickly furred tail measures 32 to 40 inches (81 to 102 centimeters). The snow leopard has thick chest muscles for climbing and large, heavily padded forepaws for walking through snow. An excellent leaper, the animal can jump as far as 50 feet (15 meters) in a single bound.

Snow leopards usually hunt at dusk or at night. Although their preferred prey is the bharal (a goatlike mammal), they also hunt yaks, marmots, musk deer, and domestic livestock. An individual snow leopard's home range extends from 5 to 15 square miles (13 to 39 square kilometers).

Like other big cats, snow leopards are solitary animals. Males and females come together only to mate in late winter. After a gestation (pregnancy) period of 98 to 103 days, a female snow leopard gives birth to one to four cubs. The cubs nurse for at least two months and remain dependent on their mother for up to a year.

Habitat and current distribution

Snow leopards inhabit mountain ranges in central Asia. Their potential range could cover as much as 1,158,000 square miles (3 million square kilometers), most of which are in China. It is not clear, however, how much of this area snow leopards actually use. Wherever they are found,

The snow leopard faces various regional threats throughout the mountains of central Asia where it is found, including the depletion of its prey, poaching, and war. © ALAN JEFFERY/SHUTTERSTOCK.COM.

these rare and endangered animals exist in only sparse populations. Scientists estimated in 2003 that there were between 4,080 and 6,590 mature snow leopards in the wild; they also estimated, however, that only about half of that population was successfully reproducing. So the species' numbers are thought to be declining.

Snow leopards are normally found in dry alpine (above the tree line of high mountains) and subalpine regions above 9,840 feet (3,000 meters). During summer months, when their prey moves to higher pastures, snow leopards may climb to an altitude of 13,000 feet (3,960 meters).

History and conservation measures

Along with other spotted cats, the snow leopard has long been hunted for its prized coat. Although current international treaties protect the animal, poachers (illegal hunters) still hunt down snow leopards and sell the hide or bones illegally. Because some of the animal's habitat is not easy to reach, officials have a difficult time enforcing the snow leopard's protective rights.

Snow leopards are also threatened by human development. As human populations have grown in the region and snow leopard habitat has been converted into agricultural land for livestock, the animal's traditional prey has become scarce. Forced to feed on domestic animals, the snow leopard has become a target for angry farm and ranch owners. Livestock can make up as much as 58 percent of the snow leopard's diet in some areas, creating serious tensions between herders and the cats.

In addition, much of the snow leopard's range is in border areas where there is political turmoil. This makes treaty agreements on conservation difficult. Military activity can also endanger leopards.

In 2008 scientists mapped out the snow leopard's range and were able to highlight areas where conservation is needed. Still, conservation remains a challenge. Unless large areas of its natural habitat are preserved, the snow leopard will continue to be in jeopardy.

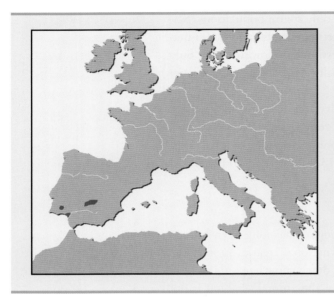

Lynx, Iberian
Lynx pardinus (also *Felis pardina*)

PHYLUM:	Chordata
CLASS:	Mammalia
ORDER:	Carnivora
FAMILY:	Felidae
STATUS:	Endangered, IUCN Endangered, ESA
RANGE:	Portugal, Spain

Lynx, Iberian
Lynx pardinus (also *Felis pardina*)

Description and biology

The Iberian lynx, also known as the Spanish lynx, has been called the most endangered wild cat species in the world. Between 2002 and 2015, when it was downlisted to endangered status, it had been listed as critically endangered by the International Union for Conservation of Nature and Natural Resources (IUCN). There are two types of lynx in Europe: the Iberian lynx and the Eurasian lynx. Iberian lynx are about half the size of Eurasian lynx, with females weighing about 20 pounds (9 kilograms) and males 29 pounds (13 kilograms). Their body length is between 30 and 40 inches (75 and 100 centimeters), and their height ranges from 18 to 28 inches (45 to 70 centimeters) at the shoulder. Iberian lynx are spotted and dark yellow or brown, with short tails and black tufts of fur at the tops of their ears.

Iberian lynx are solitary animals. Each individual, male and female, has its own home range, an area it knows thoroughly and patrols on a regular basis but does not necessarily defend. Within its home range, the lynx lives within a smaller specific territory, which may range in size from 2.5 to 6 miles (4 to 9.5 kilometers) in diameter, which it does defend from other lynx. Iberian lynx are nocturnal (active at night). In winter, their fur grows thicker, and they remain active, taking shelter in caves or trees when the weather is severe. Having keen senses of vision and smell, the Iberian lynx is a good hunter. Its diet consists almost exclusively of rabbits but may also include small deer, other small mammals, and ducks. When the lynx kills its prey, it drags it away to eat elsewhere, burying anything that is left over for the next day's meal.

Female lynx generally have only one mate per season; males may have more than one. Females give birth to two or three offspring at a time. The mother stays with her young until she mates again the next year. The offspring will then remain within the mother's territory for about another year before going off to establish their own territory. Iberian lynx have a life span of about 13 years.

Habitat and current distribution

Iberian lynx live in southern Spain and southern Portugal. They inhabit woodlands or other areas of dense vegetation (plant life) near

The Iberian lynx has experienced population growth in the early 21st century through conservation programs and other efforts after decades of hunting and trapping decimated its numbers in the wild. © ROLAND SEITRE/MINDEN PICTURES/CORBIS.

Did You Know?

As cars speed along busy Spanish highways, Iberian lynx can cross safely underneath in tunnels built for them. Such wildlife passages, both over and under roads, have saved the lives of many animals. In the United States, passageways have been built for endangered animals such as desert tortoises, jumping mice, Florida panthers, and black bears, as well as more common animals such as deer and moose. Wildlife passages do more than just save animals' lives. They allow animals to reach resources such as food and water and to mate with animals on the other side of the road.

Experts design wildlife passages carefully. Fences, walls, boulders, and trees are used to channel animals into the tunnels. Until animals become accustomed to using a new passageway, conservationists (people who work to manage and protect nature) may place food near it to lure animals inside. Some animals prefer lighted tunnels, others dark ones; animals with hooves seem to prefer overpasses. By studying how animals use passages already built, experts can design new ones that work even better.

open pastures where they can hunt for rabbits. In 2002 biologists (people who study living organisms) estimated that only 52 mature lynx remained. By 2012 the population had grown to 156 mature lynx, and in 2014 to a total of 327 lynx. The animal also occupies three times the area it did in 2002.

History and conservation measures

Iberian lynx lived throughout Spain and Portugal for centuries, particularly in cork oak forests. Several major threats have reduced the cat's population. The biggest problem is that the population of rabbits, the lynx's main food, has decreased greatly because of disease. Also, humans have built roads, railways, dams, and other structures within the species' habitat. This has not only reduced the lynx's range but also separated groups of lynx from each other. This can be harmful because smaller groups of animals have lower genetic diversity (variety of biological units that pass on inherited traits), which can make them less healthy. Lynx also are killed by motor vehicles on roads. Finally, people have hunted the animals for their fur and meat.

Biologists and conservationists (people who work to manage and protect nature) have worked hard to increase the Iberian lynx population. They have successfully bred animals in captivity and then released them into the wild. Conservationists are increasing the population of rabbits by improving their habitat. They have also purchased land where lynx live, enforced laws against hunting lynx, educated people about this cat's importance, and even built tunnels under busy roads where lynx have been killed, providing safe passageways. In Portugal the lynx had completely disappeared sometime in the 20th century, but it was reintroduced to Guadiana Valley Natural Park in 2014. These successes allowed the IUCN to change the Iberian lynx's status from critically endangered to endangered in 2015.

Threats still remain, however. Conservationists have determined that captive breeding must continue to help the species' survival. The rabbit population has collapsed further, with disease killing up to 90 percent of the rabbits in the lynx's habitat in 2013 and 2014. Climate change also poses a severe threat. Rabbits, the lynx's food source, eat certain plants whose numbers may decrease because climate change causes warmer temperatures and less rainfall. With fewer plants, fewer rabbits will survive, imperiling the lynx. Still, conservationists are cautiously optimistic about the future of this species.

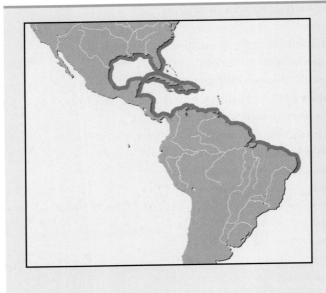

Manatee, West Indian
Trichechus manatus

PHYLUM: Chordata
CLASS: Mammalia
ORDER: Sirenia
FAMILY: Trichechidae
STATUS: Vulnerable, IUCN
Endangered, ESA
RANGE: Bahamas, Belize, Brazil, Cayman Islands, Colombia, Costa Rica, Cuba, Curaçao, Dominican Republic, French Guiana, Guatemala, Guyana, Haiti, Honduras, Jamaica, Lesser Antilles islands, Mexico, Nicaragua, Panama, Puerto Rico, Suriname, USA (Alabama, Florida, Georgia, Louisiana, Mississippi, North Carolina, South Carolina, Texas), Venezuela

Manatee, West Indian
Trichechus manatus

Description and biology

The West Indian manatee, also known as the Florida manatee, is a large marine mammal, with a rounded, heavy gray body and a horizontally flattened tail. An average West Indian manatee has a combined body and tail length of 8 to 13 feet (2.4 to 4 meters) and weighs 800 to 3,500 pounds (360 to 1,590 kilograms). It has small eyes and no ear pinnas (external flaplike portions). The animal's nostrils are on the upper surface of its snout and can be tightly closed by valves when the manatee is underwater. Manatees often rest just below the water's surface, coming up to breathe every 15 or 20 minutes. They use their flexible flippers almost like hands for eating, moving through sea grass, touching, holding a nursing calf, and even hugging other manatees.

Manatees are the only marine mammals that feed solely on vegetation (plant life). They eat a variety of aquatic plants, including wa-

The West Indian manatee, found in the tropical waters of the Atlantic Ocean, is put at risk by boat traffic, changes in water temperature, severe weather, and growing human populations near its habitat.
© GARY POWELL/SHUTTER-STOCK.COM.

ter hyacinths, hydrillas, and sea grasses. Manatees are often called "sea cows" because they graze on marine sea grass meadows. They use their split upper lip to grasp food and pull it into their mouths. Primarily a nocturnal (at night) feeder, manatees can consume up to 100 pounds (45 kilograms) of food a day.

Manatees have no particular breeding season, but most births seem to occur in spring and early summer. After a gestation (pregnancy) period of 13 months, a female manatee gives birth to one calf, which is about 4 feet (1.2 meters) long and weighs approximately 60 pounds (27 kilograms). Even though it begins grazing on vegetation within a few months, the calf continues to nurse from its mother for one to two years. Because mothers only give birth to one calf every two to five years, reproduction rates are low.

Habitat and current distribution

The West Indian manatee is found in the coastal waters and rivers of Florida and Georgia and occasionally other states in the southeastern United States. It is also found on the coasts of Central America and the West Indies. It prefers to inhabit slow-moving rivers, river mouths, bays, lagoons, coves, and other shallow coastal areas. It is at home in all types of water environments: fresh, brackish (slightly salty), and salt. The manatee requires warm water and will migrate great distances between winter and summer grounds.

The estimated population of West Indian manatees worldwide is under 5,000 animals as of 2014.

History and conservation measures

Native Americans hunted manatees for centuries, using the animals' flesh, bones (for medicine), and hide (for leather). When Spanish explorers began colonizing Caribbean islands in the 16th century, manatee hunting increased. Biologists (people who study living organisms) believe this hunting is responsible for the manatee's initial decline.

The greatest continued threat to manatees comes from humans. Many manatees drown each year from being trapped in fishing nets. Others are drowned or crushed by floodgates or canal locks. Some are injured by discarded fishing lines, hooks, and trash. The majority of manatee deaths in Florida are caused by collisions with speeding boats. Those animals that survive such collisions bear lifelong propeller scars.

In 1978 the Florida legislature designated the entire state as a refuge and sanctuary for the animal, and in 1989 key counties along the coast of Florida were directed to reduce manatee injuries and deaths. Manatee protection zones have been established in which boats are required to reduce their speed. In areas declared manatee refuges, no boats, swimmers, or divers are allowed. In other countries in the West Indian manatee's range, public education programs have been launched to raise awareness about the animal's plight. The number of manatees may be increasing slowly. As of 2014 the U.S. Fish and Wildlife Service is investigating whether the species' status may be upgraded to threatened from endangered.

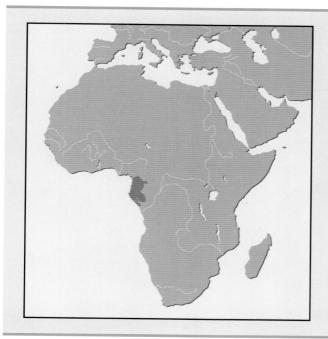

Mandrill
Mandrillus sphinx

PHYLUM: Chordata
CLASS: Mammalia
ORDER: Primates
FAMILY: Cercopithecidae
STATUS: Vulnerable, IUCN
Endangered, ESA
RANGE: Cameroon, Equatorial
Guinea, Gabon, Republic of the Congo

Mandrill
Mandrillus sphinx

Description and biology

Related to the baboon, the mandrill is the largest member of the monkey family. An average male has a head and body length of 31 inches (79 centimeters), a shoulder height of 20 inches (51 centimeters), and a tail length of 3 inches (8 centimeters). It weighs 119 pounds (54 kilograms). Females are considerably smaller.

Male mandrills are considered the most colorful of all mammals. Although the animal's body fur is mainly dark brown, its bare areas (face and buttocks) are dazzlingly colored. Bright blue ridges line its face on either side of its nose. Its doglike muzzle is bright red. Black fur surrounds its close-set, yellow-brown eyes. Its beard and the edges of its mane are pale yellow. The pads on its buttocks are bright red, blue, and purple. The coloring on females and infants is not as brilliant.

The mandrill is under threat because of the destruction of its forest habitat in western central Africa and because it is hunted for its meat. © NAGEL PHOTOGRAPHY/SHUTTERSTOCK.COM.

Mandrills are active during the day, foraging for fruits, buds, leaves, roots, insects, fungi, and seeds. When food is scarce, the animals sometimes raid crops from nearby farms and plantations. At night, they sleep in trees.

Social animals, mandrills form groups of 20 to 40 members headed by a single male. The home range of a single group may be between 12 and 19 square miles (31 and 48 square kilometers). Little is known about the mandrill's reproductive habits. Most female mandrills give birth between December and April after a gestation (pregnancy) period of about 170 days.

Habitat and current distribution

Mandrills are found in the tropical forests and thick bush areas in central west Africa, south of the Sanaga River and west of the Ogooué and Ivindo Rivers.

Since mandrills avoid contact with humans, they are difficult to observe in the wild. Biologists (people who study living organisms) are, therefore, unsure of the total number currently in existence. Scientists believe there may be as few as 3,000 mandrills alive in the wild.

History and conservation measures

The mandrill population has drastically declined due to habitat destruction and hunting. It is relatively easy to hunt mandrills because they emit loud calls. Hunters sometimes use dogs to chase the animals up trees before shooting them down.

Local populations hunt the mandrill for food or because they are considered pests in all countries in its range. Much of the animal's forest habitat has been logged for its timber or cleared to create farmland. Although the animal is found in several reserves, it receives little protection because hunting, logging, and the building of settlements continues to take place within many of these areas.

Mandrills bred in captivity have been successfully released into the wild. In the United States there are about 100 mandrills in captivity. There is a breeding program in zoos internationally that aims to increase the genetic diversity of animals in the wild, but finding successful mating pairs has been difficult. When there are too few mating pairs, offspring must mate with relatives for the species to survive. This results in less genetic diversity, and subsequent offspring can be more likely to suffer from genetic disease.

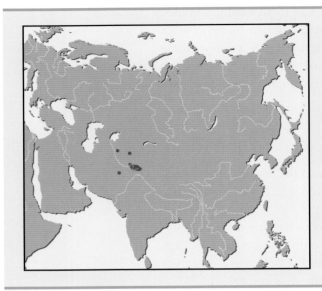

Markhor
Capra falconeri

PHYLUM: Chordata
CLASS: Mammalia
ORDER: Artiodactyla
FAMILY: Bovidae
STATUS: Near threatened, IUCN Threatened, ESA (*Capra falconeri megaceros* subspecies only)
RANGE: Afghanistan, India, Pakistan, Tajikistan, Turkmenistan, Uzbekistan

Markhor
Capra falconeri

Description and biology

The markhor is one of the largest members of the goat family. An average markhor has a head and body length of 55 to 73 inches (140 to 186 centimeters) and a shoulder height of 26 to 40 inches (66 to 102 centimeters). Its tail measures 3 to 5.5 inches (7.5 to 14 centimeters). The animal may weigh between 70 and 240 pounds (32 and 109 kilograms). Males are substantially larger than females.

Male markhors have unique corkscrew-shaped horns that are very thick and heavy. They also have a large beard and a long, shaggy mane at the base of their neck. If a female has a beard, which is rare, it is small. The coat of both sexes varies in length and color with the seasons. In the summer a markhor's coat is short and reddish brown. In the winter it is long, silky, and gray.

Markhors are active during the day, grazing on grasses and herbs or browsing (feeding on the tender shoots, twigs, and leaves) on shrubs and low trees. Wolves, leopards, and snow leopards often prey on the markhor.

Males generally live by themselves, while females and young live in groups of 10 to 12. During the winter mating season, males compete with each other over the right to mate with females. After a gestation

The markhor is found in Afghanistan, India, Pakistan, Tajikistan, Turkmenistan, and Uzbekistan. Threats to the animal in those regions include hunting and poaching, habitat loss, and war. © SOKOLOV ALEXEY/SHUTTERSTOCK.COM.

(pregnancy) period of about 155 days, a female markhor gives birth to one or two young.

Habitat and current distribution

Markhors inhabit rocky areas, open forested slopes, and meadows in the rugged mountains of central Asia. Their range extends from the western end of the Himalayas in northwestern India to southern Tajikistan and Uzbekistan.

There are three subspecies of the markhor, each with a more limited range. Only one of these three, the straight-horned markhor (*Capra falconeri megaceros*), is listed as threatened by the U.S. Fish and Wildlife Service (USFWS). The straight-horned markhor is found primarily in Afghanistan and Pakistan. The other two subspecies are the Bukharan markhor (*Capra falconeri heptneri*), which is found in Afghanistan, Turkmenistan, Tajikistan, and Uzbekistan, and the Astor markhor (*Capra falconeri falconeri*), which lives in Afghanistan, India, and Pakistan.

Overall markhor population numbers are uncertain but appear to be on the rise, at least in some areas. For example, in the Torghar Hills of Pakistan, scientists had estimated a population of only around 200 markhors until a 2011 estimate put numbers in that region at 2,829 individuals. In 2014 the USFWS estimated the number there to be over 3,500.

History and conservation measures

Excessive hunting, primarily for the markhor's horns, is the main reason for the animal's decline. As the human population increases in the markhor's range, so does the destruction of its habitat. Trees are cut down for timber, forested land is cleared to create agricultural land, and domestic sheep and goats compete with markhors for food.

Twenty-seven protected areas have been established in the markhor's range. The level of safety in these areas, however, is limited by political unrest and military activity in the region. In addition, most markhor populations are very small and often isolated from each other, making conservation efforts difficult.

Despite these challenges, there have been successful markhor conservation projects. Hunting has been restricted or outlawed in many countries, including Pakistan. The Torghar Conservation Project has also been successful in improving the habitat of both the markhor and domestic livestock owned by nearby herders, while also providing conservation jobs to local people. Funds from the program have been used to pay for game wardens, to build wells, and to purchase medical and veterinary supplies.

The success of markhor conservation efforts led the USFWS to reclassify the markhor from endangered to threatened in 2014, under the Endangered Species Act. The IUCN likewise changed the markhor's status from endangered to near threatened in 2015.

Marmoset, white-eared
Callithrix aurita

PHYLUM: Chordata
CLASS: Mammalia
ORDER: Primates
FAMILY: Callitrichidae
STATUS: Vulnerable, IUCN
Endangered, ESA
RANGE: Brazil

Marmoset, white-eared
Callithrix aurita

Description and biology

The white-eared marmoset, also known as the buffy tufted-ear marmoset, is a small monkey, about 7 to 9 inches (18 to 23 centimeters) long without the tail and weighing only about 10.5 to 17.6 ounces (300 to 500 grams). The white-eared marmoset is a member of the Callitrichidae family, which includes 26 species of marmosets and tamarins from the tropical forests of Central and South America. They are some of the world's smallest primates.

The white-eared marmoset is black with white spots on the forehead and tail and very long, white hair coming out of its ears. The species is diurnal (active during the day) and arboreal (lives in trees). Its diet consists of fruit and insects, such as ants, termites, and caterpillars, and some small animals. It has claws instead of nails on its fingers and toes

Did You Know?

The Atlantic Forest in Brazil is home to thousands of unique plant and animal species. The forest teems with life and has an extraordinarily high level of biodiversity (variety of life-forms). In fact, 8,000 of the 20,000 plant species found in this forest exist nowhere else on Earth. The luxuriant growth is due to tiny microorganisms, or fungi, from which the plant life gets its nutrients. When farmers clear portions of the rain forest to make room for agricultural crops such as coffee, cocoa, sugarcane, or soybeans, these crops grow well at first. But after the land has been cleared, the fungi that feeds the vegetation (plant life) dies, and the soil is too poor to keep up the harvests for long. The farmers then have to clear more land in order to grow better crops.

Over several centuries, the Atlantic Forest has been reduced to just 8 percent of its original land area. The forest has not been cleared for agricultural crops alone. Cattle ranching is common and requires large areas of land to be cleared for grazing. Trees are cut for their timber and to make way for growing cities and suburban areas. The reduction and fragmentation (breaking up into smaller areas that no longer border each other) of habitat represents a threat to the survival of many of the unique plant and animal species in this forest.

for climbing trees. It moves about on all four limbs when on the ground. The white-eared marmoset can also leap through the forest canopy (the uppermost layer of a forest).

The white-eared marmoset is a social animal. It usually lives in a small group consisting of 2 to 13 members. Each group has its own territory, which may be 1 to 13 acres (0.4 to 5.3 hectares) in diameter. The group sleeps together in the branches of a tree or in dense vegetation (plant life) on the ground. The white-eared marmoset is monogamous—males and females remain partners for life. Living groups are centered around one dominant monogamous couple; other members tend to come and go over time. Only the dominant female in the group breeds. She will give birth to one to four offspring—usually twins—after a gestation (pregnancy) period of 140 to 148 days. The young are then raised cooperatively by the members of the living group. Males as well as females care for the young in this family arrangement. Marmosets' life spans are about 11 to 17 years.

The white-eared marmoset has several means of communication. It makes high-pitched trills to signal alarm. It opens and closes its mouth, making a lip-smacking sound, to initiate sexual behavior or to convey aggression. Sometimes it puts its tongue in and out of its mouth

The white-eared marmoset, already a rare species, is at risk because of the destruction of its Brazilian rain forest habitat. © CLAUS MEYER/MINDEN PICTURES/CORBIS.

rhythmically along with the lip smacking. When threatened, it will raise its eyebrows. Scent is also used by a female to mark a male before mating takes place.

Habitat and current distribution

The white-eared marmoset has the southernmost range of all marmosets. It occurs in coastal mountain rain forest regions above 3,000 feet (914 meters) in altitude along the Atlantic coastline of southeastern Brazil. The area includes parts of Minas Gerais, Rio de Janeiro, and São Paulo. Marmosets in the wild are difficult for humans to observe, and their current population numbers are not known.

History and conservation measures

The largest threat to the white-eared marmoset is deforestation (large-scale removal of trees) in the Brazilian rain forests and tropical forests. Brazil's Atlantic rain forest region has long been home to hundreds of thousands of species. It is a huge area of more than a half million square miles. In the last five centuries, however, the area has been overwhelmed by an overflowing human population. Into the 1970s the Brazilian government promoted clearing the forests to harvest the lumber and to make way for sugar, coffee, and cocoa plantations, cattle grazing, and industry. As a result, nearly 93 percent of the natural forests and wilderness have been lost.

White-eared marmosets live, therefore, in small, fragmented (broken up) areas. They are at risk from human capture as well, as they are prized as pets in Europe and elsewhere, and they are used for testing in medical and scientific laboratories. During the 1990s, with severely declining populations, it appeared that the white-eared marmoset would be extinct within 20 years. Breeding-in-captivity programs were thought to be the greatest hope for the preservation of the species.

Beginning in the 1980s the Brazilian government changed its policies. Concerned citizen groups have made a tremendous difference in conservation efforts. Marmosets are now protected by the government, and cutting down the rain forests has been prohibited. A number of protected areas provide habitats for the white-eared marmoset in Minas Gerais, Rio de Janeiro, and São Paulo. With many organizations and private citizens working on behalf of the tiny primates, there was reason to hope that the marmoset populations were on the road to recovery in the early 21st century. In 2008 the International Union for Conservation of Nature and Natural Resources (IUCN) downlisted the status of the white-eared marmoset from endangered to vulnerable. However, a potential new threat is interbreeding of the vulnerable species with non-native marmosets. When two different but related species mate, their hybrid offspring carry a combination of genetic traits from each of their parent species. If this happens too often, there will be fewer and fewer offspring that can be considered white-eared marmosets, and the species could interbreed itself out of existence.

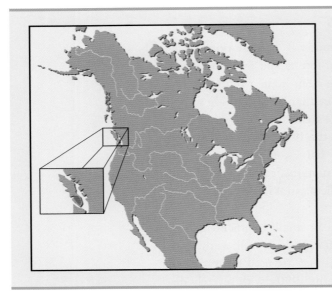

Marmot, Vancouver Island
Marmota vancouverensis

PHYLUM: Chordata
CLASS: Mammalia
ORDER: Rodentia
FAMILY: Sciuridae
STATUS: Critically endangered, IUCN
Endangered, ESA
RANGE: Canada (Vancouver Island)

Marmot, Vancouver Island
Marmota vancouverensis

Description and biology

Marmots are ground-living rodents of the squirrel family, closely related
to the chipmunk, ground squirrel, and prairie dog. The groundhog or
woodchuck is the best-known North American marmot species. The
Vancouver Island marmot has coarse fur and a bushy tail 4 to 10 inches
(10 to 25 centimeters) long. Its deep-brown coat is darker than that of
most marmots. An average Vancouver Island marmot has a head and
body length of 12 to 23.5 inches (30 to 60 centimeters) and weighs between 6.5 and 16.5 pounds (3 and 7.5 kilograms).

Vancouver Island marmots feed on plants, especially flowering parts.
They hibernate (spend the winter in an inactive state) for seven months in
a den, huddled together in a family group of about eight members. Male
and female Vancouver Island marmots mate after emerging from hibernation, usually in April or May. After a gestation (pregnancy) period of four
to five weeks, a female marmot gives birth to a litter of two to six young.

The Vancouver Island marmot is the target of conservation and protection programs that include captive breeding in order to increase its population.
© ALL CANADA PHOTOS/ALAMY.

Habitat and current distribution

This species of marmot is found only on Vancouver Island, off the southwest coast of British Columbia, Canada, and near the coast of Washington State. It inhabits the higher regions of the coastal mountains that mark the central and southern parts of the island. In 2011 there were 320 to 380 of these marmots living in the wild.

These marmots prefer to inhabit steep, rocky slopes and open meadows at elevations between 3,280 and 6,560 feet (1,000 and 2,000 meters).

History and conservation measures

The Vancouver Island marmot was discovered in 1911. Since that time, its population has declined. The 1990s brought a population crash for the animals, and in 1998 only 70 of these marmots remained. Biologists (people who study living organisms) are not sure of the reasons for the decline but a probable cause is logging activity, which reduced the habitat area for the animals. After trees were cut down, the Vancouver Island marmots moved into the newly treeless areas, but those living in these areas have lower survival rates than those in their original habitat. The Vancouver Island marmots' biggest threat is being eaten by predators, especially wolves, cougars, and golden eagles. The population of these predators has greatly increased since 1980.

In 2004 the population of Vancouver Island marmots had declined by more than 80 percent in the previous 18 years, and only 35 such marmots were alive in the wild. The situation began to improve with the help of a nonprofit group. The Vancouver Island Marmot Recovery Foundation has led efforts to save the species, joined by the Canadian government and local landowners. The group's three goals are to monitor the Vancouver Island marmot population, breed these marmots in captivity, and restore the population in the wild. The first two steps have been successful. Vancouver Island marmots bred in captivity and released were surviving and breeding. The group aims to have 400 to 600 Vancouver Island marmots living in three separate areas on the island by 2020.

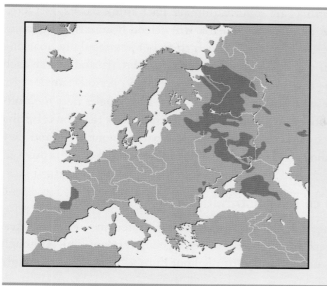

Mink, European
Mustela lutreola

PHYLUM: Chordata
CLASS: Mammalia
ORDER: Carnivora
FAMILY: Mustelidae
STATUS: Critically endangered, IUCN
RANGE: France, Romania, Russia, Spain, Ukraine

Mink, European
Mustela lutreola

Description and biology

Minks belong to the weasel family, which also includes ermines, skunks, martens, wolverines, and otters. There are two types of mink within the family, the European and the American mink. The European mink, now very rare, is smaller than the American and has a wide white area around its mouth. European minks have blackish-brown to light-brown fur. They molt (change their fur) twice a year. Males weigh about 1.6 pounds (740 grams) and females weigh about 1 pound (440 grams). Minks live near water. They have partly webbed feet that aid them in swimming and diving. They are nocturnal (active at night) creatures that hunt on ground and under water for their food. Their diet consists of small mammals, birds, frogs, mollusks, crabs, fish, and insects. They have a keen sense of smell that helps in their hunting. European minks live in burrows taken from water voles (small, semiaquatic rodents) or among the roots of trees.

European minks are solitary animals. Each mink has its own territory near a river or a stream, which it will defend from intruding members of its species. The minks check their borders regularly, marking them with their scent. Mating takes place in February and March each year. After a 5- to 10-week gestation (pregnancy) period, females give birth to two to seven young in April or May. The females raise their offspring for the first 3 or 4 months of their lives. After that the offspring go off on their own. They are mature at about 10 months old and they generally live about 6 years in the wild, and up to 12 years in captivity.

Habitat and current distribution

European minks live on the banks of fresh waterways, such as lakes, creeks, and rivers, where there is heavy vegetation (plant life). Although the species was once common throughout Europe, today it exists mainly

The European mink, which once could be found across most of Europe, is now limited to small patches of Spain, France, Romania, Ukraine, and Russia due to habitat loss and competition with the American mink. © WILDLIFE GMBH/ALAMY.

in parts of Russia and a few other eastern European countries, where it is rapidly declining. In 2006 scientists estimated there were 20,000 European minks in Russia, although this may be far higher than the actual number, according to the International Union for Conservation of Nature and Natural Resources (IUCN).

Small populations of minks can be found in France—a 2006 study found several hundred in the country. Conservation efforts have also helped to create a stable population in Spain along the Mediterranean Sea. In 2003 researchers estimated the total Spanish population of European minks as being between 500 and 1,000 animals.

History and conservation measures

The European mink is threatened chiefly by destruction of its habitat. It has also been damaged by overhunting; mink are highly valued for their fur.

The mink's valuable fur has threatened it in other ways as well. When the number of European minks declined, fur farmers imported American mink into the European mink's native areas. Since its introduction in 1926, various American mink have escaped from farms and entered the wild. There they have outcompeted the European mink, pushing the species further toward extinction.

The European mink range has been reduced by more than 85 percent since the mid-1800s. Since the 1990s predictions of the extinction of the species have motivated numerous conservation efforts to preserve the European mink in the wild and to breed it in captivity. Crucial to the survival of the species is the protection of its original habitats in Russia, France, and Spain, along with the creation of new habitats and conservation areas. Efforts are under way to remove the population of American mink in the wild in some European areas. In Spain, in particular, reduction of American mink populations have helped to stabilize the numbers of European mink. However, overall, the population of European mink is declining and extinction in part or all of its remaining range is a possibility.

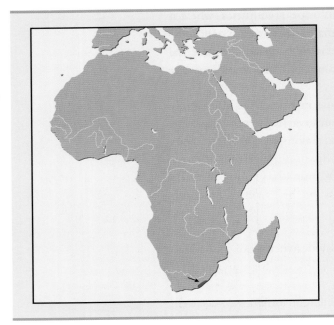

Mole, giant golden
Chrysospalax trevelyani

PHYLUM: Chordata
CLASS: Mammalia
ORDER: Afrosoricida
FAMILY: Chrysochloridae
STATUS: Endangered, IUCN
RANGE: South Africa

Mole, giant golden
Chrysospalax trevelyani

Description and biology

There are 17 species of golden moles, all found in Africa. The giant golden mole, the largest, rarest, and most endangered of the golden moles, is about 8 inches (20 centimeters) long and weighs as much as 19 ounces (538 grams). Its fur is shiny and reddish brown. Giant golden moles have tiny eyes that are covered by skin, making them blind. Their ears, too, are tiny and hidden in fur.

The giant golden mole spends most of its time below ground, where it digs systems of tunnels. It builds hills in the ground that serve as doors into its underground chambers. The giant golden mole eats crickets, cockroaches, grasshoppers, worms, snails, and other invertebrates. One of the items on its diet is the giant earthworm, found only in South Africa and the longest known species of earthworm in the world at 4 or 5 feet (1.5 meters) long. The giant golden mole rarely comes up from underground, except when heavy rains wash out its tunnels and force it to the surface. At these times, the mole is particularly vulnerable to dogs. The giant golden mole hibernates in winter, burrowing among the roots of trees. It moves slowly but stays in motion all the time it is awake in order to keep its body temperature normal. When it sleeps, its body twitches to maintain its body temperature. A mother giant golden mole generally gives birth to two, but sometimes only one, offspring at a time.

Habitat and current distribution

The giant golden mole is native to the forests of the Eastern Cape Province of South Africa, where it was known to have lived in 17 areas. However, it is now believed to be extinct in most of its former range and to remain only in groups along the eastern slopes of the Amathole Mountains in South Africa that are fragmented (broken into smaller areas that no longer border each other). Because these moles are so rare and remain underground and hidden most of the time, they are difficult to study. Wildlife biologists (people who study living organisms in the wild) do not know how many giant golden moles remain in the world today.

History and conservation measures

Most of the giant golden mole's natural habitat forests have been cut down and replaced with plantations. Although South Africa has sought to protect the indigenous forests, these areas are often under the control of tribal chiefs.

The primary threat to the giant golden mole's habitat is ongoing deforestation (large-scale removal of trees). Stripping bark from trees for traditional medicines (health practices used by specific cultures since before the time of modern medicine), cutting down trees for firewood, controlled burning of unprotected sections of forest, tourism, and urbanization all contribute to the reduction of forest area where the animal may live. Other threats to the giant golden mole include cattle, which may trample and damage habitats, and hunting by people and wild dogs.

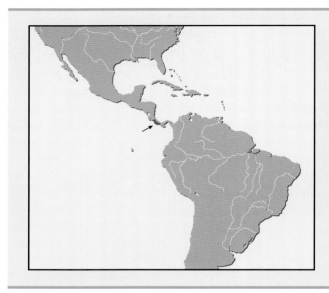

**Monkey, Central American
squirrel**
Saimiri oerstedii

PHYLUM: Chordata
CLASS: Mammalia
ORDER: Primates
FAMILY: Cebidae
STATUS: Vulnerable, IUCN
Endangered, ESA
RANGE: Costa Rica, Panama

Monkey, Central American squirrel
Saimiri oerstedii

Description and biology

The Central American squirrel monkey is also known as the red-backed squirrel monkey because of the short, thick, reddish fur covering its back, limbs, and tail. The face and chest are white or yellowish, and the animal has a black or dark-gray crown atop its head. An average Central American squirrel monkey has a head and body length of 9 to 14 inches (23 to 36 centimeters) and weighs between 1 and 2.4 pounds (0.5 and 1.1 kilograms). The tail, which is not prehensile (adapted for grasping or holding, especially by wrapping around something), measures 14 to 18 inches (36 to 46 centimeters) long.

The Central American squirrel monkey spends most of its time in trees and feeds on fruit and insects. Groups of 20 to 70 monkeys live together, often combining with other groups to form very large societies.

The Central American squirrel monkey, native to Costa Rica and Panama, has seen its habitat affected by logging and agriculture activities. © EDUARDO RIVERO/SHUTTERSTOCK.COM.

Some groups inhabit forest areas as small as 2 acres (0.8 hectares). Others may occupy as much as 50 to 100 acres (20 to 40 hectares).

Males and females breed in September. Males do not fight over mating rights; the females choose their mates, preferring the biggest males. Thus, at the beginning of breeding season, males will put on extra weight to become temporarily larger to attract females. After a gestation (pregnancy) period of seven months, a female Central American squirrel monkey gives birth to a single infant. It clings to its mother after birth and remains dependent on her for almost a year.

Habitat and current distribution

Central American squirrel monkeys are found only on and near the Pacific coast of Costa Rica and Panama. One subspecies, *Saimiri oerstedii*

oerstedii (the black-crowned Central American squirrel monkey), lives in southern Costa Rica and the western Pacific coast portion of Panama. The other subspecies, *Saimiri oerstedii citrinellus* (the gray-crowned Central American squirrel monkey), inhabits the coast of Costa Rica, in and near one national park. The animals prefer forests, woodlands, and areas dominated by shrubs and low, bushy trees. A 2006 study estimated that about 4,000 Central American squirrel monkeys remained.

History and conservation measures

The population of Central American squirrel monkeys has decreased greatly since the 1950s mainly because of deforestation (large-scale removal of trees). Much of the squirrel monkey's habitat has been converted to banana plantations, cattle ranches, and rice and sugarcane farms. The Panamanian government passed a land reform law in the 1950s that required landowners to make profitable use of their forested land or be forced to give up that land. As a result, forests—and squirrel monkey habitat—were destroyed to create moneymaking farms. A lesser threat has been capture for the pet trade or medical research. The Central American squirrel monkey was listed as "endangered" by the International Union for Conservation of Nature and Natural Resources (IUCN) in 1982.

However, the situation has improved for these animals. They are protected in many wildlife reserves throughout their range. Conservation groups have been working to reforest habitats and educate local residents about the species' importance. The rise of ecotourism (tourism aimed at raising awareness of environmental threats to the toured area) has been a boon for Central American squirrel monkeys and other species in Costa Rica. The country has benefited economically from such tourism, creating a reason to limit environmentally harmful development. As a result of these conservation efforts, the IUCN moved the species to the less serious "vulnerable" status in 2008.

Muriqui
Brachyteles spp. (both species)

PHYLUM: Chordata
CLASS: Mammalia
ORDER: Primates
FAMILY: Atelidae
STATUS: Endangered, IUCN
(*Brachyteles arachnoides*)
Critically endangered, IUCN
(*Brachyteles hypoxanthus*)
Endangered, ESA
(*Brachyteles arachnoides*)
RANGE: Brazil

Muriqui
Brachyteles spp. (both species)

Description and biology

The muriqui, or woolly spider monkey, is the largest species of New World (Western Hemisphere) monkey. It has an average head and body length of 18 to 25 inches (46 to 64 centimeters) and weighs between 26 and 33 pounds (12 and 15 kilograms). Its prehensile (adapted for grasping or holding, especially by wrapping around something) tail is 25 to 32 inches (64 to 81 centimeters) long, which is longer than its body. The animal's head is round and small in relation to its body. Its limbs are long. The fur on its body is thick and golden in color, and its face is black and hairless. There are two species of muriqui: the southern muriqui (*Brachyteles arachnoides*) and the northern muriqui (*Brachyteles hypoxanthus*). In most respects these species are quite similar, but the southern muriqui lacks a small thumb that is present in the northern species.

A muriqui rests on a branch in a forest in Brazil, where its already sparse population is threatened by hunters and the loss of habitat. © AGE FOTOSTOCK/ALAMY.

The muriqui lives in the crown of the tallest trees and has never been seen on the ground. It moves through the trees by swinging from branch to branch with its long arms. It feeds during the day on leaves, seeds, fruits, and insects.

Most muriquis form social groups of 2 to 4 members, although groups of up to 20 or more have been observed in the wild. Mating between males and females may take place at any time of year. After a gestation (pregnancy) period of four to five months, a female muriqui gives birth to a single infant.

Habitat and current distribution

The muriqui prefers to inhabit undisturbed tropical rain forests of the Brazilian coastal areas. The range of the southern muriqui is limited to the southeastern Brazilian states of São Paulo, Rio de Janeiro, and Paraná. Brazilian officials estimate that fewer than 2,000 southern muriquis remain in the wild.

As its name would suggest, the northern muriqui inhabits a range slightly farther north, but one that is still within the coastal forest. It can be found in the Brazilian states of Minas Gerais, Espírito Santo, and Bahia. The northern muriqui is classified as critically endangered by the International Union for Conservation of Nature and Natural Resources (IUCN), with fewer than 1,000 believed to exist in the wild, while the southern muriqui is classified as endangered.

History and conservation measures

Muriquis once ranged over all the Atlantic coastal forests of eastern and southeastern Brazil. Since the 1800s the human population in this region of Brazil has swelled enormously. To feed the growing numbers of people, large tracts of forest have been cleared over the years to provide pastureland for cattle and to create coffee, sugarcane, and cocoa plantations. Logging of these forest areas for their valuable timber has also taken its toll. Less than 7 percent of the species' original forest habitat remains in this region. Muriquis are also in increasing danger of being infected with deadly diseases because they have become more likely to have contact with humans, domestic animals, and polluted water.

In the past, muriquis were hunted for food. Although currently protected by law, they are still hunted for sport in some areas.

Small, isolated groups of the southern muriqui exist in protected conservation areas in the states of São Paulo and Rio de Janeiro. In 2010 Brazil prepared a national action plan to save the muriqui from extinction. Conservation programs are expected to raise public awareness of the threats to both species and provide more protection for the remaining populations. One goal is for the southern muriqui to be downlisted to vulnerable from endangered and the northern muriqui to be downlisted from critically endangered to endangered by 2020.

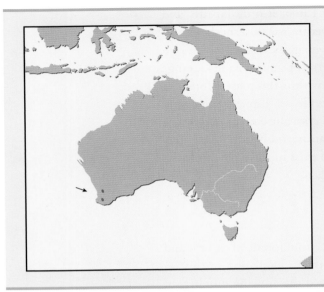

Numbat
Myrmecobius fasciatus

PHYLUM: Chordata
CLASS: Mammalia
ORDER: Dasyuromorphia
FAMILY: Myrmecobiidae
STATUS: Endangered, IUCN
Endangered, ESA
RANGE: Australia

Numbat
Myrmecobius fasciatus

Description and biology

The numbat, also known as the banded anteater, is a very unusual Australian marsupial. Marsupials are mammals whose young continue to develop after birth in a pouch on the outside of the mother's body. Most marsupials are nocturnal (active at night). The numbat, however, does not have a true pouch in which its young develop and is diurnal (active during the day).

Resembling a squirrel in size, an average numbat has a head and body length of 9 inches (23 centimeters) and a tail length of 7 inches (18 centimeters). It weighs between 14 and 21 ounces (397 and 595 grams). The numbat's coat is reddish brown with white flecks. A series of white stripes stretches across its back all the way to its bushy tail. A dark stripe runs across the animal's eye from its ear to its long, flattened snout.

The numbat feeds chiefly on termites. It uses its sharp-clawed forefeet to dig into termite colonies it finds in fallen branches. It then uses its long, sticky tongue to remove the termites, which it swallows whole. The animal has a home range of 50 to 120 acres (20 to 48 hectares). At night, numbats build a sheltering nest of leaves, grass, and bark in hollow logs or they dig burrows for themselves.

The normally solitary male and female numbat come together only to mate. A female numbat gives birth to four young, usually in January or February, after a gestation (pregnancy) period of about two weeks. Since the mother does not have a pouch, her young attach themselves to her nipples and cling to the surrounding hair. They stay attached for six months. Afterward, the female places her young in various nests she has built, moving them between those nests by carrying them on her back. The young numbats eventually leave their mother's home range by November or December.

The numbat, native to western Australia, is at risk of seeing its already small numbers decline because of predators and habitat losses. © FRANS LANTING/LATITUDE/CORBIS.

Habitat and current distribution

Numbats tend to live in forests dominated by eucalyptus trees that are prone to attack by termites. The animals are currently found only in southwestern Western Australia, in the Dryandra Woodland and Perup Nature Reserve. It is extremely difficult for humans to observe and count numbats. Biologists (people who study living organisms) estimate that fewer than 1,000 numbats exist in the wild; they fear that numbats may become extinct without effective conservation programs. The International Union for Conservation of Nature and Natural Resources (IUCN) changed the status of the numbat from vulnerable to endangered in 2008 because of a drastic decline in the Dryandra Woodland population.

History and conservation measures

The numbat once ranged throughout southern Australia. Slowly it began to disappear from eastern areas until, by the 1960s, it was found only in the southwestern region of the country. The numbat population continued to decline until 1980, when the Australian government realized that red foxes that had been introduced into numbat habitat were preying on the animals. Since then, the government has made attempts to control the number of foxes in the region and the numbat population has recovered slightly.

The Australian government is also trying to relocate numbats to their former eastern habitats. According to the government, releases of numbats into the open areas are usually not successful because the animals can be eaten by natural predators. However, numbats bred in captivity can be released in areas with no feral (once domesticated, now wild), nonnative animals, called exclosures. It is hoped that such exclosures will improve the chances for the numbat's survival and will also help other species that share the numbat's habitat.

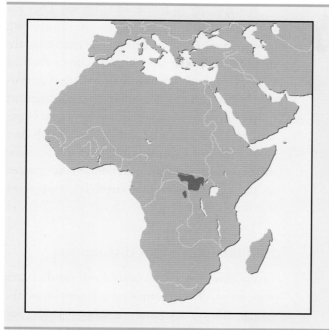

Okapi
Okapia johnstoni

PHYLUM: Chordata
CLASS: Mammalia
ORDER: Artiodactyla
FAMILY: Giraffidae
STATUS: Endangered, IUCN
RANGE: Democratic Republic of the Congo

Okapi
Okapia johnstoni

Description and biology

The only other member of the giraffe family, the okapi looks somewhat like a cross between a giraffe, a deer, and a zebra. Its forehead, long neck, and body are chocolate brown, and its upper legs have horizontal (side to side) white and black stripes. The lower legs are white with a black band near the hoof. The okapi has large, flexible ears and gray cheeks. Like a giraffe, it has a tongue that is long, black, and prehensile (adapted for grasping or holding, especially by wrapping around something). It uses its tongue to strip leaves from trees. Male okapis have short, hair-covered horns. The okapi's body is about 6.5 feet (2 meters) long, and the animal stands around 5.25 feet (1.6 meters) at the shoulder. It weighs between 460 and 550 pounds (210 and 250 kilograms).

Did You Know?

Wars hurt more than just people; they are bad for animals, too. Because people in war zones often cannot carry out their traditional activities, such as farming and trade, they turn to other ways to survive. They may eat endangered animals such as the okapi for food or capture endangered animals to sell illegally. Armed groups pose a particular threat to wildlife because they can kill many animals with their high-powered weapons. Animals also suffer when people fleeing dangerous areas move through the species' habitat. People may chop down trees, destroy plants the animals eat, or pollute the water and air. Deprived of their own land, people may settle in wildlife areas, cutting down trees to make farmland.

Okapis live in forests of tall trees. They eat more than 100 species of plants, consuming leaves, grass, fruit, and fungi. To get minerals, they eat river clay and charcoal from burned trees. This species is mostly diurnal (active during the day). Okapis are solitary, coming together only to mate. After a gestation (pregnancy) period of 15 months, the female gives birth to a single calf. It is weaned (given solid food instead of the mother's milk) in 6 months and reaches its full size in 3 years. In captivity, okapis can live for 33 years.

Habitat and current distribution

Okapis live only in the central and northeastern rain forest of the Democratic Republic of the Congo (DRC), a country in central Africa. Scientists do not know the total population size but estimate that 35,000 to 50,000 okapis remain, although many believe the number is much lower.

History and conservation measures

For centuries, native African peoples told of a shy creature living in the rain forest, its camouflage making it almost impossible to find. European explorers were curious about the secretive creature, which they called the African unicorn. Early in the 20th century, the British explorer Harry Johnston (1858–1927) obtained skin and skulls of the animal and sent them to England, where biologists (people who study living organisms) identified the animal as a member of the giraffe family.

The okapi has been a protected species in the Democratic Republic of the Congo since 1933 and appears on the country's money. But from 1995 to 2013, its population decreased by more than 50 percent. Deforestation (large-scale removal of trees) and human settlement pose the greatest threats to the okapi. Since 1996 the DRC has suffered through two civil wars that killed millions of people. The country is still unstable as well as desperately poor. Armed militia groups have settled in pro-

The okapi has experienced a dramatic loss of its forest habitat in its native Democratic Republic of the Congo in Africa since the 1980s. © JUNIORS BILDARCHIV GMBH/ALAMY.

tected rain forests where okapis live. The militias farm and log illegally and hunt the okapi and other endangered animals for food. In 2012 armed militia members opened fire on the headquarters of the Okapi Wildlife Reserve, killing 6 people and 14 okapi.

Both African and international conservation groups are planning strategies to protect the okapi. The International Union for Conservation of Nature and Natural Resources (IUCN) listed the species as endangered in 2013 and formed the IUCN Giraffe and Okapi Specialist Group to develop a conservation strategy. Protecting okapi within the Okapi Wildlife Reserve and another large national park in the DRC is the most important objective. One group, the Okapi Conservation Project, supports the government personnel who patrol the wildlife reserve and educates people living near the reserve about forest conservation. Conservationists (people who work to manage and protect nature) believe that raising worldwide awareness about okapis—and raising funds for protection efforts—is essential for this species' survival.

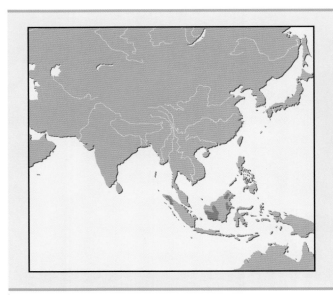

Orangutan
Pongo spp. (both species)

PHYLUM: Chordata
CLASS: Mammalia
ORDER: Primates
FAMILY: Hominidae
STATUS: Critically endangered, IUCN
(*Pongo abelii*)
Endangered, IUCN (*Pongo pygmaeus*)
Endangered, ESA
RANGE: Indonesia, Malaysia

Orangutan
Pongo spp. (both species)

Description and biology

The only great ape found in Asia, the orangutan is the largest living arboreal (living in trees) ape. In the Malay language, its name means "forest person" or "man of the woods." With its long, powerful arms and hands and feet that can grasp branches, the animal moves easily from tree to tree. The orangutan's reddish-brown coat is long and soft. It has small ears, a bulging snout, and a high forehead. An average orangutan has a head and body length of 30 to 40 inches (76 to 102 centimeters) and a shoulder height of 45 to 60 inches (114 to 152 centimeters). It weighs between 85 and 220 pounds (39 and 100 kilograms). Males are much larger and heavier than females.

There are two species of orangutan: the Bornean orangutan (*Pongo pygmaeus*) and the Sumatran orangutan (*Pongo abelii*). The two species look very much alike and have similar behaviors. In fact, they were both classified as subspecies of *Pongo pygmaeus* until the 21st century.

The orangutan has suffered a drop in population as its habitat in the forests of Borneo and Malaysia have shrunk due to logging activity and farming in the late 20th century. © VINCENT ST. THOMAS/SHUTTERSTOCK.COM.

Sumatran orangutans have narrower faces, longer beards, and lighter-colored coats.

Orangutans spend 95 percent of their lives in trees. During the day, the animals feed primarily on fruit. They also eat leaves, insects, bark, and young birds and squirrels. Each night they build a nest in a tree 35 to 80 feet (11 to 24 meters) above the ground. The home range of individuals varies from 1 to 4 square miles (2.5 to 10 square kilometers).

The orangutan is a solitary animal. The only bond formed is between a mother and her infant. Mating, which can occur at any time during the year, is the only time males and females interact. They stay together for a few days to a few months until the female is pregnant, then they split up. After a gestation (pregnancy) period of 233 to 270 days, a female gives birth to one young. She raises the infant alone, keeping it constantly with her for the first year. She nurses the infant for up to three years. During her normal life span of 40 years, a female will bear only four or five offspring.

Habitat and current distribution

The orangutan inhabits a variety of forest habitats, including swampy coastal forests, mangrove forests, and mountain forests. *Pongo pygmaeus* is found on Borneo (an island in Southeast Asia divided among the countries of Indonesia, Malaysia, and Brunei). *Pongo abelii* is found on Sumatra, an island west of Borneo that is part of Indonesia. Biologists (people who study living organisms) estimate that there are about 54,000 Bornean orangutans and about 6,600 Sumatran orangutans left in the wild. In contrast, at the beginning of the 20th century there were about 315,000 orangutans over a wide area of Southeast Asia.

History and conservation measures

For thousands of years, the orangutan has been a victim of human abuse. Early humans considered it a food source and hunted it to the point of extinction in many areas. Orangutans now live on only 2 percent of their original range.

The greatest threat to orangutans is habitat destruction. The relentless clearing of rain forests to create plantations on Borneo and Sumatra has greatly reduced the habitat available to orangutans. The animals are driven into forest areas that are too small to support them. Seeking food, the orangutans often wander onto nearby plantations. There, many are then killed or injured by workers protecting the crops.

Orangutans and other wildlife in Southeast Asia suffer terribly from devastating wildfires and smoke that frequently sweep across the region. The fires result from both human-made and natural causes. Farmers in the region rely on slash-and-burn agriculture, a process whereby a forest is cut down and all trees and vegetation (plant life) are burned to create cleared land. Private companies also set fires to clear forestland to create palm oil plantations.

The periodic weather pattern known as El Niño also impacts orangutans. It delays seasonal monsoons (heavy rains), resulting in hot and dry conditions that fan forest fires. Many orangutans die in the fires or from smoke inhalation. Others are killed by frightened villagers as the orangutans try to escape burning forests.

Another major threat to orangutans is capture. Thousands of females have been slaughtered so their offspring could be captured and sold as pets. Some childless couples even raise the animals like children, dressing them in human clothes. In the late 1980s and early 1990s, for example, the demand for orangutans as pets was especially strong in some parts of Asia, where a children's television show featured a pet orangutan. Of those infants that are captured in the wild, up to 50 percent die during transport.

Several protected reserves have been established in the orangutan's range, including the Gunung Leuser National Park in northern Sumatra and the Tanjung Puting National Park in Borneo. In 2015 the last unprotected tropical forest in central Sumatra was set aside for conservation. An area covering 154 square miles (400 square kilometers) began being protected from forest clearing and was expected to provide a much-needed habitat for Sumatran orangutans as well as for endangered elephants.

Did You Know?

Orangutans are among the most intelligent nonhuman animals on the planet. Some tests indicate that the intelligence of the great apes can reach the same level as a three-and-a-half-year-old human, and orangutans are some of the smartest apes. They carefully find solutions to problems instead of jumping to conclusions.

This intelligence led to a landmark decision in 2014, when a 28-year-old orangutan was legally recognized as having basic human rights. Lawyers were successful in arguing that Sandra, an orangutan living at the Buenos Aires zoo in Argentina, was being illegally detained. As of 2015, another court had yet to decide on whether Sandra should be transferred to an animal sanctuary where she would have more freedom. The zoo, meanwhile, has set about improving Sandra's living space.

Conservationists (people who work to manage and protect nature) and wildlife researchers have also established camps to help train orangutans that were once pets to return to their natural habitat. However, most of these orangutans have spent too much time among humans and cannot adapt to live in the wild.

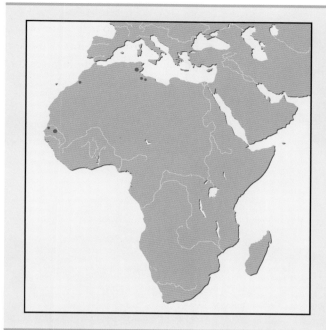

Oryx, scimitar-horned
Oryx dammah

PHYLUM: Chordata
CLASS: Mammalia
ORDER: Artiodactyla
FAMILY: Bovidae
STATUS: Extinct in the wild, IUCN
Endangered, ESA
RANGE: Morocco, Senegal, Tunisia

Oryx, scimitar-horned
Oryx dammah

Description and biology

The scimitar-horned oryx is a small, horselike antelope. It is so-named because its two horns, which extend back from its head in a long sweeping arc, are similar in shape to scimitars, which are curved, single-edged Asian swords. Most of its body is nearly white in color. Its neck and small portions of its face are dark brown. This oryx has short, rounded ears, large hooves, and a tuft of hair below its chin and at the end of its tail. It also has a short mane extending from its head over its shoulders.

An average scimitar-horned oryx has a head and body length of 60 to 90 inches (152 to 229 centimeters) and weighs 250 to 460 pounds (114 to 209 kilograms). Its tail measures 18 to 35 inches (46 to 89 centimeters) long, while its horns extend 30 to 55 inches (76 to 140 centimeters).

A herd of scimitar-horned oryx is one of several in captivity in North Africa, as conservationists work to reintroduce the species to the wild. © WOLF AVNI/SHUTTERSTOCK.COM.

Scimitar-horned oryx often gather in herds of 20 to 40 members. During the day, the herds travel over great distances to feed on grass and other desert vegetation (plant life). The animals are often preyed upon by hyenas and large cats.

Mating may take place between males and females at any time, but births appear to peak during early spring and early fall. Female scimitar-horned oryx give birth to a single infant after a gestation (pregnancy) period of 220 to 253 days.

Habitat and current distribution

More than one million scimitar-horned oryx once inhabited the rolling dunes and grassy plains of the desert regions in northern Africa. In 1985 there were about 500 scimitar-horned oryx in Chad and Niger, and by 1988 only a few survived in the wild. The last confirmed sighting of the animal in the wild was in 1988. The species has been listed as extinct in the wild by the International Union for Conservation of Nature and Natural Resources (IUCN) since 2000.

Worldwide, 1,735 scimitar-horned oryx live in 226 institutions such as zoos and wildlife parks as of 2014. North America has the largest number of captive scimitar-horned oryx.

History and conservation measures

Scimitar-horned oryx were once quite common in the areas surrounding the Sahara Desert in northern Africa. Herds sometimes joined together to form groups that numbered in the thousands. By the mid-1900s, however, desertification, drought, competition from domestic livestock, and uncontrolled hunting by humans all combined to eliminate this oryx from much of its original habitat.

Desertification is the gradual transformation of productive land into that with desertlike conditions. Even a desert can become desertified, losing its sparse collection of plants and animals and becoming a barren wasteland. Much of the scimitar-horned oryx's habitat has been desertified by natural and human-made actions. Droughts have plagued the region, and overgrazing by farm animals has depleted what little vegetation has been able to grow.

The greatest threat to the scimitar-horned oryx, however, was hunting. Wanton (merciless) killing by humans brought the animal to near extinction in several parts of its range during various times of the 20th century. By the mid-1970s almost all of the region's scimitar-horned oryx were confined to a single place: the Ouadi Rimé-Ouadi Achim Faunal Reserve in Chad. Established in 1969, the reserve was a suitable, well-protected habitat area for the oryx. By 1978 the oryx population in the reserve numbered about 5,000. However, that same year, civil war broke out in the country and protection for the reserve ceased.

In addition to the reserve in Chad, other programs to breed the scimitar-horned oryx in captivity began in the 1960s. The oryx are managed in three coordinated captive programs with participating institutions in North America, Europe, and Australia. Breeding programs have been very successful and reintroduction programs in which scimitar-horned oryx are released in wildlife reserves are ongoing in Senegal, Morocco, and Tunisia. The goal is for these new populations to begin to reproduce and sustain themselves, so that the species will once again exist in the wild.

Otter, marine
Lontra felina

PHYLUM: Chordata
CLASS: Mammalia
ORDER: Carnivora
FAMILY: Mustelidae
STATUS: Endangered, IUCN
Endangered, ESA
RANGE: Argentina, Chile, Peru

Otter, marine
Lontra felina

Description and biology

Otters are members of the weasel family. The marine otter, sometimes called the sea cat, has a long body, a flat head, small ears, and a broad, whiskered muzzle. Its short legs and webbed feet help make it an agile swimmer. Thick, glossy dark-brown hair covers its body. An average marine otter has a head and body length of 22 to 31 inches (59 to 79 centimeters) and a tail length of 12 to 14 inches (30 to 36 inches). It weighs 7 to 31 pounds (3 to 14 kilograms).

Marine otters feed mainly on crustaceans (such as crabs and shrimp) and mollusks (such as snails, clams, and oysters). While swimming on their backs, they often lay their prey on their chests and use rocks to smash open the hard shells. The otter's main predator is the killer whale (*Orcinus orca*).

Otters are primarily solitary animals, but groups of three or more have been observed in the wild. Male and female marine otters typically mate during December or January. After a gestation (pregnancy) period that lasts between 60 and 65 days, female marine otters usually give birth to a litter of two to four pups.

Habitat and current distribution

The marine otter ranges along the Pacific coast of South America from northern Peru to the southern tip of Chile. Because the otters are only seen alone or in very small groups, their numbers are difficult to estimate. Biologists (people who study living organisms) estimate that there are fewer than 2,000 marine otters worldwide.

Marine otters prefer to inhabit exposed rocky coastal areas and secluded bays and inlets near estuaries (coastal waters where a freshwater

The marine otter is found along South America's Pacific coast in Chile, Peru, and Argentina, all of which have programs protecting the animal from the effects of a dwindling habitat. © KEVIN SCHAFER/MINDEN PICTURES/CORBIS.

Did You Know?

The preservation of otters is important for all species, including humans. There are 13 species of otters. They are found on all continents except Australia and Antarctica, live both in water and on land, and are near the top of the food chain. For this reason, they are an important indicator species (plants or animals that, by their presence or chemical composition, give some distinctive indication of the health or quality of the environment). A drop in the number of otters could indicate that the areas they inhabit (water meadows, rivers, estuaries, lakes, coastal zones) or the food they eat (fish, crustaceans, mollusks, frogs) may be in poor condition. As of 2015, all but one of the 13 otter species were listed by the International Union for Conservation of Nature and Natural Resources (IUCN) as near threatened, vulnerable, or endangered.

river empties into a saltwater sea or ocean). Habitats suitable for the marine otter include caves in rocky sections of the seashore and even sometimes docks and abandoned or shipwrecked boats. While searching for freshwater shrimp, marine otters have been known to swim 2,000 feet (610 meters) up a river from the ocean.

History and conservation measures

Marine otters were once plentiful throughout their entire range. In the 20th century otter hunters nearly killed the species out of existence. The marine otter is now a protected species throughout its range countries. Illegal hunting for fur and sport, however, continues in some areas because protection laws are not enforced properly.

In the 21st century, the major threat to the marine otter is the destruction of its habitat by the increase in human development along the South American coast. Marine otters compete with humans for fish, oysters, and shrimp, resulting in conflict and the killing of marine otters who may disrupt commercial fishing operations. Marine otters are also killed accidentally when they become entangled in fishing nets or when illegal techniques such as dynamite fishing (a fishing practice in which explosives are used to kill many fish at once) are used.

Water pollution also destroys the marine otter's habitat and poses a direct threat to the animal. Waste from factories, industrial fishing, and human settlements flows into the ocean directly and through rivers. Heavy metals, pesticides, and other toxic materials from this polluted water are then consumed by the marine otters.

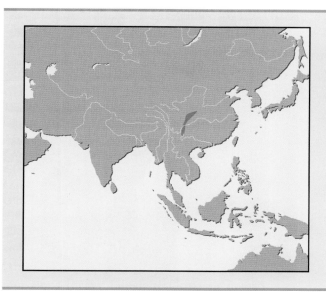

Panda, giant
Ailuropoda melanoleuca

PHYLUM: Chordata
CLASS: Mammalia
ORDER: Carnivora
FAMILY: Ursidae
STATUS: Endangered, IUCN
Endangered, ESA
RANGE: China

Panda, giant
Ailuropoda melanoleuca

Description and biology

Recognized worldwide, the giant panda has become a symbol in the fight to save endangered species from extinction. The animal shares many characteristics with both bears and raccoons, but genetic tests reveal it is more closely related to the bear. Thus, scientists classify it as a member of the bear family (Ursidae).

An average giant panda has a head and body length of 4 to 6 feet (1.2 to 1.8 meters) and weighs between 165 and 350 pounds (75 and 160 kilograms). Its tail measures 5 inches (13 centimeters) in length. The animal's thick, woolly coat is primarily white. Its legs, shoulders, ears, and eye patches are black.

Bamboo stalks and roots make up 95 percent of the giant panda's diet. One of its wrist bones is enlarged and elongated, and the animal uses it like a thumb when grasping stalks of bamboo. The giant panda also has strong jaws and teeth to crush bamboo. The remainder of its

The giant panda, beloved in its native China, has benefited from conservation and preservation programs led by the Chinese government and other wildlife organizations to eliminate poaching and improve its habitat. © DON MAMMOSER/SHUTTERSTOCK.COM.

diet is made up of grass, bulbs, insects, rodents, and fish. The animal spends 10 to 16 hours eating the 20 to 40 pounds (9 to 18 kilograms) of food it needs each day.

Giant pandas are solitary and territorial. They have a home range of 1.5 to 2.5 square miles (4 to 6.5 square kilometers), which they mark with secretions from scent glands. Males and females come together to mate between March and May. After a gestation (pregnancy) period of 125 to 150 days, a female giant panda gives birth to one to two cubs in a sheltered den. The cubs are very fragile at birth, weighing only 3 to 5 ounces (85 to 142 grams). If two cubs are born, usually just one survives. It remains with its mother for up to a year. The average life span of a giant panda in the wild is 15 years.

Habitat and current distribution

Among the rarest mammals in the world, giant pandas are found only in the mountains of central China, in the Sichuan, Shaanxi, and Gansu Provinces. The animals prefer to inhabit dense bamboo and coniferous (cone bearing) forests at elevations between 5,000 and 10,000 feet (1,525 and 3,050 meters). Biologists (people who study living organisms) estimate that about 1,800 giant pandas existed in the wild as of 2014, a significant increase since the late 1970s when the estimate was 1,000 pandas. There are 49 pandas in 18 zoos outside China.

History and conservation measures

The giant panda has existed in China for hundreds of thousands of years. It was once common throughout the country, but over the last 2,000 years it has disappeared from the Henan, Hubei, Hunan, Guizhou, and Yunnan Provinces. In 1869 the French missionary and naturalist Armand David (1826–1900) became the first European to describe the giant panda. The species was not well known in the West until a captive specimen was brought to the United States in the 1930s. As a gesture of goodwill, the Chinese government presented U.S. president Richard Nixon (1913–1994) with a pair of giant pandas (Ling-Ling and Hsing-Hsing) in 1972. The animals were kept at the National Zoo in Washington, D.C., until their deaths in the 1990s.

Habitat destruction is the primary danger to giant pandas. Since bamboo grows slowly, the pandas need a large range in which to feed. This range is constantly being threatened by China's growing human population—estimated at more than 1.3 billion people in 2015. To help save the dwindling giant panda population, the Chinese government has set aside 50 panda preserves that protect almost 45 percent of the animal's natural habitat.

Another threat to the giant panda is poaching, or illegal hunting. The animal is protected by international treaties, and the Chinese government sentences those convicted of poaching a giant panda to life in prison. Nonetheless, the animal is still hunted for its fur, which is sold illegally in Southeast Asian markets at a high price.

Giant pandas are often difficult to breed in captivity. The first giant panda bred in captivity was born in 1963 in Beijing, China. Since then, fewer than 10 have been born in zoos outside of China. The first giant panda birth outside China occurred at the Mexico City Zoo in 1980. Successful births in captivity have increased since then. With hundreds of giant pandas in captivity, a long-term goal of panda preservation programs in China is to eventually release captive-born pandas into the wild.

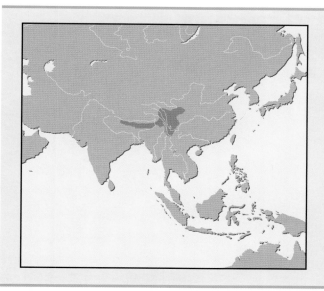

Panda, red
Ailurus fulgens

PHYLUM: Chordata
CLASS: Mammalia
ORDER: Carnivora
FAMILY: Ailuridae
STATUS: Vulnerable, IUCN
RANGE: Bhutan, China, India, Myanmar, Nepal

Panda, red
Ailurus fulgens

Description and biology

The red panda, also known as the lesser panda, has rust-colored fur with chocolate-brown markings. The Chinese call this striking animal "firefox" because of its flame-colored fur. The red panda has short, pointed ears and a mask similar to that of a raccoon. Taxonomists (biologists who classify species on the basis of their genes, characteristics, and behavior) have been uncertain whether to classify red pandas as part of the bear family or part of the raccoon family. As of the 2010s, it has been classified as its own family, the Ailuridae.

An average red panda has a head and body length of 20 to 23.5 inches (51 to 60 centimeters) and weighs between 7.7 and 11 pounds (3.5 and 5 kilograms). Its banded tail measures 12 to 20 inches (30 to 51 centimeters) in length. The animal is most active at dawn and at dusk. Although it spends most of its time in trees, it feeds on the ground. Its diet consists mainly of bamboo leaves, but it also eats grasses, berries, fruits, roots, and other plant matter.

The red panda, which is native to China, India, Myanmar, Nepal, and Bhutan, is at risk because of depletion of its bamboo-forest habitat. © JOE RAVI/SHUTTERSTOCK.COM.

Red pandas are solitary and territorial. A male red panda will often patrol the boundary of his territory, while a female will often remain in the center of hers. The territory of a single male will overlap the territories of several females. Males and females come together to mate in January and February. During the courtship period, males and females will groom each other. After mating is complete, the male leaves and will not care for the female or her young.

A female red panda gives birth to 1 to 4 cubs in a secure den (hollow tree, cave, or rock crevice) after a gestation (pregnancy) period of 90 to 145 days. The newborn pandas are tan in color, blind, and totally dependent on their mother. They nurse for about 5 months, then begin eating bamboo leaves. A month later, they leave to stake out their own territories.

Habitat and current distribution

The red panda is found in the Himalayas and other mountains in northern India, southern China, Nepal, Bhutan, and northern Myanmar. It inhabits mountain spruce and fir forests at elevations between 6,500 and 13,000 feet (1,980 and 3,960 meters). Because it is shy, nocturnal (active at night), and difficult to find in the wild, the red panda has been difficult to study. However, scientists in the first decade of the 2000s estimated that there were about 10,000 red pandas in the wild worldwide. Around 5,000 to 6,000 are estimated to live in China, and 3,000 to 7,000 in India.

History and conservation measures

The major threat to red pandas is the loss of their habitat. Forests throughout much of the animal's range have been cleared to create farmland to feed a growing human population. In areas where forests have not been completely cleared, many trees have been cut down for use as fuel or building materials. The little "islands" of forest that remain are often not large enough to support the number of red pandas that have been forced to live there. With limited food sources, many of the animals starve to death.

Because of its attractive fur, the red panda has been hunted for its coat. Traps set for other animals in its range, such as the musk deer, have also taken their toll on the red panda. International treaties prohibit the trading of red panda pelts, and the animal is protected in China, Nepal, Bhutan, and in India, where it has the highest protection possible for an endangered species. However, enforcement of protective legislation in India is very weak. Some of the panda's protected habitat, however, is in remote areas where humans do not disturb the animals.

In China, a number of red pandas also benefit by inhabiting the parks and reserves that have been set up for giant pandas. Displayed in zoos worldwide, red pandas have been bred in captivity with reasonable success. The International Red Panda Management Group is leading an effort to unite breeding programs around the world into a single global program.

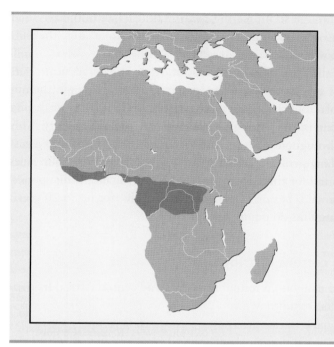

Pangolin, long-tailed
Phataginus tetradactyla (also *Manis tetradactyla*)

PHYLUM: Chordata
CLASS: Mammalia
ORDER: Pholidota
FAMILY: Manidae
STATUS: Vulnerable, IUCN
RANGE: Cameroon, Central African Republic, Côte d'Ivoire, Democratic Republic of the Congo, Equatorial Guinea, Gabon, Ghana, Liberia, Nigeria, Republic of the Congo, Sierra Leone

Pangolin, long-tailed
Phataginus tetradactyla (also *Manis tetradactyla*)

Description and biology

Encased in overlapping scales that look like an artichoke or pinecone and able to curl into a tight ball to escape predators, the pangolin is an unusual mammal. The long-tailed pangolin, also called the black-bellied pangolin, is the smallest of the eight pangolin species. Its 24- to 28-inch (60- to 70-centimeter) tail dwarfs its 14- to 18-inch (35- to 45-centimeter) body and its small head. The animal weighs 4.4 to 5.5 pounds (2 to 2.5 kilograms). Most of its body is covered in brown scales with yellowish edges, and its underside has dark fur. The long-tailed pangolin has a prehensile tail, which means it is adapted for grasping and holding, especially by wrapping around something. Its tail has a patch on its bare tip that senses branches strong enough to hold the animal's weight. It eats ants, finding them through scent, tearing their nests apart with its claws, and lapping them up with its long, sticky tongue. Because of its diet, the pangolin is also known as the scaly anteater.

The long-tailed pangolin lives in moist, tropical habitats near rivers and swamps. It spends almost all its time in the forest canopy (the uppermost layer of a forest) but also swims well. It is diurnal (active during the day), sleeping in trees at night. Pangolins are shy and solitary. This species mates throughout the year, producing one baby, born after a gestation (pregnancy) period of about 140 days. The young pangolin rides on its mother's tail for three months. Little is known about this species' life span in the wild, but other pangolin species live for up to 20 years. Long-tailed pangolins do poorly in captivity.

Habitat and current distribution

The long-tailed pangolin is found in western and central Africa. Its population numbers are unknown.

The long-tailed pangolin is hunted for its meat and for medicinal purposes in the areas of west and central Africa where it is found. © FRANS LANTING/LATITUDE/CORBIS.

History and conservation measures

Pangolins have been captured for human use for many centuries. In African myth and legend, offering a pangolin to an authority figure, such as the village chief, was said to bring blessings to the community. In traditional medicine (health practices used by specific cultures since before the time of modern medicine) in Africa, China, and Vietnam, pangolin scales are believed to treat many illnesses. Chinese and Vietnamese diners eat pangolins as a delicacy, and Africans consume them as a source of protein. Pangolins are the most illegally smuggled and sold animals in the world.

Out of the eight pangolin species, the International Union for Conservation of Nature and Natural Resources (IUCN) lists two Asian species as critically endangered, two other Asian species as endangered, and all four African species (including the long-tailed) as vulnerable. Pollution, such as oil spills, and habitat loss threaten this species as well. In 2014 the IUCN listed the long-tailed pangolin's status as vulnerable, stating that without protection, its population would decrease by at least 30 percent to 40 percent by 2035. The species is protected in most countries where it is found. It appears on Appendix II of the Convention on International Trade in Endangered Species of Wild Fauna and Flora (CITES; an international treaty to protect wildlife), indicating that its trade should be controlled to prevent it becoming threatened by extinction. Nonetheless, pangolin trafficking (illegal trading) continues.

Nonprofit groups worldwide are working to conserve pangolins. In 2014 the IUCN launched a major campaign to promote the conservation of all pangolin species. The plan includes breeding and rehabilitating pangolins and reintroducing them into the wild; monitoring pangolin habitats; working with law enforcement to discourage hunting; and conducting media campaigns to increase worldwide awareness about pangolins. According to the IUCN, the most important task is to reduce consumer demand. Conservationists (people who work to manage and protect nature) are beginning by targeting restaurants and traditional Chinese medicine shops in China and Vietnam.

Porcupine, thin-spined
Chaetomys subspinosus

PHYLUM:	Chordata
CLASS:	Mammalia
ORDER:	Rodentia
FAMILY:	Erethizontidae
STATUS:	Vulnerable, IUCN Endangered, ESA
RANGE:	Brazil

Porcupine, thin-spined
Chaetomys subspinosus

Description and biology

The thin-spined porcupine, also known as the bristle-spined rat, gets its common names from the thin, bristly spines that cover its body. The animal is not considered a member of the family of true porcupines, but a member of the family of spiny rats. Unlike true porcupines, the thin-spined porcupine has no spines on its lower back. The spines on the animal's head and shoulders are kinky and short, just 0.6 inch (1.5 centimeters) in length. Those on its upper back, legs, and tail are wavier and longer, up to 2 inches (5 centimeters) in length. The spines are usually tricolored, ranging from pale yellow at the base to dark brown in the middle and back to pale yellow at the tip. The animal's body is brownish gray in color, while its feet and tail are darker.

The thin-spined porcupine lives in limited numbers in small areas of the Brazilian rain forest, a habitat that continues to shrink because of human activity. © MARK MOFFETT/MINDEN PICTURES/CORBIS.

An average thin-spined porcupine has a head and body length of 15 to 18 inches (38 to 46 centimeters) and a tail length of 10 inches (25 centimeters). All four of the animal's limbs have four digits resembling human fingers or toes, which end in long, curved claws. These sharp claws help make the thin-spined porcupine an excellent climber, able to scale stone walls.

The thin-spined porcupine is nocturnal (active at night), feeding on fruits and cocoa tree nuts. Biologists (people who study living organisms) have been unable to study the animal well enough to learn its social structure or its reproductive habits.

Habitat and current distribution

The thin-spined porcupine is found only in the Atlantic Forest, which runs along the coast of eastern and southeastern Brazil. It inhabits the edges of open, coastal rain forest areas in the states of Bahia and Espírito Santo. The number of thin-spined porcupine existing in the wild is unknown, but the animal is believed to be quite rare.

History and conservation measures

The main threat facing the thin-spined porcupine is the loss of its habitat due to forest clear-cutting (the process of cutting down all the trees in a forest area). Because scientists and conservationists (people who work to manage and protect nature) know very little about the habits of the animal, saving its forest ecosystem (an ecological system including all of its living things and their environment) is the best strategy to preserve the thin-spined porcupine. Brazil issued a national action plan in 2011, aimed at protecting the species and reversing the decline in the thin-spined porcupine population. The plan's goals include reducing habitat loss, expanding forest areas in the species' range, reducing hunting, and increasing local knowledge about the species and policies aimed at conservation.

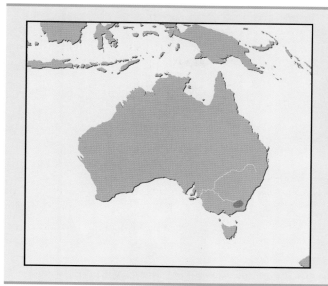

Possum, mountain pygmy
Burramys parvus

PHYLUM: Chordata
CLASS: Mammalia
ORDER: Diprotodontia
FAMILY: Burramyidae
STATUS: Critically endangered, IUCN
Endangered, ESA
RANGE: Southeastern Australia

Possum, mountain pygmy
Burramys parvus

Description and biology

The mountain pygmy possum is a small marsupial (mammal whose young continue to develop after birth in a pouch on the outside of the mother's body). It has an average head and body length of 4 to 5 inches (10 to 13 centimeters) and weight of just 1 to 2 ounces (28 to 57 grams). Its 5.5-inch (14-centimeter) tail is prehensile, meaning it can hold onto items such as tree limbs by wrapping around them. The animal is covered with brownish-gray fur that ends at the base of its tail.

Nocturnal (active at night), the mountain pygmy possum's main diet item is a species of moth. It also eats other insects, seeds, and fruit. It is the only marsupial that stores seeds for use during the winter.

Male and female mountain pygmy possums mate in late October to early November. After a gestation (pregnancy) period of only 13 to 16 days, a female mountain pygmy possum gives birth to a litter of four.

The young remain in the mother's pouch for at least three weeks and are nursed for up to nine weeks.

Habitat and current distribution

Mountain pygmy possums inhabit three areas in the mountains of southeastern Australia. The animals are most often found at elevations between 5,000 and 6,000 feet (1,525 and 1,830 meters), living among the loose stones or rocky debris at the base of a slope or cliff. Only about 2,000 of these animals remain, occupying a total area of less than 2.7 square miles (6.9 square kilometers).

History and conservation measures

Before the mid-1960s, the mountain pygmy possum was known only from fossilized remains found in New South Wales. A live mountain pygmy possum was then found and identified in Victoria. Additional living specimens were also found in New South Wales.

The most severe threat to the mountain pygmy possum is habitat destruction caused by the development of ski resorts. In particular, human activity at ski resorts, including vibrations from snow sports and slope maintenance machinery, can result in the possum waking up too early from hibernation. Climate change is another major threat. Warmer temperatures will cause the animals to emerge early from hibernation. In both cases, the animals are endangered because their main food source, moths, have not yet arrived from migration.

The species faces other threats as well. One is predators, especially foxes and feral (once domesticated, now wild) cats. Introduced foreign species, such as pest plants and animals, especially habitat competition from rabbits, can affect the possums' natural environment, as can garbage from the resorts. Wildfires have destroyed some of the species' habitat and some of the plants it uses for food. Listed as endangered by the International Union for Conservation of Nature and Natural Resources in 1996, the mountain pygmy possum was given the more severe critically endangered listing in 2008 because its population has continued declining.

The Australian government's recovery plan for the mountain pygmy possum includes studying its population and habitat; protecting remaining habitat; restoring lost habitat; reducing the impact of human activity at ski resorts; controlling predators and introduced species; and increasing community awareness of the animal's plight. Mountain pygmy possums are being bred in captivity but with limited success. The animal is protected in two national parks, the Kosciuszko National Park and Victoria's Alpine National Park.

Prairie dog, Mexican
Cynomys mexicanus

PHYLUM: Chordata
CLASS: Mammalia
ORDER: Rodentia
FAMILY: Sciuridae
STATUS: Endangered, IUCN
Endangered, ESA
RANGE: Mexico

Prairie dog, Mexican
Cynomys mexicanus

Description and biology

The Mexican prairie dog is a large, stout member of the squirrel family, closely related to ground squirrels, chipmunks, and marmots. An average Mexican prairie dog measures 12 to 16 inches (30 to 41 centimeters) in length and weighs 1.5 to 3 pounds (0.7 to 1.4 kilograms). The animal's buff-colored fur is tinted with black, white, red, and yellow. The tip of its short tail is black. Twice a year, its fur is shed and replaced by a new coat (a process called molting).

Like other prairie dogs, the Mexican prairie dog is active above ground during the day. It feeds on grasses and other plants. Badgers, coyotes, weasels, eagles, hawks, and snakes are its main predators.

Mexican prairie dogs live in coteries, or groups, in large burrows they have dug with several entrances. A coterie is made up of one or two adult males, one to four adult females, and a number of young. Mating

A Mexican prairie dog peeks from its burrow in its grassland habitat, which is threatened by the development of agriculture. © BLICKWIN-KEL/ALAMY.

between males and females usually takes place between late January and July. After a gestation (pregnancy) period of about 30 days, a female Mexican prairie dog gives birth to a varying number of pups.

Habitat and current distribution

The Mexican prairie dog is found only in north-central Mexico, in the states of Coahuila and San Luis Potosí. It previously occurred in the states of Nuevo León and Zacatecas. More than 60 percent of the species' natural habitat has been lost, and in 2015 the animal's range covered about 193 square miles (500 square kilometers). The animal prefers the open plains and valleys of the central Mexican Plateau at elevations between 5,200 and 7,200 feet (1,600 and 2,200 meters). Biologists (people who study living organisms) do not know the total number of Mexican prairie dogs currently in existence.

Did You Know?

Prairie dogs greet each other with a kiss. All members of a coterie (social group) press their mouths together and lock teeth with each other as a way of confirming their kinship within a coterie. If the two parties belong to the same coterie, their kiss will be simple and quick and they will then part ways or go about their usual activities. When two prairie dogs discover through their kiss that they in fact belong to separate coteries, they may break out into a wrestling match or a standoff before one chases the other out of its territory.

History and conservation measures

The greatest threat to the Mexican prairie dog is habitat loss. Much of its former habitat has been destroyed to create farmland to feed a growing human population. Some colonies of Mexican prairie dogs have been intentionally poisoned by humans who view the animals as pests that destroy crops and grazing land. Soil erosion caused by cattle herding and the loss of grassland also contributed to the animal's habitat loss.

The Mexican prairie dog is rarest in the southern part of its range. Moving individuals from northern areas may help increase the population in southern areas. The Mexican prairie dog is protected by law, but the laws are not strongly enforced.

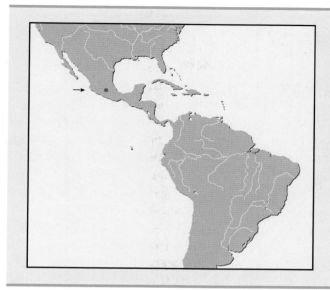

Rabbit, volcano
Romerolagus diazi

PHYLUM: Chordata
CLASS: Mammalia
ORDER: Lagomorpha
FAMILY: Leporidae
STATUS: Endangered, IUCN
Endangered, ESA
RANGE: Mexico

Rabbit, volcano
Romerolagus diazi

Description and biology

The volcano rabbit, also known as the Mexican pygmy rabbit, has short, thick, dark-brown hair. It is one of the few species of short-eared rabbits. Its rounded ears measure just 1.6 inches (4 centimeters) long. The animal also has short hind legs and feet and a very short tail. An average volcano rabbit has a head and body length of 10.5 to 13 inches (26.5 to 33 centimeters) and weighs between 14 and 18 ounces (397 and 510 grams).

Active mainly during the day, the volcano rabbit feeds on the tender young leaves of zacaton or bunchgrass (various wiry grass species that grow in low clumps in Mexico and the southwestern United States). Its main predators are long-tailed weasels, bobcats, and rattlesnakes.

Volcano rabbits construct elaborate burrows in deep sandy soil. Entrances are hidden in the base of grass clumps. For temporary shelter during the day, the animals sometimes use abandoned pocket-gopher burrows or the hollows between rocks and boulders.

The volcano rabbit is at risk because of the destruction of its habitat and hunting. © GEORGE D. LEPP/ENCYCLOPEDIA/CORBIS.

Scientists know little about the social structure of volcano rabbits. Groups of two to seven animals have been observed in the wild. Male and female volcano rabbits mate year-round with activity peaking during the rainy summer months. After a gestation (pregnancy) period of 38 to 40 days, a female gives birth to a litter of one to five kittens or kits (baby rabbits).

Habitat and current distribution

The volcano rabbit is found only in central Mexico on the slopes of four volcanoes: Popocatépetl, Iztaccíhuatl, El Pelado, and Tlaloc. The animal inhabits pine forests on those slopes at elevations between 9,000 and 14,000 feet (2,740 and 4,270 meters). The species' range is approximately 149 square miles (386 square kilometers). These areas are often dry in the winter and rainy in the summer. Biologists (people who study living organisms) are unsure of the total number of volcano rabbits currently in existence, and estimate that about 7,000 volcano rabbits were alive in the wild as of the late 1990s.

History and conservation measures

The volcano rabbit has traditionally been hunted for food and sport. Although laws have been passed making it illegal to hunt these animals, they are seldom enforced.

Forest fires, the conversion of forestland into farmland, the overgrazing of cattle and sheep, and the cutting of trees for timber have all contributed to the destruction of volcano rabbit habitat. Many of the forest fires result when farmers burn bunchgrass areas in hopes of promoting new growth for their livestock (a process known as slash-and-burn agriculture). Part of the volcano rabbit's present-day range lies within the Izta-Popo Zoquiapan National Park. However, habitat destruction continues even within these protected areas.

The volcano rabbit is a "habitat specialist," meaning that it cannot move and adapt to a different type of habitat. Each of the remaining volcano rabbit populations lies within a 45-minute drive of Mexico City. One of the largest cities in the world, its metropolitan area has a rapidly growing population of more than 21 million people. As the city and rural settlements around it continue to expand, volcano rabbit habitat continues to decrease.

As of the early 21st century, a very low number of habitat areas exist that are suitable for the volcano rabbit. Scientists have determined that the species is more threatened than was previously thought. Conservation programs are being considered that would focus on educating the local residents of central Mexico about the species and the urgent need to save its habitat from further destruction.

Rat, giant kangaroo
Dipodomys ingens

PHYLUM: Chordata
CLASS: Mammalia
ORDER: Rodentia
FAMILY: Heteromyidae
STATUS: Endangered, IUCN
         Endangered, ESA
RANGE: USA (California)

Rat, giant kangaroo
Dipodomys ingens

Description and biology

The kangaroo rat, a desert rodent related to the pocket mouse, is so named because it uses its long legs and tail to leap like a kangaroo. There are about 20 kangaroo rat species, the largest of which is the giant kangaroo rat. This species can have a head and body length of up to 14 inches (36 centimeters) and weigh up to 6 ounces (170 grams). Its tail can measure up to 8 inches (20 centimeters) long. The animal has a mouselike head, large eyes, and cheek pouches in which it stores food. Its body is covered with long, silky fur that is pale brown above and white underneath. Its tail ends in a tuft of black-and-white hair.

The giant kangaroo rat eats seeds, leaves, stems, and buds of young plants. Like other desert animals, the kangaroo rat seldom drinks water, but obtains the moisture it needs from the food it eats. It also conserves the water it takes in by foraging only at night.

Giant kangaroo rats live in underground burrows, where they store food for the winter months. The normally solitary male and female kangaroo rats come together only to mate, which may occur at any time during the year. After a gestation (pregnancy) period of about 30 days, a female giant kangaroo rat gives birth to a litter of two to five young.

Habitat and current distribution

The giant kangaroo rat is native to California in the United States. It is now restricted to the southwestern border of the San Joaquin Valley, and some other nearby valleys in central California. Although there are likely more than 100,000 adults in California as of the 2010s, the population is greatly reduced from historical numbers and continues to decline.

The giant kangaroo rat has experienced an extreme loss of habitat in its native California because of industrial, agricultural, and urban development. COURTESY OF THE U.S. FISH AND WILDLIFE SERVICE.

History and conservation measures

The giant kangaroo rat, like all kangaroo rat species, is threatened by habitat destruction due to a growing human population. Its former habitat has been turned into farmland, oil fields, or residential areas. The animal also faces the risks of pesticide poisoning (from overspraying on nearby farms) and attacks by domestic cats.

The International Union for Conservation of Nature and Natural Resources (IUCN) changed the status of the giant kangaroo rat from critically endangered to endangered in 2008. The species is also on the U.S. and California endangered species lists, and some parts of their range fall in protected areas. According to conservationists (people who work to manage and protect nature), studies of population distribution and land management will be required if the giant kangaroo rat is to be preserved.

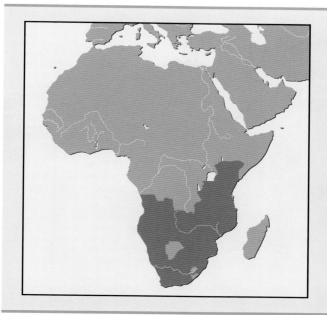

Rhinoceros, black
Diceros bicornis

PHYLUM: Chordata
CLASS: Mammalia
ORDER: Perissodactyla
FAMILY: Rhinocerotidae
STATUS: Critically endangered, IUCN Endangered, ESA
RANGE: Angola, Botswana, Ethiopia, Kenya, Malawi, Mozambique, Namibia, South Africa, Swaziland, Tanzania, Zambia, Zimbabwe

Rhinoceros, black
Diceros bicornis

Description and biology

The black rhinoceros is one of two species of rhinoceros found in Africa (the other is the white rhinoceros). Despite its name, the animal is actually gray in color. An average black rhinoceros has a head and body length of 9 to 12 feet (2.7 to 3.7 meters), stands 4.5 to 5.25 feet (1.4 to 1.6 meters) tall at its shoulder, and weighs between 2,000 and 4,000 pounds (908 and 1,816 kilograms). The animal's huge size is deceiving, as it can move quite quickly when it decides to charge. It has very poor eyesight—it can see clearly only up to 30 feet (9 meters) away—but has acute senses of hearing and smell.

Rhinoceros means "horn nosed." The black rhinoceros has two horns on its snout. The front one is longer and can measure up to 53 inches (135 centimeters). The animal uses its horns (made of keratin fibers, the same substance as in human fingernails) to dig in the ground

The black rhinoceros has a distinctive horn that is prized by poachers for use in traditional medicines and for decoration, which was a major factor in the animal's drop in population in the 20th century. © DANITA DELMONT/SHUTTERSTOCK.COM.

for mineral salt, to defend its territory against other rhinos, and to defend itself against predators such as lions and hyenas.

The black rhinoceros protects itself against the intense African heat by sleeping during the day in a patch of brush. It awakens in the cool of the evening to begin feeding. The animal is an herbivore (animals that eat mainly plants), eating branches, leaves, and bark. Its pointed upper lip is prehensile, meaning the lip can actually grasp branches to help pull and break them.

Black rhinos are mostly solitary animals, and males and females come together only to mate. Mating may take place at any time during the year. Males will often fight over the right to mate with a female, and males and females often fight during their courtship. After a gestation (pregnancy) period of 15 to 18 months, a female black rhinoceros gives birth to a single calf, which weighs about 90 pounds (41 kilograms).

The calf nurses for up to two years and remains dependent on its mother for another year. Black rhinos have an average life span of 30 to 35 years.

Habitat and current distribution

The black rhinoceros lives in a variety of habitats, from deserts to wet forests, but most live in savannas (flat, tropical or subtropical grasslands). It is found only in small pockets in eastern and southern Africa. In 1995 the estimated population of the species was an all-time low of 2,410 animals. The number had risen to 4,880 by the end of 2010 thanks to conservation measures in some countries within its range.

History and conservation measures

There were more than 850,000 black rhinos in the first half of the 20th century, and it was the most numerous rhino species in the world. However, as a result of hunting and the clearing of large tracts of land to make way for human settlements and agriculture, the black rhino population was reduced to approximately 100,000 by 1960. Another dramatic decrease in numbers followed, and by 1995 the black rhinoceros was disappearing faster than any large animal on the planet, with an estimated population of just over 2,000 animals. Although the black rhinoceros once ranged widely throughout the savannas of Africa, biologists (people who study living organisms) estimate that the species number dropped by over 95 percent between 1970 and 1995. At this rate, all black rhinos would have been extinct by the early 21st century. It has been determined that the large populations of free-ranging rhinos have disappeared for the most part. Because they traveled over vast areas, they could not be adequately protected. The rhinos surviving in the early 21st century live within more concentrated areas in which they can be protected from hunters.

The direct cause of the decline of black rhinos has been the demand for their horns. For centuries, people in Asia have believed that the powder of ground rhino horns can cure fevers, nosebleeds, measles, food poisoning, and other illnesses. Many believe it increases sexual desire and stamina, as well. Rhino horns have also been used to make handles for the traditional *jambiya* daggers worn by men in Yemen.

International treaties outlaw the trade or sale of any rhino products. Nonetheless, poaching (illegal hunting) continues. A pound of rhino horn powder can sell for as much as $2,000. The animal's skin, blood, and urine are also sold. War and civil unrest also have a negative effect on the black rhino. During times of human conflict, horn and ivory may be traded for weapons, desperately poor people may turn to poaching for income, and legal protections are not enforced. In 1994 the U.S. Congress passed the Rhinoceros and Tiger Conservation Act. This measure provides financial assistance for the development of conservation measures for rhinos and tigers.

In the 1990s a number of conservation initiatives were launched to help conserve the rhino population. As a result, many remaining rhinos are now located in protected sanctuaries, where the animal populations can be easily monitored and controlled for rapid growth. In some cases, this has resulted in surplus animals, which are then relocated to other suitable, protected areas where the populations can continue to grow.

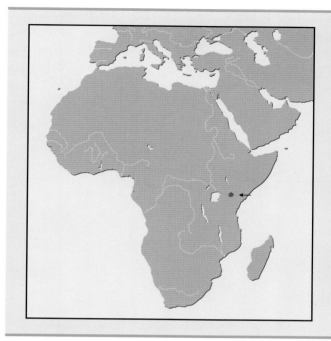

Rhinoceros, northern white
Ceratotherium simum cottoni

PHYLUM: Chordata
CLASS: Mammalia
ORDER: Perissodactyla
FAMILY: Rhinocerotidae
STATUS: Critically endangered, IUCN
Endangered, ESA
RANGE: Kenya (not original range)

Rhinoceros, northern white
Ceratotherium simum cottoni

Description and biology

The northern white rhinoceros is also called the northern square-lipped rhinoceros. The animal likely derives its color-related name from the Afrikaans (the language of white South Africans of Dutch descent) word *weit* meaning "wide." The reference is to the animal's wide snout. However, the word *weit* was misinterpreted by English speakers as "white," and so the animal is now known as the white rhinoceros.

The white rhinoceros is not white in color. It is a light gray, although it can also appear yellowish-brown. The northern white rhinoceros is one of two subspecies of white rhinoceroses in Africa, the other being the southern white rhinoceros. Recent studies have suggested that the northern white rhino may actually be a separate species, but scientists do not agree on this.

Hunters have driven this species to the edge of extinction because they wanted the animals' horns. Shown here is a northern white rhino that is missing one of its prized horns. © IMAGEBROKER/ALAMY.

The northern white rhinoceros is the world's second-largest land animal. Only the elephant is larger. The white rhino has a large, square-shaped mouth that allows it to graze on short grass. The male is slightly larger than the female. He has a head and body length of 12 to 13 feet (3.7 to 4 meters) and stands 5 to 6.5 feet (1.5 to 2 meters) tall at his shoulder. The tail measures 20 to 28 inches (51 to 71 centimeters) long. On average, males weigh about 5,000 pounds (2,270 kilograms) while females weigh around 3,750 pounds (1,700 kilograms). Despite its large size, the northern white rhinoceros can gallop as fast as 25 miles (40 kilometers) per hour.

Northern white rhinoceroses have short legs, broad ears, and two horns on their snout (*rhinoceros* means "nose horn"). White rhinos have the largest horns of any rhinoceros species, averaging 23.6 inches (60 centimeters) in length. They use their horns to fight other males over territory and females, to defend themselves against predators such as lions and hyenas, and to dig in the ground for mineral salts. The animals have poor vision, but highly developed senses of hearing and smell.

During the heat of the day, northern white rhinoceroses rest in shady spots. To keep cool, they often wallow in mud. When no water is available, they roll in dust to keep cool and to keep insects from biting. They feed in the evening and in the early morning. The average feeding territory for males is about 0.75 square miles (2 square kilometers), while the average feeding territory for females is from 2.3 to 7.7 square miles (6 to 20 square kilometers).

Male and female northern white rhinoceroses come together only to mate. Mating can take place any time of the year but occurs most frequently in February and June. After a gestation (pregnancy) period of about 16 months, a female gives birth to a single calf. The mother tends to the calf for two years. The species can live for 50 years.

Did You Know?

The white rhinoceros is separated into two subspecies: the northern and southern white rhinos. Although there are only three known northern rhinos left on the planet, the southern rhino is a conservation success story. It was thought to have gone extinct at the end of the 19th century, but a small population of not more than 100 individuals was discovered in South Africa in 1895. After more than a century of careful management, more than 20,000 southern white rhinoceroses live in the wild and are the only rhinos that are not classified as endangered. Despite this success, a surge of poaching (illegal hunting) in recent years has begun to threaten their numbers again.

Habitat and current distribution

The northern white rhinoceros used to range over parts of Uganda, Chad, Sudan, the Central African Republic, and the Democratic Republic of the Congo. It prefers to inhabit open grasslands and savannas (flat, tropical or subtropical grasslands). The last wild group of rhinos lived in Garamba National Park in the Democratic Republic of the Congo until the middle of the first decade of the 2000s, when poaching (illegal hunting) destroyed that population. Although there are unconfirmed reports of wild rhinos in South Sudan, there are only three known northern white rhinos left on the planet. These are in a private reserve in Kenya called the Ol Pejeta Conservancy.

History and conservation measures

The northern white rhinoceros is one of the most endangered animals in Africa. It has been driven to the brink of extinction by hunting, specifically for its horns. For hundreds of years, people in Asia have used powdered rhino horn in medicines and as aphrodisiacs (af-row-DEEZ-ee-aks; substances that stimulate sexual desire). In many Middle Eastern cultures, ceremonial daggers made with rhino-horn handles are highly valued. Despite efforts to enforce animal protection laws, poaching of rhinos has increased in recent years. Some conservationists (people who work to manage and protect nature) have gone as far as to capture rhinos and remove their horns without killing the rhinos so that the animals will not be poached just for their horns.

All international commercial trade in African rhino species and their products was prohibited in 1977 by the Convention on International Trade in Endangered Species of Wild Fauna and Flora (CITES; an international treaty to protect wildlife). In 1980 as many as 821 of the animals existed in the wild; however, six years later only 17 remained. Officials at Garamba National Park in the Democratic Republic of the Congo began intensive conservation efforts to protect the species and managed to keep a population of around 30 rhinos from the late 1980s to 2003. Despite these efforts, poaching has eliminated the rhino from the park.

In the mid-2010s, of the three known northern white rhinos, there is only one male, and he may be too old to mate successfully. The two remaining females are also elderly and unable to reproduce naturally. Scientists have considered crossing the northern white rhinoceros with the more numerous southern white rhinoceros or using the southern white rhino as a surrogate (substitute) parent for in vitro fertilization. (In vitro fertilization is a process in which scientists combine the eggs and sperm of a species in a laboratory in order to cause reproduction.) This could help keep the northern's genetic material in existence. As of November 2015, the San Diego Zoo had set aside $2 million for in vitro fertilization efforts. The necessary northern white rhino genetic material (eggs and sperm) for this project is preserved in the zoo's cold-storage facility. However, even if successful, the low number of remaining rhinoceroses would ensure that any future generations would be highly inbred (closely interrelated). This is a problem because the more genetic diversity a species has, the better its chances of surviving. Inbreeding can also lead to a variety of genetic diseases.

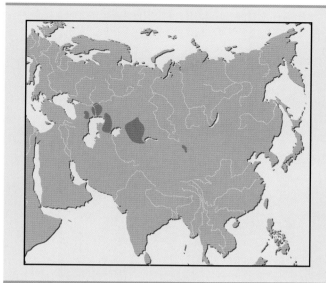

Saiga
Saiga tatarica

PHYLUM: Chordata
CLASS: Mammalia
ORDER: Artiodactyla
FAMILY: Bovidae
STATUS: Critically endangered, IUCN Endangered, ESA (*Saiga tatarica mongolica* subspecies only)
RANGE: Kazakhstan, Mongolia, Russia, Turkmenistan, Uzbekistan

Saiga
Saiga tatarica

Description and biology

The saiga is an antelope with a body about the size of a goat's. It is about 53 inches (135 centimeters) long and 28 inches (71 centimeters) tall and weighs an average of 77 pounds (35 kilograms). The animal's legs are long and thin. In the summer its coat is tan, but in winter it becomes white and very thick. Males have almost vertical horns, about 9 inches (23 centimeters) long, that are ringed most of the way to the top.

The saiga has a very unusual nose. Its nose is long, flexible, and wrinkled, curving downward and ending in large nostrils. The nose's shape and size serve useful functions. When the saiga herd migrates, the nose filters out dust the animals' hooves kick up. In winter, the nose warms up the cold air before it reaches the saiga's lungs.

Saigas live on the steppe (large, semi-arid, grass-covered plains found in southeastern Europe and Siberia). In herds of up to 2,000 animals, they migrate north in the summer and south in the winter, moving 48 to

The saiga, native to the steppes and deserts of southeastern Europe and central Asia, has seen its population depleted by poachers seeking the animal's horns and meat. The saiga has an unusual nose. © WILD WONDERS OF EUROPE/SHPILENOK/NATURE PICTURE LIBRARY/CORBIS.

72 miles (77 to 116 kilometers) a day. Saigas can run up to 48 miles (77 kilometers) per hour and can swim across rivers. As they travel, they graze on many species of plants. At night they dig shallow circles to sleep in.

Every November the saiga mating season begins. Males gather a group of 5 to 15 females and fiercely fight other males that try to mate with these females. During this period, males' noses swell up, sticky mucus covers the hair beneath their eyes, and they eat very little. Many die from starvation and exhaustion. Surviving males mate with up to 30 females. At the end of April, males begin migrating north. Females give birth to one or two foals, and several days later the females and foals join the males. When the herd reaches the summer feeding grounds, the animals form smaller groups. In autumn they gather in large groups to move south once again.

Habitat and current distribution

Most saigas live in Kazakhstan, a country in central Asia. Others live in Russia. During winter some migrating animals reach the neighboring countries of Uzbekistan and Turkmenistan. In 2014 the population was estimated at 262,000, but a May 2015 epidemic killed almost half the population. A small population of saigas in Mongolia is considered a subspecies (*Saiga tatarica mongolica*).

History and conservation measures

Saigas roamed Europe during the last ice age (a time when large parts of Earth were covered in ice that ended about 12,000 years ago). In Kazakhstan they are cultural symbols and appear on the country's paper money. The saiga population reached 1.25 million in the mid-1970s. After Kazakhstan gained its independence in 1991 after the collapse of the Soviet Union, however, the country suffered from severe poverty and people began hunting saiga. They sold the animals' meat as well as the males' horns, which have medicinal value in China. The population of male saigas was greatly reduced, and so fewer saigas were born, reducing the population further. By 2008 only 50,000 saigas remained.

Since 2008 Kazakhstan and other countries where saigas live have banned hunting the species. Kazakhstan has created a nature preserve for the animal. Nonprofit groups monitor illegal hunting and educate local communities about the importance of saiga preservation. By 2014 the population had rebounded to around 262,000. In May 2015, however, a mysterious epidemic killed at least 127,000 saigas. Scientists think that the animals' immune systems were weakened for some reason; this allowed them to fall prey to a type of bacteria that is normally found in healthy saigas. The epidemic, however, brought this interesting animal's cause greater worldwide publicity.

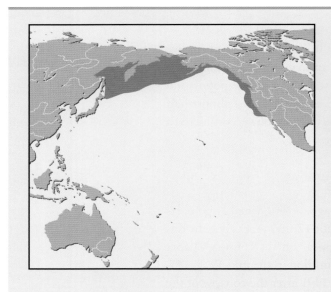

Sea lion, Steller
Eumetopias jubatus

PHYLUM: Chordata
CLASS: Mammalia
ORDER: Carnivora
FAMILY: Otariidae
STATUS: Near threatened, IUCN
Endangered, ESA (Alaska
west of Cape Suckling)
Delisted, ESA (Alaska east
of Cape Suckling, California,
Oregon, Washington)
RANGE: Canada, Japan, Russia, USA
(Alaska, California, Oregon, Washington)

Sea lion, Steller
Eumetopias jubatus

Description and biology

Sea lions and fur seals are members of the family of eared seals. They differ from true seals in that they have external ear flaps, a flexible neck, and hind flippers that can be turned forward for walking on land.

The Steller sea lion, also known as the northern sea lion, is one of the largest species of sea lion. Males may grow up to 13 feet (4 meters) in length and weigh as much as 2,200 pounds (1,000 kilograms). Females are much smaller, weighing about half as much. The sea lion's thin coat of short, coarse hair is tawny brown in color.

Steller sea lions feed primarily on fish, squid, octopi, and crustaceans (shellfish such as shrimp and crabs). They hunt in relatively shallow waters, but can make 20-minute dives down to depths of about 650 feet (198 meters).

During the spring breeding season, the sea lions gather in large groups called rookeries. The Aleutian Islands, a chain of volcanic islands curving in an arc about 1,200 miles (1,931 kilometers) west off the Alaska Peninsula, are one of the animals' principal gathering places. Males come ashore first and stake out their individual territories, occasionally through fighting. They will try to mate with females that pass through their territory. A dominant male who is able to defend his territory successfully may mate with as many as 30 females over a two-month period.

Females arrive on the islands shortly after the males. They first give birth to pups that had been conceived during the previous breeding season. A few weeks later, they are ready to mate again. The pups remain dependent on their mothers for about a year.

Habitat and current distribution

Steller sea lions inhabit the coastal waters around rocky islands. They occasionally come on shore to rest and sun themselves on the beaches. Their range extends from the Aleutian Islands west into the Bering Sea

Steller sea lions, found in the Pacific Northwest region of the United States and Canada as well as Russia and Japan, are protected by laws and conservation efforts in their native states. © NATUREDIVER/SHUTTERSTOCK.COM.

and down the Asian coast to northern Japan, and east into the Gulf of Alaska and down the Canadian and American coasts to Southern California. Wide-ranging individual sea lions have been sighted as far away as China.

A 2011 study of Steller sea lions estimated that there were around 143,000 adults in the wild, a decline of 28 percent since 1981. However, it is an increase over the number of animals since the 1990s. As of the 2010s Steller sea lion populations were increasing at about 4 percent per year. As a result, scientists estimate there is less than a 10 percent chance of extinction in the next 100 years.

History and conservation measures

Steller sea lions, along with other sea lions, were hunted extensively in the 19th century for their hides and blubber (fat that was melted down to make oil). In the 20th century they were killed by fishers who blamed the animals for robbing their catch of fish.

In 1972 the U.S. Congress passed the Marine Mammal Protection Act, which prohibited the hunting of sea lions in U.S. territorial waters. The Steller sea lion received further protection in 1990 when it was placed on the U.S. Endangered Species List. The National Marine Fisheries Service has acted to protect breeding spots from shipping and to reduce the number of accidental deaths of sea lions during commercial fishing operations. Sea lions are also protected in Japan, where there is a quota on hunting, and in Russia, which regulates access to rookeries (areas where the sea lions breed). Governments have also funded research to promote management and understanding of the sea lions.

As a result of conservation efforts, sea lion populations have slowly recovered, and the animals are no longer considered in danger of extinction. Consequently, the United States took eastern populations of Steller sea lions off the Endangered Species List, although populations in the western part of Alaska are still protected.

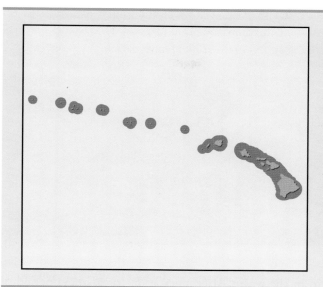

Seal, Hawaiian monk
Neomonachus schauinslandi (also
Monachus schauinslandi)

PHYLUM:	Chordata
CLASS:	Mammalia
ORDER:	Carnivora
FAMILY:	Phocidae
STATUS:	Endangered, IUCN Endangered, ESA
RANGE:	USA (Hawaii)

Seal, Hawaiian monk

Neomonachus schauinslandi (also *Monachus schauinslandi*)

Description and biology

The Hawaiian monk seal is a large, warm-water seal. It is a member of the family of true seals because it does not have external ear flaps as fur seals and sea lions do. An average Hawaiian monk seal measures 7 to 7.5 feet (2.1 to 2.3 meters) long and weighs 450 to 550 pounds (204 to 250 kilograms). Unlike most other species, female Hawaiian monk seals are larger than their male counterparts. The color of a monk seal's body varies slightly, from slate gray on top to silver gray underneath.

Hawaiian monk seals eat a variety of aquatic animals, including fish, eels, and octopi. They feed mainly along the shorelines of the islands they inhabit. Sharks often prey upon the seals.

Male Hawaiian monk seals choose a mate by wandering the beaches where females sun themselves. Since there are three times as many males as females, the females are often disturbed. When a male and female

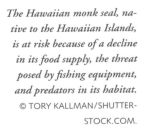

The Hawaiian monk seal, native to the Hawaiian Islands, is at risk because of a decline in its food supply, the threat posed by fishing equipment, and predators in its habitat.
© TORY KALLMAN/SHUTTER-STOCK.COM.

mate, they do so in the water. After a gestation (pregnancy) period of about 330 days, a female Hawaiian monk seal gives birth on the beach to a single pup. She nurses the pup for five weeks, during which time she fasts (does not eat). At birth, the pups are weak swimmers, and they must practice under their mother's supervision until they are weaned (given solid food instead of the mother's milk).

Habitat and current distribution

The Hawaiian monk seal inhabits the islands and atolls (ring-shaped reefs surrounding lagoons) of the Hawaiian Islands. Breeding takes place primarily around Kure Atoll, Midway Atoll, Pearl and Hermes Reef, Lisianski Island, Laysan Island, and French Frigate Shoals. The area of land habitat available for the seals is extremely limited on and around the Hawaiian Islands. Although some Hawaiian monk seals move between islands, most remain fairly close to their home beaches.

As of 2011, only about 1,200 Hawaiian monk seals remain in the wild. Their worldwide population has declined more than 20 percent since the early 1980s.

History and conservation measures

Hawaiian monk seals evolved in an environment totally free of humans. Since they did not know humans, they had no fear of them when contact was made. This made them easy prey for 19th-century hunters who sought their fur and blubber (fat that was melted down to make oil). Hunting was so rampant during this period, the species was pushed to the brink of extinction.

The population of Hawaiian monk seals increased slightly, however, in the early 20th century as the animals sought out undisturbed, remote areas. After World War II (1939–1945), humans began occupying more and more of the Hawaiian Islands, and the seals suffered. Any intrusion into their range has a negative effect on the seals. When disturbed by humans, a pregnant female may abort her fetus. If a nursing female is disturbed, she may be unable to continue nursing, and her pup may die.

Fishing activity in the Hawaiian monk seal's range is among the primary threats to the species. Seals can be injured by fishing hooks or become entangled in fishing nets and drown. Fishers may kill or harass the seals, believing the animals steal their catch and damage their fishing nets. Other threats include sharks, which prey on pups, and infections spread by wild animals, pets, and livestock.

Since the 1980s a variety of programs and regulations have aimed to ensure the survival of the Hawaiian monk seal. The species population has continued to decline during this period. However, without these aggressive conservation efforts there would be even fewer Hawaiian monk seals left in the wild. Interactions between humans and seals have been minimized. The marine habitat for the animals is cleaner. Sharks are removed or seal pups are relocated to reduce the number of seals killed. Adult seals are moved to other parts of the habitat to improve their likelihood of survival. Commercial fishing regulations help prevent interaction with the seals that could cause conflicts or accidents.

The land and water of the Hawaiian monk seal's habitat in the northwestern Hawaiian Islands are all within protected refuges and reserves. Strict controls in these areas limit or prohibit human activities that might harm the seals or their habitat, to ensure that Hawaiian monk seals—among the most endangered seals in the world—remain as undisturbed as possible.

Newer conservation efforts will focus on educating the public about the Hawaiian monk seal and its habitat. In 2014 a hospital was established to provide care for sick and injured seals. A program to vaccinate Hawaiian monk seals against two deadly viral diseases was expected to begin in 2015. Officials are also working on strategies to modify seals' behavior around fisheries and around domesticated animals.

Tamarin, golden lion
Leontopithecus rosalia

PHYLUM: Chordata
CLASS: Mammalia
ORDER: Primates
FAMILY: Callitrichidae
STATUS: Endangered, IUCN
Endangered, ESA (*Leonto-pithecus spp.*)
RANGE: Brazil

Tamarin, golden lion
Leontopithecus rosalia

Description and biology

Tamarins are unique New World (Western Hemisphere) monkeys that have a golden mane and long, silky fur. The most striking of the tamarins is the golden lion tamarin, which has a flaming reddish-gold coat and a luxuriant mane. Its face is dark and hairless. This monkey has an average head and body length of 8 to 13 inches (20 to 33 centimeters) and weighs between 21 and 28 ounces (595 and 794 grams). Its furry tail measures 12 to 16 inches (30 to 41 centimeters) long.

Golden lion tamarins are tree dwellers. Active during the day, they travel from tree to tree, feeding on fruit, insects, plant matter, and small animals.

The animals often form family groups ranging from two to eight members. A male-female pair forms the center of the group. After a gestation (pregnancy) period of 126 to 132 days, female golden lion tamarins normally give birth to twins. Most births occur between September and March. Both mother and father share responsibility for raising their young.

Habitat and current distribution

The golden lion tamarin prefers to inhabit tropical forests along the Atlantic coast at altitudes below 984 feet (300 meters) above sea level. The animal is usually found 10 to 33 feet (3 to 10 meters) above the ground in trees where dense vines and interlacing branches provide cover.

The animal is limited to the Brazilian state of Rio de Janeiro. In 1992 biologists (people who study living organisms) estimated that only about 560 golden lion tamarins existed in the wild. Since then, with much work from conservationists (people who work to manage and protect nature), the population has increased to 3,200 as of 2014.

History and conservation measures

The golden lion tamarin lives in one of the most densely populated parts of Brazil. The major cause of the animal's decline was deforestation (large-scale removal of trees). Less than 2 percent of the animal's original habitat remains. As a result, only pockets of forest provide suitable habitat for the golden lion tamarin. The separation of these areas from each other, called fragmentation, also reduces genetic diversity (variety of biological units that pass on different traits). Less genetically diverse populations are less healthy. In 1996 the International Union for Conservation of Nature and Natural Resources (IUCN) listed the species as critically endangered.

The Poço das Antas and União Biological Reserves were established in the state of Rio de Janeiro specifically to protect the golden

Did You Know?

Before 1500, golden lion tamarins lived in a vast forest. Then Europeans arrived. The people cut down trees for timber and cleared land for sugarcane, coffee plantations, roads, and towns. These activities split up the tamarins' habitat into small pieces, or fragments, that do not border each other. Habitat fragmentation such as this is the main reason why many species are endangered. Fewer animals can live in these smaller areas. When there is a smaller population, one natural disaster or contagious disease can destroy the entire species. And if animals cannot move between these isolated areas to mate, their offspring are less genetically diverse. People working to save animals harmed by fragmentation have several options. Sometimes, as with the golden lion tamarin, they can buy land in between fragments to create a larger, continuous area. But sometimes, they must concentrate on preserving the smaller areas that remain.

The golden lion tamarin has benefited from protection and conservancy efforts in its native Brazil, including breeding programs and habitat restoration. © ERIC GEVAERT/SHUTTERSTOCK.COM.

lion tamarin. Conservationists have brought back the species from the verge of extinction by breeding tamarins in captivity and reintroducing them into the wild. They also move these tamarins from isolated, unsafe forests to larger, protected ones. In addition, they have educated local people about the species, and deforestation of the area has almost entirely stopped. As a result of these efforts, the golden lion tamarin population has increased, and the IUCN downlisted the animal to endangered in 2003.

Conservationists celebrated the 2014 count of 3,200 golden lion tamarins. Their goal is to create forest corridors between the separate fragments of forests where these tamarins live. This will allow the golden lion tamarins to safely travel the whole extent of their range. Conservationists are forming these connections by planting forest areas on privately owned land. They expect that the reconnected forest will help to improve the future of the species, and they plan to continue monitoring the golden lion tamarin and managing its habitat.

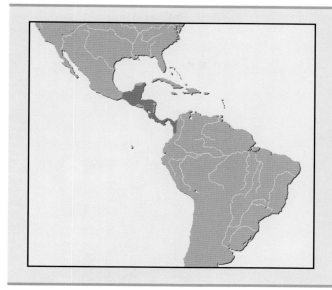

Tapir, Central American
Tapirella bairdii (also *Tapirus bairdii*)

PHYLUM: Chordata
CLASS: Mammalia
ORDER: Perissodactyla
FAMILY: Tapiridae
STATUS: Endangered, IUCN
Endangered, ESA
RANGE: Belize, Colombia, Costa Rica, Guatemala, Honduras, Mexico, Nicaragua, Panama

Tapir, Central American
Tapirella bairdii (also *Tapirus bairdii*)

Description and biology

The Central American or Baird's tapir is a large animal with a medium to dark brown coat. Related to the horse and rhinoceros, it is almost as large as a donkey. An average Central American tapir has a head and body length of 6.5 to 8 feet (2 to 2.4 meters) and weighs between 550 and 660 pounds (250 and 300 kilograms). It stands 36 to 42 inches (91 to 107 centimeters) tall at its shoulder.

The animal has short legs and a stout body that narrows in front, which allows it to move quickly through the forest. A good swimmer, it spends much time in water or in mud. With small, deeply set eyes, the animal has poor vision, but its senses of hearing and smell are acute. Its nose and upper lip extend to form a short trunk, which the animal uses to shovel food into its mouth. Its diet consists of grass, leaves, and a variety of fruit. Jaguars and mountain lions are the Central American tapir's main predators.

A Central American tapir roams at a national park in Costa Rica. The species, native to southern Mexico and Central America, is at risk because of loss of habitat and hunting. © THOMAS MARENT/ENCYCLOPEDIA/CORBIS.

Male and female Central American tapirs mate at any time during the year. After a gestation (pregnancy) period of 390 to 405 days, a female tapir gives birth to a single calf. At birth, the calf is covered with protective colored markings that allow it to blend easily into its forest environment. These markings begin to fade within a few months. The calf may remain dependent on its mother for up to a year.

Habitat and current distribution

The Central American tapir is found from southern Mexico to northern Colombia. It lives in a variety of humid habitats, including marshes, mangrove swamps, and tropical rain forests. Biologists (people who study living organisms) estimate the total population of the species to be fewer than 5,000 animals in the wild.

History and conservation measures

The Central American tapir once ranged as far south as Ecuador. In the past, the animal was hunted for its meat and hide and for sport. Now legally protected, the tapir nevertheless continues to be the target of poaching (illegal hunting). Despite this problem, the most serious threat to the Central American tapir today is habitat destruction. At least half of the Central American tapir's forest habitat has been lost to deforestation (large-scale removal of trees) since the mid-20th century. Vast tracts of land in the tapir's range have been cleared for farmland to feed the growing human population in the area and for oil palm plantations. New highways and roads in former forest areas also threaten the species. They decrease the area available for the Central American tapir, as well as separate and isolate the remaining habitats. A number of tapirs have also been killed accidentally during construction. Guerrilla warfare within the range presents another threat, particularly because it impedes research and conservation measures.

Many Central American tapirs live in protected parks and natural reserves in its habitat range. Although there are national laws that protect the animal in the range countries, the laws are often not enforced in some areas. Important efforts to save the Central American tapir are ongoing, however. Scientists are conducting research to better understand the animal and the areas where it might thrive. They are also testing improved techniques to count the animals using camera traps and to track them in the wild using GPS collars. Species reintroduction—that is, moving animals born in captivity from zoos to natural habitats where they can reproduce—is also being explored. To that end, the Nicaragua Tapir Project opened the country's first tapir rescue, rehabilitation, and reintroduction center in the Wawashang Reserve in 2014.

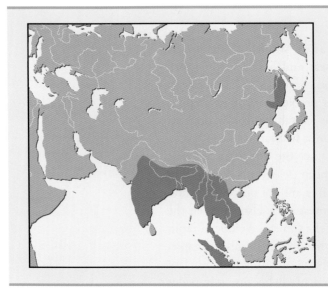

Tiger
Panthera tigris

PHYLUM: Chordata
CLASS: Mammalia
ORDER: Carnivora
FAMILY: Felidae
STATUS: Endangered, IUCN
Endangered, ESA
RANGE: Bangladesh, Bhutan, Cambodia, China, India, Indonesia, Laos, Malaysia, Myanmar, Nepal, North Korea, Russia, Thailand, Vietnam

Tiger
Panthera tigris

Description and biology

Tigers are members of the cat family. They are the biggest of the big cats, a group that includes leopards, lions, and jaguars. There are nine subspecies of tiger. Three of these—the Bali, Caspian, and Javan—all became extinct in the 20th century. The remaining six subspecies are the Bengal (or Indian), Indo-Chinese, Malayan, Siberian (or Amur), South Chinese, and Sumatran.

The color, size, and general appearance of tigers varies according to the subspecies. On average, a male tiger has a head and body length of 5 to 9 feet (1.5 to 2.7 meters) and a tail length of 2 to 3 feet (0.6 to 0.9 meters). It stands about 3.5 feet (1 meter) tall at its shoulder and weighs between 220 and 660 pounds (100 and 300 kilograms). Because the animal is found in a variety of climates, from the snowy forests of Siberia to the jungles of Indonesia, the length of its coat varies. In general, its coat is orange-yellow in color, with numerous black stripes. Its under-

The tiger, threatened by poaching and loss of habitat across its Asian habitat, is the target of several programs to protect and increase its population.
© HELEN E. GROSE/SHUTTER-STOCK.COM.

parts are white. The striping pattern varies not only among subspecies but with each individual tiger.

Tigers are mainly nocturnal (active at night). They are able climbers, good swimmers, and fast runners. Tigers can leap up to 32 feet

(10 meters) and swim up to 18 miles (29 kilometers). They are carnivores (animals that eat mainly meat), preying on deer, antelope, wild pigs, cattle, and other mammals. Their senses of hearing, sight, and smell are all keen. Tigers stalk or ambush their prey, pouncing on it from the rear or the side. The prey is usually killed by a bite to the neck or spine. Despite their abilities, tigers are successful hunters only about 10 percent of the time. Because of this, most tigers travel between 10 and 20 miles (16 and 32 kilometers) a night in search of food. Though uncommon, tigers do attack and eat humans; however, those that do are generally too old or sick to hunt wild animals.

Tigers are solitary animals with home ranges that vary between 4 and 1,500 square miles (10 and 3,885 square kilometers). They are not entirely loners, as they will band together to hunt and to share their kill. Males and females come together to mate at any time during the year, though primarily between November and April. After a gestation (pregnancy) period of just over 100 days, a female gives birth to a litter of two to four cubs. The cubs are blind and helpless for the first two weeks. They nurse for six to eight weeks, then begin accompanying their mother on hunting trips. After almost two years, they leave their mother's territory to establish their own.

Habitat and current distribution

Tigers occupy a wide variety of habitats, including rain forests, evergreen forests, mangrove swamps, marshlands, grasslands, and savannas.

As of 2010, only about 2,100 tigers remained in the wild. The Bengal tiger has the largest population of any tiger subspecies. It is found in India, Bangladesh, Myanmar, Nepal, and Bhutan. The Indo-Chinese tiger is found in Laos, Malaysia, Thailand, Myanmar, and Vietnam. The South Chinese tiger is found only in southern China and is believed to be extinct. The Siberian tiger, the largest of all subspecies, is found in North Korea, northern China, and the far east of Russia. The Sumatran tiger, the smallest of all living tiger subspecies, is found on the island of Sumatra, Indonesia.

History and conservation measures

The protection of tigers has been an international concern since the 1970s. At the beginning of the 20th century, an estimated 100,000 tigers roamed the Asian forests and grasslands. That population has since decreased by about 95 percent in the early 21st century. The Bali tiger, the smallest of the eight subspecies, became extinct in 1937. The Caspian tiger, once found as far west as Turkey, disappeared in the 1970s. The Javan tiger was last seen in 1983.

Historically, the tiger has been hunted as a trophy and for its beautiful coat. For centuries, many Asian cultures have used other tiger parts (bones, eyes, teeth, nails) in medicines, believing they cure diseases such as rheumatism and dysentery. Some people even believe that a soup made from the genitals of a male tiger can increase sexual ability. International treaties now protect tigers, but because of these ancient beliefs, the animals are still hunted and traded.

The primary threats to the tiger's survival are poaching (illegal hunting) and habitat destruction. As forests throughout Asia are cleared for human settlement, for timber or to create farmland, tigers are forced into smaller and smaller areas. These tiny islands of forest do not hold enough prey for the animals, and they are forced to feed on livestock and even humans. Increased contact with humans has only resulted in more tiger deaths.

The Tiger Summit of 2010 in St. Petersburg, Russia, was the first-ever international summit convened to save an endangered species. It was attended by representatives, including a few heads of state, from the countries in the tiger's habitat range. At the summit, countries agreed to "a 12-year recovery program to double the population of tigers in the wild by 2022." The conservation plans include strategies for protecting habitats, fighting illegal hunting and consumer demand for tiger parts, restoring populations in their former range, and engaging local communities in efforts to save the tiger from extinction.

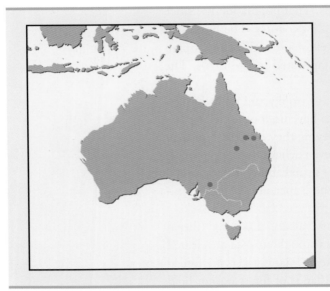

Wallaby, bridled nail-tailed
Onychogalea fraenata

PHYLUM: Chordata
CLASS: Mammalia
ORDER: Diprotodontia
FAMILY: Macropodidae
STATUS: Endangered, IUCN
Endangered, ESA
RANGE: Australia

Wallaby, bridled nail-tailed
Onychogalea fraenata

Description and biology

A member of the kangaroo family, the bridled nail-tailed wallaby gets its name from the white line that runs like a bridle from under its forearms to the back of its neck (bridled) and from the horny spur on the end of its tail (nail-tailed). An average bridled nail-tailed wallaby has a head and body length of 17.5 to 23.5 inches (44.5 to 59.7 centimeters) and weighs about 11 pounds (5 kilograms). Its tail is almost as long as its body, measuring 13.5 to 19.5 inches (34.3 to 49.5 centimeters).

This wallaby is a solitary animal that rests in a shallow depression under a shrub, tree, or log during the day. At night, it feeds on a variety of grasses and herbs. Dingoes, wild Australian dogs, are the animal's main predator.

Wallabies are marsupials, or mammals whose young continue to develop after birth in a pouch on the outside of the mother's body. Bridled nail-tailed wallaby females are able to conceive while they have a joey

A bridled nail-tailed wallaby roams in its grassy habitat in Queensland, Australia, where the species is protected. © DAVE WATTS/ALAMY.

(infant) in the pouch, with the development timing being such that the next baby is born just after the previous one leaves permanently, typically around 17 weeks. The animals breed year-round, with an average life expectancy of around six years. Biologists (people who study living organisms) know very little about the breeding habits of this particular species of wallaby in the wild; most available data on bridled nail-tailed wallabies are based on observation of these animals in captivity.

Habitat and current distribution

The only naturally occurring population of bridled nail-tailed wallabies lives in a 42-square-mile (110-square-kilometer) area in Taunton National Park near the town of Dingo in the northeastern Australian state of Queensland. There are also populations that have been reintroduced in two other protected areas in Queensland and one in New South Wales. The population of bridled nail-tailed wallabies varies each year, depending on rainfall. Estimates vary from 600 to 1,900.

During the day, bridled nail-tailed wallabies prefer to inhabit forest areas dominated by trees or shrubs. At night, they feed in open woodland or grassland areas.

History and conservation measures

The bridled nail-tailed wallaby was once common throughout eastern and southeastern Australia. In the early 1800s farmers and ranchers moved into the animal's range, bringing with them domestic livestock. The bridled nail-tailed wallaby was then forced to compete for food with these grazing animals, especially sheep. The farmers and ranchers soon considered the wallaby a pest and began paying to have the animal killed. They were also killed by foxes, which were brought to British colonies in Australia for sport hunting. By 1930 the species was considered extinct.

In 1973 a small population of bridled nail-tailed wallabies was discovered near the town of Dingo. The wallabies likely survived in this area because it is free of foxes. Later that decade, the Taunton Scientific Reserve was established to protect this newly discovered population. The majority of surviving bridled nail-tailed wallabies now exist there. Park managers provide food during periods of low rainfall and remove feral (once domesticated, now wild) cats. They also monitor and support the park's natural environment to suit the wallabies' needs for nutrition and shelter. Since the recovery effort began, the bridled nail-tailed wallaby has also been reintroduced to Idalia National Park and Avocet Nature Refuge in Queensland and to the Scotia Sanctuary in New South Wales.

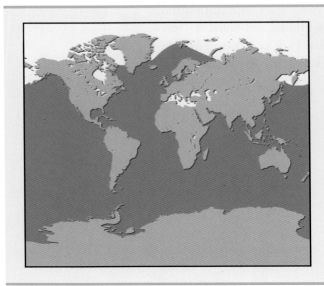

Whale, blue
Balaenoptera musculus

PHYLUM: Chordata
CLASS: Mammalia
ORDER: Cetacea
FAMILY: Balaenopteridae
STATUS: Endangered, IUCN
Endangered, ESA
RANGE: Oceanic except the Arctic
Ocean

Whale, blue
Balaenoptera musculus

Description and biology

Scientists consider the blue whale to be the largest animal that has ever lived on Earth. An average adult measures 79 to 88 feet (24 to 27 meters) long and weighs between 200,000 and 300,000 pounds (91,000 and 136,000 kilograms). In the Antarctic, blue whales can grow up to 110 feet (33 meters), but they are smaller in the North Atlantic and North Pacific. The blue whale has a wide, U-shaped head and a dorsal (on its back) fin. Its body is slate blue in color. Sometimes, microorganisms accumulate on the whale's body, giving it a faintly yellow sheen. This is why it is also called the sulfur-bottomed whale.

The blue whale feeds mainly on krill, which are small, shrimplike shellfish. Like all whales in its family, the blue whale uses the fringed baleen (whalebone) plates that line its mouth to strain krill from seawater. The animal has 80 to 100 furrows (called ventral grooves) lining its narrow neck. When it sucks in seawater, the grooves allow its throat to expand like a pouch. As it expels the large volume of water from its mouth, its baleen plates trap the krill.

Blue whales mate at the end of winter. After a gestation (pregnancy) period of 300 to 330 days, a female blue whale gives birth to one calf, which measures 20 to 23 feet (6 to 7 meters) long. The calf nurses for up to seven months.

Habitat and current distribution

Blue whales are found in all of the major oceans. Most blue whales prefer cold waters and open seas. In summer, they inhabit subarctic and Antarctic waters, feeding on krill in the water of melting ice packs. In winter, they migrate to warmer waters near the equator, where they will mate. Some blue whales, however, do not appear to migrate, residing year-round in tropical coastal areas. Such whales have been observed off the coast of Peru and in the northern Indian Ocean.

The blue whale, found in all oceans, is currently protected in many parts of the world after decades as a target of commercial whalers. Here, one rises to the surface near the coast of Norway. © KEVIN SCHAFER/TERRA/CORBIS.

Did You Know?

Humans have hunted whales—such as the blue whale—for thousands of years. All parts of the animal were useful; one whale could provide nutrition, building materials, clothing, and even oil for lamps. However, the advance of technology meant that hunting became more efficient in the modern age, and it is thought that more whales were killed in the early 1900s than in the previous four centuries combined. Many whale species became endangered. The International Whaling Commission (IWC) ordered a moratorium (temporary halt) of whaling in 1982; since then, only Japan, Norway, and Iceland have continued hunting whales for various cultural and scientific reasons. Today, certain whale populations have managed to at least partially recover from almost certain extinction.

Scientists are not sure how many blue whales currently exist in the world's oceans. Population estimates range from 10,000 to 25,000 whales, which is about 10 percent of the population thought to exist at the beginning of the 20th century.

History and conservation measures

When large-scale whaling began in the 17th century, blue whales were considered too difficult to hunt because of their size, speed, and strength. This view changed in the mid-19th century with the development of the exploding-head harpoon and the factory ship (which could completely process whales caught at sea). Blue whales were now a prime prey, and their numbers decreased drastically, especially in the 20th century. Between 1920 and 1970, an estimated 280,000 blue whales were slaughtered.

In 1966 the International Whaling Commission (IWC; body that regulates most of the world's whaling activity) banned the hunting of blue whales. Whaling is no longer considered a threat to the species' survival. The primary threats to the blue whale are ship strikes, which can severely injure or kill the animal, and interactions with fishing operations, where the whales may become entangled in nets or injured. Ongoing conservation efforts include strategies to prevent both types of accidents.

The blue whale also faces the loss of its main food source, krill. Scientists have discovered that the krill population has decreased by as much as 80 percent since the 1970s. Krill feed on algae that grow underneath sea ice. As temperatures have risen in Antarctica, melting a sizable portion of sea ice, the algae population has diminished. In a domino effect, this loss could affect the entire Antarctic food chain. Scientists believe this situation is the result of global warming—the rise in Earth's temperature that is attributed to the buildup of carbon dioxide and other pollutants in the atmosphere.

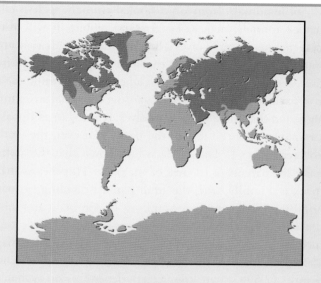

Wolf, gray
Canis lupus

PHYLUM: Chordata
CLASS: Mammalia
ORDER: Carnivora
FAMILY: Canidae
STATUS: Least concern, IUCN
Endangered, ESA (most U.S. states)
Threatened, ESA (Minnesota)
Delisted, ESA (Idaho, Montana, and
parts of Oregon, Washington, and
Utah)
RANGE: Afghanistan, Albania, Armenia, Azerbaijan, Belarus, Bhutan, Bosnia
and Herzegovina, Bulgaria, Canada,
China, Croatia, Czech Republic, Estonia,
Finland, France, Georgia, Germany, Greece, Greenland, Hungary, India, Iran, Iraq, Israel, Italy,
Jordan, Kazakhstan, Kyrgyzstan, Latvia, Libya, Lithuania, Macedonia, Mexico, Moldova, Mongolia, Montenegro, Myanmar, Nepal, North Korea, Norway, Oman, Pakistan, Poland, Portugal,
Romania, Russia, Saudi Arabia, Serbia, Slovakia, Slovenia, South Korea, Spain, Sweden, Syria,
Tajikistan, Turkey, Turkmenistan, Ukraine, United Arab Emirates, USA, Uzbekistan, Yemen

Wolf, gray
Canis lupus

Description and biology

The gray wolf, also known as the timber wolf, is the largest member
of the Canidae (dog) family and was once the world's most widely distributed land mammal. An average adult measures 5 to 6 feet (1.5 to
1.8 meters) from nose to tip of tail and stands 26 to 32 inches (66 to
81 centimeters) at its shoulder. It can weigh between 70 and 155 pounds
(32 and 70 kilograms). Females are slightly smaller than males. The
wolf's coat can be a number of different colors, such as gray, red, brown,
tan, black, or pure white.

The gray wolf is well adapted for hunting. It has long legs and keen
senses of hearing and smell. The wolf is a carnivore, or meat eater. It

feeds on a variety of mammals, from large, hoofed animals, such as elk and deer, to smaller animals, such as beavers and rabbits. It will also eat small rodents, such as mice. Wolves generally kill animals that are young, old, diseased, or deformed—those that are easy to capture. If the opportunity arises, however, the wolf will kill a healthy adult animal.

Wolves live in packs. Previous theories regarding the social structure of wolf packs suggested that there were two wolves, referred to as alphas, that exerted dominance over the rest of the pack. However, the work of American wolf researcher L. David Mech has shown that the alpha wolves are actually the parents of the rest of the pack. This means that a typical wolf pack is a family, with the adult parents dividing various tasks among the group. The hierarchy, or ranking, of dominant and subordinate animals within a pack helps it function as a unit.

A pack generally hunts within a specific territory. Territories may be as large as 50 square miles (130 square kilometers) or even extend to 1,000 square miles (2,590 square kilometers), depending on available food. Wolves communicate with pack members and other wolf packs through facial and body postures, scent markings (urine and feces), and vocalizations, which include barks, whimpers, growls, and howls.

Gray wolves begin mating when they are two to three years old. A female digs a den or uses an existing shelter or structure in which to rear her pups for the first six weeks of their lives. In early spring she gives birth to an average litter of six pups. The pups depend completely on their mother's milk for the first month, and then they are gradually weaned off the mother's milk and begin to eat solid food. By six to eight months of age, when they are almost fully grown, the young wolves begin traveling and hunting with the adults. Often, a young wolf of one or two years of age will leave and try to form its own pack.

Habitat and current distribution

The gray wolf has one of the largest ranges of all mammal species, existing in most of the Northern Hemisphere. However, it currently occupies only two-thirds of its original range as a result of habitat fragmentation (breaking up of habitat into smaller areas that no longer border each other) and hunting by humans. Its range is still widespread enough and its population stable enough in most of the world that it has been given a status of least concern by the International Union for Conservation of Nature and Natural Resources (IUCN).

The gray wolf, once found in many parts of the world, is the focus of many programs to reintroduce the species in regions where its population dropped or had been eliminated.
© MIREK SRB/SHUTTERSTOCK .COM.

In the United States, however, the gray wolf is still listed as endangered in most states. It is found primarily in Alaska and Wyoming (listed as endangered); Minnesota (listed as threatened); and Montana, Idaho, north-central Utah, eastern Oregon, and eastern Washington (delisted). Approximately 65,000 wolves remain in Canada and Alaska. There are 3,722 total in the western Great Lakes states, 1,782 in the northern Rocky Mountains, and 109 in Arizona and New Mexico, where it has recently been reintroduced after 30 years of local extinction.

Worldwide, the gray wolf population is found mostly in the northernmost wilderness forests and tundra areas of Canada, Alaska, Europe, and Asia. Isolated pockets of gray wolves also exist farther south.

History and conservation measures

Gray wolves once lived everywhere north of about 15°N latitude, a parallel that runs through southern Mexico and southern India. They occupied an array of climates and ecosystems (ecological systems including all of their living things and their environment), from dry deserts to deciduous (made up of trees whose leaves fall off annually) forests to frozen tundra. On the North American continent, they ranged from coast to coast and from Canada to Mexico.

As settlers moved west across America in the 19th century, they killed off most of the populations of bison, deer, elk, and moose—animals that were important prey for wolves. With little natural prey left, wolves then turned to sheep and cattle. To protect livestock, ranchers and government agencies began a decades-long campaign to eliminate the animals. Wolves were trapped, shot, and hunted with dogs. Animal carcasses (dead bodies) poisoned with strychnine (pronounced STRICK-nine) were left out for wolves to eat. This practice also killed eagles, ravens, foxes, bears, and other animals that fed on the poisoned carcasses. By the time the gray wolf became protected in 1974 under the U.S. Endangered Species Act, only a few hundred were left in the contiguous United States (the connected 48 states); they were located in northern Minnesota.

At present, gray wolves occupy a fraction of their former range. In 1995 and 1996 the U.S. government relocated about 65 gray wolves from Canada to Yellowstone National Park (mostly in Wyoming) and central Idaho. The wolves adjusted quickly. Within two years, they had reshaped the Yellowstone ecosystem, improving the overall balance of species in the park. The wolves killed many of the park's coyotes, which allowed the rodent population to increase. This, in turn, allowed animals that feed on rodents to increase in number. Other animals, such as grizzly bears, benefited by feeding on the remains of elk killed by wolves.

From the beginning, however, ranchers and farm groups have opposed the reintroduction of gray wolves, claiming that wolves are a threat to livestock in the area. To ease the concerns of ranchers, the U.S. government changed the species' status in Idaho from endangered to threatened. This change gave ranchers the legal right to shoot wolves that attack their livestock. This compromise was still not enough for some livestock groups, and they sued to stop the reintroduction efforts. In December 1997 a federal judge ruled that the government had violated parts of the Endangered Species Act when it reintroduced wolves to Yellowstone and central Idaho. The judge did delay his decision, allowing federal agencies and other environmental groups time to file an appeal. A U.S. appeals court reversed the decision, and the gray wolves were allowed to remain in Yellowstone. If the judge's decision had been upheld, all the gray wolves in Yellowstone would have had to be killed or removed.

Since then, there have been several other legal battles over the reintroduction of the gray wolf and its protection under the Endangered Species Act. A number of states with large livestock populations continued to oppose the endangered listing of the gray wolf. In 2011 U.S. senators from Idaho and Montana helped pass a controversial law that delisted the gray wolf in Idaho, Montana, eastern Oregon, eastern Washington, and north-central Utah. As a result, hunting of gray wolves is legal in these states, according to each state's laws. Efforts to delist the wolf in other states have been reversed by U.S. courts, but states where wolves are found continue to seek a delisted status. In 2012 the Wyoming population was removed from the U.S. Endangered Species List, but environmental groups challenged the decision, and a 2014 court ruling allowed the wolves in that state to return to protected status.

Before the ruling reversing the delisting of the species in Wyoming, conservationists (people who work to manage and protect nature) had criticized the U.S. Fish and Wildlife Service for removing wolves from endangered status in some states where populations were still small or nonexistent. Furthermore, the gray wolf's endangered status is not secure; members of the U.S. Congress have made several efforts to delist the species without regard to the scientific evidence of its recovery. If the protection provided by endangered status were removed, it is likely that the species would be limited to the isolated areas it now inhabits and would not fully recover to roam its former North American range.

Wolf, maned
Chrysocyon brachyurus

PHYLUM: Chordata
CLASS: Mammalia
ORDER: Carnivora
FAMILY: Canidae
STATUS: Near threatened, IUCN
Endangered, ESA
RANGE: Argentina, Bolivia, Brazil,
Paraguay, Peru

Wolf, maned
Chrysocyon brachyurus

Description and biology

The maned wolf is related to dogs, wolves, and foxes but has a look all its own. It has a pointed fox-like face but large, 7-inch (18-centimeter) ears that swivel to pick up sounds of potential prey. Reddish-orange fur covers most of the maned wolf's body, contrasting with long, black hairs on its shoulder and neck. These hairs stand up when the animal feels threatened, which makes it look bigger. Its throat and the tip of its tail are white. Long, black legs raise the animal above the tall grasslands it inhabits, helping it spy prey. These unusually long legs make it look like a fox on stilts. The maned wolf stands about 35 inches (90 centimeters) at the shoulder, with a head and body length of around 41 inches (105 centimeters) and an 18-inch (45-centimeter) tail. It weighs on aver-

The maned wolf has seen the grasslands and woodlands of its habitat in central South America depleted by agricultural development. Increasing human populations have put the animal at risk of becoming roadkill along highways and prey for domestic dogs.
© DMITRI GOMON/SHUTTERSTOCK.COM.

age 50 pounds (23 kilograms). By contrast, the gray wolf is shorter but weighs more than twice as much.

The maned wolf does not form packs. An individual wolf shares its territory with one mate, with the two interacting only to breed and rear young. The wolf hunts from dusk to midnight. It barks loudly to warn other wolves of its presence and marks its territory with strong-smelling urine. Half of its diet consists of small mammals, mostly rodents and rabbits. The other half is made up of plants, such as sugarcane, and fruits, such as bananas, guavas, and the wolf apple, which resembles a tomato. Maned wolves avoid humans.

Maned wolves mate anytime from November to April. Gestation (pregnancy) lasts 60 to 65 days, and two to six pups are born. They weigh about 1 pound (0.45 kilogram) at birth and have dark fur for several months. Pups are fully grown at 1 year. The life span of a maned wolf in the wild is unknown, but captive animals live 12 to 15 years.

Habitat and current distribution

The maned wolf inhabits central and southeastern Brazil, Paraguay, eastern Bolivia, northern Argentina, and a small area of southeastern Peru. It prefers habitats with both patches of forest and open grassland. It can also live in swampy areas and scrublands. Biologists (people who study living organisms) estimate that there are about 20,000 maned wolves in Brazil and a few thousand in other countries.

History and conservation measures

Maned wolves evolved during the Pleistocene epoch (1.8 million years ago to 11,700 years ago) or earlier. They were already there when the first humans arrived in South America. In Brazil, some people have traditionally believed that maned wolves can kill chickens just by looking at them and that hearing the bark of a maned wolf indicates a change in the weather. Some people have also believed that the maned wolf's body parts, especially its eyes, brought good luck. This led to the hunting of the animals for those parts. The maned wolf is on the Brazilian government's endangered species list, and some live in the country's national parks, where they are protected from hunters.

The main threat to this species is habitat loss that results when its territory is converted to use for farming. Such habitat loss also isolates animals from each other, causing more inbreeding (animals mating with relatives) and thus lower genetic diversity (variety of biological units that pass on inherited traits). Because many roads run through the species' habitat, maned wolves are frequently killed by motor vehicles. Another threat comes from domestic dogs. They chase and sometimes kill maned wolves; dogs can also spread parasites and diseases.

North American zoos have had a species survival plan for the maned wolf since 1985. The goals are to keep a healthy captive population in zoos, educate people worldwide about the species, and study the animals. In the United States, about 90 maned wolves live in captivity, but captive-born pups often do not survive. Researchers in Brazil and other South American countries are studying the maned wolf's population in the wild and educating local communities about the importance of this unique animal.

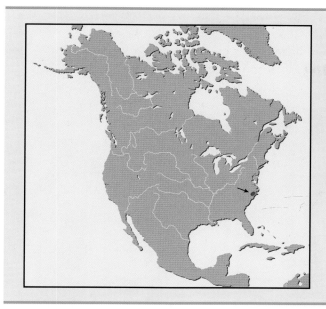

Wolf, red
Canis rufus

PHYLUM: Chordata
CLASS: Mammalia
ORDER: Carnivora
FAMILY: Canidae
STATUS: Critically endangered, IUCN
Endangered, ESA
RANGE: USA (North Carolina)

Wolf, red
Canis rufus

Description and biology

Despite its name, the red wolf has a coat that varies in color from cinnamon-brown to nearly black. Smaller than its relative the gray wolf, the red wolf is about the size of a large dog. It has an average head and body length of 37 to 47 inches (94 to 119 centimeters) and a tail length of about 10 inches (25 centimeters). It weighs between 45 and 65 pounds (20 and 29 kilograms). The animal's most distinguishing features are its long ears and legs.

The red wolf feeds on swamp rabbits, raccoons, birds, white-tailed deer, and other small mammals. It is also known to eat chickens and, sometimes, calves and piglets. A male and female pair hunts on a territory averaging 30 to 40 square miles (78 to 104 square kilometers).

The wolves have a complex social order centering on family groups called packs. Individual males and females form a mating pair that is

The red wolf, once extinct in wild, was reintroduced in eastern North Carolina in 1987. © RICHARD HIGGINS/ALAMY.

long-lasting. During the mating season (January to April), the pair establishes a den, usually in hollow logs, in ditch banks, or under rock outcrops. Here they raise their young year after year. A female red wolf gives birth to a litter of two to eight pups after a gestation (pregnancy) period of 61 to 63 days. The pups, which are born with their eyes closed, are completely dependent on their mother for the first two months. They remain with their parents for about two to three years.

Habitat and current distribution

Although it was once common throughout the eastern and southern United States, the red wolf was declared extinct in the wild in 1980. All the animals currently in existence are descendants of animals raised in captivity. In 1987 a small population of captive-bred red wolves was reintroduced into the wild in North Carolina. According to the U.S. Fish and Wildlife Service, as of 2015 there were 50 to 75 red wolves living in natural habitats in eastern North Carolina and about 200 in captivity throughout the United States.

The animals prefer to inhabit swamps, wetlands, bushlands, and forests.

History and conservation measures

The red wolf once ranged from central Texas east to the Atlantic coast and from the Gulf of Mexico north to southern Pennsylvania. In the early 20th century, it began disappearing from much of that range. By the middle of the century, only scattered populations of the animal survived. Its decline was brought about by human settlers moving into its habitat. Forests were cleared for their timber or to create farmland, and the settlers killed the red wolf out of fear and ignorance.

As forests were cut down in eastern Texas and Oklahoma, the separate ranges of the red wolf and the coyote began to meet. The red wolves, whose numbers were very low, started to interbreed with the coyotes. As a result, the number of genetically pure red wolves in the wild became even smaller.

In 1973 the U.S. Fish and Wildlife Service (USFWS) established a captive-breeding program in hopes of reintroducing the red wolf into the wild. It was the first recovery plan developed by the USFWS for an endangered species. Over a six-year period, more than 400 animals believed to be red wolves were captured in the wild. Only 17 of those were found to be true red wolves, and only 14 of these were able to breed successfully in captivity.

In 1987, four pairs of captive-bred red wolves were reintroduced to the wild on the 120,000-acre (48,550-hectare) Alligator River National

Did You Know?

Red wolves are of the genus *Canis*, making them closely related to coyotes and gray wolves, who share this genus. It was previously thought that the animals were only capable of living in the wilderness. *Canis* animals have proven, however, that they can survive anywhere there is sufficient food and human tolerance. Cities and towns have many rats and other prey, and over the past few decades *Canis* predators have followed this food source into urban areas. Coyotes in particular have moved into cities. It is estimated that over 2,000 of them live in metropolitan Chicago alone. Coyotes prefer to hunt wildlife such as rabbits and songbirds rather than eat garbage and leftover human food. Scientists studying these ecosystem interactions are a part of a relatively new field of ecology, called urban ecology.

Wildlife Refuge in northeastern North Carolina. Although disease and conflicts with humans took their toll on this small population, wild births and additional releases of captive-bred animals have kept it going. The reintroduction area has been expanded to include several additional sites that together cover almost 2,700 square miles (7,000 square kilometers) in North Carolina.

Another small group was reintroduced into the Great Smoky Mountains National Park in Tennessee in 1992. Most of the red wolves born in the wild in Tennessee did not survive, however, and the program ended there in 1998.

The red wolf captive-breeding program continues to be the most important component of the survival plan for this species. Interbreeding with coyotes is the biggest threat to the survival of the species in its current habitat area. Reducing the threat of coyotes, which are not native to North Carolina, and continuing to build the red wolf population in the wild are current priorities for the USFWS.

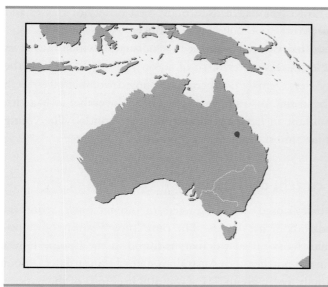

Wombat, northern hairy-nosed

Lasiorhinus krefftii

PHYLUM: Chordata
CLASS: Mammalia
ORDER: Diprotodontia
FAMILY: Vombatidae
STATUS: Critically endangered, IUCN
Endangered, ESA
RANGE: Australia

Wombat, northern hairy-nosed
Lasiorhinus krefftii

Description and biology

The northern hairy-nosed wombat is also variously known as the Queensland hairy-nosed wombat or Barnard's hairy-nosed wombat. The animal does indeed have a hairy nose, or muzzle. Its body is covered with a soft, silky brown coat. It has a large head, small eyes, pointed ears, and powerful legs with strong claws. The animal's poor eyesight is offset by its keen senses of hearing and smell. An average northern hairy-nosed wombat has a stocky body measuring 3.25 feet (1 meter) in length and weighing between 42 and 70 pounds (19 and 32 kilograms).

The animal uses its strong front claws to excavate a series of connected burrows called a warren. It generally digs its burrows in sandy soils that are supported by tree roots. Each burrow may be up to 66 feet (20 meters) long, and each warren may have several entrances. The animal's home range surrounding its warren may extend over 6.5 acres (2.6 hectares) in summer and 15.4 acres (6.2 hectares) in winter. The northern hairy-nosed wombat feeds at night on a variety of grasses and sedges (grasslike plants).

The northern hairy-nosed wombat is a marsupial, which means its young continue to develop after birth in a pouch on the outside of the mother's body. After a female northern hairy-nosed wombat gives birth to a single infant in the Australian summertime (November to March), she carries her infant in her pouch for about six months. The young wombat nurses for almost nine months.

Habitat and current distribution

The northern hairy-nosed wombat prefers to inhabit open, semi-arid (semidry) woodlands or grasslands. The only known surviving population of northern hairy-nosed wombats is found in the Epping Forest National Park in the northeastern Australian state of Queensland. About 90 of these animals live in about 741 acres (300 hectares) of the park.

History and conservation measures

The northern hairy-nosed wombat was probably already quite rare when Europeans began settling in Australia in the late 18th century. By 1909

A northern hairy-nosed wombat exits its burrow at Epping Forest National Park in Queensland, Australia. © DAVE WATTS/ALAMY.

the species was considered extinct. In 1937, however, a small group of the animals was discovered west of the city of Clermont in east-central Queensland.

The area inhabited by these remaining wombats was declared a national park in the 1970s. At first the animals were not fully protected, as cattle in the park grazed on the wombat's food source. Although steps have been taken since then to eliminate cattle from the park, the number of surviving northern hairy-nosed wombats continues to be very low. A major recovery program has been in effect in Australia since 1992 to increase the species' population in the wild and in captivity. The goal is to reestablish the northern hairy-nosed wombat throughout its historic range.

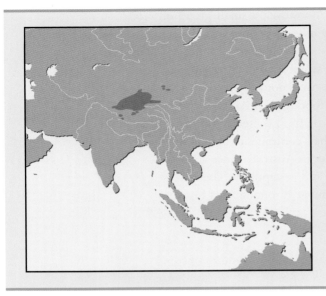

Yak, wild
Bos grunniens mutus (also *Bos mutus*)

Description and biology

The wild yak is a rare and mysterious animal. Its huge body is covered with coarse, shaggy, dark-brown hair that hangs almost to the ground. Its muzzle is white. The animal has a large, drooping head, humped shoulders, and short legs. The average male wild yak has a head and body length of 10.75 feet (3.3 meters) and stands 5.5 to 6.5 feet (1.7 to 2 meters) tall at its shoulder. It weighs between 1,800 and 2,200 pounds (820 and 1,000 kilograms). Its upward curved horns are dark and may grow up to 3 feet (0.9 meters) long. Females are substantially smaller.

Wild yaks feed on mosses and lichens (organisms composed of a fungus and an alga) while inhabiting areas at high elevations. At lower elevations, they feed on mosses, herbs, and grasses. Because vegetation (plant life) is often scarce in their habitat, the animals often cover great distances looking for food. A known predator is the Tibetan wolf.

Poaching is considered the main threat against the wild yak. © DANIEL PRUDEK/SHUTTERSTOCK.COM.

Males and females form separate herds. During mating season, which begins in September, the herds come together and the males compete with each other over the right to mate with available females. After a gestation (pregnancy) period of 258 days, a female wild yak gives birth to a single calf. The calf then nurses for up to a year.

Habitat and current distribution

Although there are more than 12 million domesticated yaks in central Asia, wildlife biologists (people who study living organisms in the wild) estimate that there were fewer than 10,000 wild yaks alive in 2014. These animals inhabit isolated patches on Qingzang Gaoyuan, a high plateau in southwestern China, at elevations between 13,500 and 20,000 feet (4,115 and 6,096 meters).

History and conservation measures

The wild yak's range once extended into northern Siberia. Biologists believe the animal's population was still quite large at the beginning of the 20th century. Since that time, excessive hunting has reduced the number of wild yaks to a dangerously low level. Humans have always valued the animal's meat, hide, and coat. Even though the wild yak is protected by international treaties and by Chinese laws, hunting continues. Because of the wild yak's remote mountain habitat, the enforcement of existing laws and the development of conservation plans are almost impossible. As a result, the surviving animals remain in grave danger.

The wild yak is also threatened by the spread of humans into their habitat areas. People bring livestock that compete with the yaks for grazing land; they also put up fences that shut out the yaks from their former grazing areas. Wild yaks can also contract diseases from livestock and mate with domestic yaks. The offspring of such pairs are hybrids, carrying a mix of genes and traits from both parents, so they can no longer be called true wild yaks.

Biologists are also concerned about the effects of global warming on the wild yak population. Scientists believe that rising temperatures in Qingzang Gaoyuan in southwestern China will likely result in less snow, which is the wild yaks' source of water.

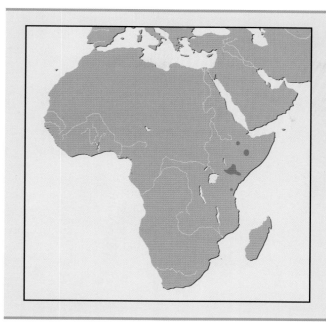

Zebra, Grevy's
Equus grevyi

PHYLUM:	Chordata
CLASS:	Mammalia
ORDER:	Perissodactyla
FAMILY:	Equidae
STATUS:	Endangered, IUCN Threatened, ESA
RANGE:	Ethiopia, Kenya

Zebra, Grevy's
Equus grevyi

Description and biology

A member of the horse family, the Grevy's zebra is similar in appearance to a mule. It has an average head and body length of 8 to 10 feet (2.4 to 3 meters) and a shoulder height of 4.5 to 5 feet (1.4 to 1.5 meters). It weighs between 800 and 950 pounds (360 and 430 kilograms). The animal has a large head; rounded ears; a tufted tail; and a short, stiff mane. It feeds primarily on grass. Lions, hyenas, and crocodiles are the Grevy's zebra's main predators.

A beautiful pattern of narrow black and white vertical stripes covers most of the Grevy's zebra's head and body. A dark stripe runs down the top of its back. Its belly is white. Scientists once thought that the stripes on zebras served to camouflage or protect the animals from predators. Some researchers now believe the stripes help the animals recognize other members of their group and, thus, form social bonds.

A Grevy's zebra grazes in Kenya, which along with Ethiopia, is one of the two African countries where the species remains. © PAPA BRAVO/SHUTTERSTOCK.COM.

Grevy's zebras are unique among zebras in that they do not form permanent groups. Nursing females and their foals (young), other females, and solitary males sometimes gather in temporary herds. Breeding males can establish territories ranging between 1 and 5 square miles (2.5 and 12.9 square kilometers) and will compete with other males over the right to mate with females in their territory. Mating takes place any time of the year, but peaks in mid-summer and mid-fall. After a gestation (pregnancy) period of 390 days, a female Grevy's zebra gives birth to a single foal. The newborn foal is brown and black in color, and its mane extends down its back to its tail. After four months, it develops adult coloring. The foal may remain with its mother for up to three years.

Habitat and current distribution

Grevy's zebras inhabit arid and semi-arid (dry and semidry) scrublands and grasslands with permanent water sources in southern Ethiopia and

Kenya. It is possible that they may also be found in South Sudan, but sightings there have not been verified. Scientists estimate that there are between 2,000 and 2,500 Grevy's zebras in existence.

History and conservation measures

In the late 20th century, the Grevy's zebra population in Ethiopia decreased by 94 percent and by up to 66 percent in Kenya. Once populous in Somalia, the animal is now extinct there. Hunting for its beautiful skin was the main reason for its decline in early years. The animal is now legally protected, and poaching (illegal hunting) is not considered a major problem.

The principal threat to the Grevy's zebra is the loss of its habitat and diminishing access to water. Increasing numbers of domestic livestock now graze on the animal's food source. Much of the water that flowed through its semiarid habitat in Kenya has been diverted to irrigate nearby developing farmland. Both Kenya and Ethiopia are taking steps to develop their conservation efforts for the species. Conservationists (people who work to manage and protect nature) suggest that programs include protection of water supplies, monitoring the number of Grevy's zebras in the wild, and involving local communities in saving the species.

Critical Thinking Questions

1. Why might conservationists specializing in trying to protect a specific animal species have mixed feelings about that animal becoming downlisted (given a less endangered status) under the Endangered Species Act (ESA) or the Red List of the International Union for Conservation of Nature and Natural Resources (IUCN)?

2. Describe three reasons why it is important that species not become extinct. Consider possible effects on other species and on humans.

3. Some species face a greater risk of endangerment than others. What are some characteristics of species and their particular habitats that can lead to greater risks of extinction?

4. What are four effects that increased carbon dioxide emissions can have on the planet's climate and weather patterns? What are some of the impacts on living organisms?

5. Scientists have extracted DNA from the bodies of extinct animals such as the woolly mammoth and are exploring possible ways to use this DNA to create new animals, a process known as "de-extincting." Do you think this scientific pursuit is a good idea? Why or why not? Does your answer depend on which species would be "de-extincted"?

6. In 2012 the United States spent $1.7 billion to conserve endangered species. Do you think this investment is worthwhile? Why or why not? Is it too much or too little? (For comparison, consider that in 2015, the lowest state budget was $4.3 billion and the U.S. military budget was approximately $600 billion.)

7. Some conservation groups focus on a small number of endangered species that people find appealing. These "flagship species" include

tigers, leopards, elephants, chimpanzees, gorillas, giant pandas, polar bears, dolphins, sea turtles, and whales. What characteristics do these animals have that might account for their public appeal? Does focusing on these animals help or hurt other endangered species that might not be as appealing?

8. Traditional practices or customary behaviors in a culture can contribute to the endangerment of species. What are some practices that do so? Think about practices in developed countries, such as the United States, and in less-developed countries.

9. What are three ways that nonnative species can be introduced into an environment? What effects can nonnative species have on native species?

10. What are some actions that you and other students could take that would help preserve endangered species?

Classroom Projects and Activities

1. Investigate a Species

Research an endangered species in your state and write a report about it. First describe the animal's appearance, social behavior, food sources, reproduction, and raising of its young. Then discuss where it lives, what its total population is, and why it is endangered. Detail conservation efforts undertaken to save it, if any. Mention interesting facts about the animal and its behavior. Include pictures of the animal and links to websites discussing the animal or videos showing it.

2. Impersonate a Conservationist

Pick an important biologist or conservationist such as Charles Darwin, Jane Goodall, Jeff Corwin, Steve Irwin, Dian Fossey, Jacques Cousteau, John Muir, or Henry David Thoreau. Research this person's life and his or her work with animals and plants. Then, either:

1. Perform a 5–10 minute monologue for your class in the character of this person. Tell stories of "your" life and conservation work. Dress up as the character if you like.
2. Present a 5–10 minute play dramatizing events from the person's life, with you and classmates acting the roles.

3. Immerse Yourself in an Issue

It can be difficult to balance people's needs and wants with the needs of animals. Consider this situation: A conservation group applies to have a bird listed as endangered. The bird's habitat includes areas where natural oil and gas are found, as well as land used for grazing livestock. Divide into groups of six, each person taking a role representing a specific point of view, then debate whether the bird should be listed. The roles are:

1. A representative of a conservation group.
2. The head of an oil and gas company that plans to drill for oil and gas on land within the bird's habitat.
3. A rancher who grazes cattle on land within the bird's habitat.
4. A local birdwatcher who enjoys observing this bird in its habitat.
5. The governor of the state where the bird is found.
6. The government official who must make the decision whether to list the bird. (This person asks questions, makes a decision at the end of the debate, and explains why she or he made that decision.)

Once the debate is done, look up the case of the greater sage grouse online. How did the decision that was made balance these different interests?

4. Invent an Animal

Invent a new animal species—a mammal, bird, amphibian, or reptile that lives on land or in the sea. Write a description and draw a picture of the animal. Describe what it looks like; its habitat (air, land, water, climate) and how it has adapted to this environment; what it eats and how it protects itself against predators; its social behavior, reproduction, and care of its young. Is the animal endangered? If so, why?

5. Invite Others to Save a Species

In a small group, choose an animal or plant from *U•X•L Endangered Species, 3rd Edition*, that is not well known. Brainstorm and write down ideas for an advertising campaign educating people about this species and the need to preserve it. Create a slogan, think about which facts and issues you would emphasize, and discuss what kind of pictures you would choose to present. Consider ways to use social media, such as Facebook, Instagram, and Snapchat, in your campaign. For inspiration, look up World Wildlife Fund's campaigns online.

6. Inspire Awareness

Create a YouTube video for other students about an endangered species topic. You could focus on one of the reasons for endangerment (habitat loss, overexploitation, invasive species, climate change), a specific species, or ways people can help save endangered species.

7. Imagine Saving the Day

Create a comic book about endangerment of species. One option: create a superhero who tries to fight endangerment, villains who put species at risk, and animals to be rescued.

8. Examine the Five Deciding Factors

Some species are listed as endangered or threatened by the International Union for Conservation of Nature and Natural Resources (IUCN), but not under the Endangered Species Act (ESA). Examples include the addax, axolotl, European mink, Ganges River dolphin, giant sequoia, and Grand Cayman blue iguana. Look up the five factors for listing a species under the Endangered Species Act. Pick and research one of the six species listed above focusing on why it is at risk. Use *U•X•L Endangered Species, 3rd Edition*; the IUCN site; and at least two other sites as sources. Then, using the 5 factors, write an argument that this animal should—or should not—be listed under the ESA.

9. Explore Ecotourism: Pros and Cons

Ecotourism is a form of tourism in which people travel to natural areas to view wildlife and other aspects of the natural environment. It has some positive aspects, but also some negative ones. Research ecotourism and list the benefits and possible disadvantages of this practice. Describe some factors that should be considered in order for ecotourism to be done in a responsible way.

10. Evaluate Common and Endangered Animals

Many endangered animals resemble similar animals that are not endangered. In the United States, for example, the American bullfrog, black bear, whitetail deer, gray squirrel, and common garter snake are not at risk, but other species of bullfrog, bear, deer, squirrel, and garter snake are endangered or threatened under the Endangered Species Act. Pick one of the animals above, and on the U.S. Fish and Wildlife Service Endangered Species website, find the similar species that are endangered. Compare and contrast the common and endangered animals. Look at geographic ranges, adaptations, habitats, value to or relationship with humans, predators and prey, and other differences. Then, in a small group, discuss your findings with students who chose other animals. Do the endangered species share characteristics in common?

11. Expand Focus

Biologist Colin Stevenson argues that conservationists' focus is often too narrow. In a March 6, 2015, interview with the BBC, a British news service, he said, "The traditional approach is to . . . study the animal, tell people about the declining numbers and the threats, and then call for people to stop doing the things causing the threats. But this approach doesn't work. The real problem is usually that the people in these areas have nothing and are just trying to survive." Choose the gharial, the giant catfish, the okapi, the dama gazelle, the markhor, or the carossier palm (a plant) and research the reasons for endangerment. In a small group, discuss how Stevenson's statement applies (or does not apply) to your species' situation.

Where to Learn More

Books

Corwin, Jeff. *100 Heartbeats: The Race to Save Earth's Most Endangered Species*. New York: Rodale, 2009. Television host and biologist Corwin interweaves personal stories of animal encounters with serious discussions of why animals face danger from humans. The book includes powerful sections on global warming and pollution.

Danson, Ted, and Michael D'Orso. *Oceana: Our Endangered Oceans and What We Can Do to Save Them*. New York: Rodale, 2011. Actor Danson traces his journey as an environmental activist, describes how actions such as deep-sea drilling and overfishing endanger the ocean and its inhabitants, and offers suggestions for reclaiming the seas. Illustrated with helpful charts and graphics.

Garbutt, Nick. *100 Animals to See Before They Die*. Buckinghamshire, UK: Bradt Travel Guides, 2007. Published by a travel company, this book profiles 100 endangered species, listed by regions where they live. Each entry offers photos, a distribution map, and a discussion of reasons for endangerment, conservation efforts, and how travelers can visit the region.

Goodall, Jane. *Hope for Animals and Their World*. New York: Hachette, 2009. Renowned chimpanzee researcher and conservationist Goodall traces ways that dedicated conservationists have worked and are working to save specific species of endangered animals.

Hoare, Ben. *DK Eyewitness: Endangered Animals*. London: DK, 2010. This guide for students aged 8 to 12 discusses why species become endangered, profiles threatened animals, and describes efforts to save species in danger. Numerous photos, pictures, charts, and graphs enliven the book.

Hoose, Phillip. *The Race to Save the Lord God Bird*. New York: Farrar, Straus, and Giroux, 2014. Using extensive archival research, Hoose traces the late-19th-century decline of the legendary ivory-billed woodpecker, a victim of habitat loss and eager hunters, and chronicles conservationists' desperate efforts to save the species.

IUCN Red List. *Species on the Edge of Survival*. London: HarperCollins UK, 2012. The International Union for Conservation of Nature and Natural

Resources (IUCN), which issues the official *Red List of Threatened Species*, describes 365 species on its list. Entries include reasons for endangerment, location maps, and photographs.

Kolbert, Elizabeth. *The Sixth Extinction: An Unnatural History*. New York: Henry Holt, 2014. Science writer Kolbert won the Pulitzer Prize for this book, which argues that humans' consumption of fossil fuels has led to a sixth period of widespread species extinctions paralleling the first five naturally caused extinction periods.

Mackay, Richard. *The Atlas of Endangered Species*, 3rd ed. Berkeley: University of California Press, 2008. A resource suitable for young adults and older readers, this atlas provides vital information on ecosystems, identifying wildlife, the importance of biodiversity, the transplanting of plants and animals across continents, and more. Also included in its 128 pages are case studies illustrating the major threats to biodiversity and the measures being taken to conserve the species.

McGavin, George. *Endangered: Wildlife on the Brink of Extinction*. Buffalo, NY: Firefly, 2006. This volume aimed at young adults explains that after five great extinction periods caused by natural events, human disregard for the environment is causing a sixth period of extinction. It describes endangered species and includes more than 400 photographs.

Montgomery, Sy. *Kakapo Rescue: Saving the World's Strangest Parrot*. New York: Houghton Mifflin Harcourt, 2010. Author Montgomery traveled to New Zealand to accompany biologists trying to save a critically endangered parrot species. It is part of the publisher's "Scientists in the Field" series, which includes books on many different animals, often endangered.

Neme, Laurel A. *Animal Investigators: How the World's First Wildlife Forensics Lab Is Solving Crimes and Saving Endangered Species*. New York: Simon & Schuster, 2009. Neme profiles a laboratory at the U.S. Fish and Wildlife Service where scientists use the bodies of animals to investigate wildlife crimes and curb trafficking in endangered species.

Pobst, Sandra. *National Geographic Investigates: Animals on the Edge*. Washington, DC: National Geographic, 2008. This short book for students ages 10 to 14 describes threats to animal species, outlines conservation efforts and what young people can do to help, and discusses formerly endangered animals now off the endangered species list.

Rogers, Kara. *The Quiet Extinction: Stories of North America's Rare and Endangered Plants*. Tucson: University of Arizona Press, 2015. Science writer Rogers explores why thousands of North American plants face possible extinction, why their survival is important, and how conservationists are working to save them.

Sartore, Joel. *Rare: Portraits of America's Endangered Species*. Washington, DC: National Geographic, 2010. National Geographic photographer Sartore presents haunting photographs of endangered animals and plants. The book is organized according to the size of the populations remaining of the photographed species, counting down to those on the edge of extinction.

Scardina, Julie, and Jeff Flocken. *Wildlife Heroes: 40 Leading Conservationists and the Animals They Are Committed to Saving.* Philadelphia: Running Press, 2012. This volume profiles 40 conservationists and the animal each works to save. Often in the conservationists' own words, entries reveal the backgrounds and experiences of these activists and describe the animals that are the focus of their efforts.

Turner, Pamela. *A Life in the Wild: George Schaller's Struggle to Save the Last Great Beasts.* New York: Farrar, Straus, and Giroux, 2008. Written for readers ages 10 to 14, this biography of noted biologist and conservationist Schaller explores his early life and his work studying gorillas and lions in Africa and tigers in India, among others. It richly describes the joys and challenges of studying endangered species in remote regions.

Watt, Simon. *The Ugly Animals: We Can't All Be Pandas.* Gloucestershire, UK: The History Press, 2014. Biologist and TV presenter Watt founded the Ugly Animal Preservation Society to humorously introduce endangered animals that are often ignored. His book features photographs and descriptions of animals such as the dromedary jumping-slug.

Periodicals

Endangered Species and Wetlands Report
P.O. Box 5393
Takoma Park, MD 20913
http://www.eswr.com/

Endangered Species Bulletin
U.S. Fish and Wildlife Service
Endangered Species
5275 Leesburg Pike
Falls Church, VA 22041
http://www.fws.gov/endangered/news/bulletin.html

World Wildlife
World Wildlife Fund
1250 24th St. NW
Washington, DC 20037
http://www.worldwildlife.org/magazine

Websites

Bagheera: An Education Website about Endangered Species and the Efforts to Save Them
www.bagheera.com/

BirdLife International
http://www.birdlife.org/

Convention on International Trade in Endangered Species of Flora and Fauna
www.cites.org

Defenders of Wildlife: Endangered Species Act 101
www.defenders.org/endangered-species-act/endangered-species-act

Defenders of Wildlife Kids' Planet: Especies Fact Sheets
www.kidsplanet.org/factsheets/map.html

Ecology: Ecology Global Network
www.ecology.com/

International Union for Conservation of Nature and Natural Resources
(IUCN) Red List of Threatened Species
www.iucn.org/about/work/programmes/species/our_work/the_iucn_red
_list

International Wild Cat Conservation Directory—Big Cats Wild Cats: Endangered Wild Cats
http://bigcatswildcats.com/endangered-wild-cats

Kids Discover Spotlight: Endangered Species
www.kidsdiscover.com/spotlight/endangered-species

National Geographic Education: Endangered Species
http://education.nationalgeographic.com/topics/endangered-species/

National Oceanic and Atmospheric Administration (NOAA) Fisheries: Endangered and Threatened Marine Species
www.nmfs.noaa.gov/pr/species/esa

Species in Pieces (online interactive exhibition)
http://species-in-pieces.com

University of Michigan: Animal Diversity Web
http://animaldiversity.org

U.S. Department of Agriculture: Threatened and Endangered Plants
http://plants.usda.gov/threat.html

U.S. Fish and Wildlife Service: Endangered Species
www.fws.gov/Endangered/index.html

Wildscreen Arkive
www.arkive.org

World Wildlife Fund: Wildfinder
www.worldwildlife.org/pages/wildfinder

The Xerces Society for Invertebrate Conservation: Endangered Species
www.xerces.org/endangered-species

Young People's Trust for the Environment: Endangered Animals of the World
https://ypte.org.uk/factsheets/endangered-animals-of-the-world/you-can
-help-too

Zoological Society of London: EDGE (Evolutionarily Distinct and Globally
Endangered) of Existence
www.edgeofexistence.org

Other Sources

Selected Organizations

[Note: The following is an annotated compilation of organizations and advocacy groups relevant to the topics found in U•X•L Endangered Species, 3rd Edition. Although the list is comprehensive, it is by no means exhaustive and is intended to serve as a starting point for assembling further information. Gale, a part of Cengage Learning, is not responsible for the accuracy of the addresses or the contents of the websites, nor does it endorse any of the organizations listed.]

African Wildlife Foundation
Ngong Road, Karen
P.O. Box 310, 00502
Nairobi, Kenya
Phone: +254 (0) 711 630 000
Fax: +254 20 2765030

U.S. office:
1400 Sixteenth St. NW, Suite 120
Washington, DC 20036
Phone: (202) 939-3333
Fax: (202) 939-3332
Email: africanwildlife@awf.org
Website: www.awf.org
The African Wildlife Foundation is an organization that works to craft and deliver creative solutions for the long-term well-being of Africa's remarkable species and habitats. It also maintains offices in the Democratic Republic of the Congo, South Sudan, Tanzania, the United Kingdom, and Zambia.

Australian Marine Conservation Society
P.O. Box 5815
West End Queensland 4101
Phone: +61 07-3846-6777
Email: amcs@amcs.org.au
Website: http://www.marineconservation.org.au/
The Australian Marine Conservation Society is the only nonprofit Australian organization focused exclusively on protecting ocean wildlife and habitats. It creates large marine national parks, promotes sustainable fishing, and protects threatened ocean animals such as sharks, seals, and whales. Its programs also combat climate change and reduce ocean pollution.

Australian Wildlife Conservancy
P.O. Box 8070 Subiaco East
Western Australia 6008
Phone: +61 8-9380-9633

Email: info@australianwildlife.org
Website: http://www.australianwildlife.org/
Organized because Australia's animals face a particularly high extinction and endangerment rate, this nonprofit is Australia's largest private owner of conservation land, protecting endangered wildlife in 23 sanctuaries spanning more than 3.15 million hectares (7.78 million acres).

Bat Conservation International
P.O. Box 162603
Austin, TX 78716
Phone: (512) 327 9721
Website: www.batcon.org
Bat Conservation International works worldwide to save, conserve, and protect the 1,300 species of bats and their ecosystems, including 77 endangered species. Its approaches include preventing extinctions, protecting areas with large bat populations, addressing major threats to species, and sponsoring research.

Canadian Wildlife Federation
Ottawa—Head Office
c/o Customer Service
350 Michael Cowpland Dr.
Kanata, Ontario K2M 2W1
Phone: (800) 563-9453
Website: http://www.cwf-fcf.org/en/
This nonprofit's mission is to conserve and inspire the conservation of Canada's wildlife and habitats for the use and enjoyment of all. Its Endangered Species Program is the biggest nongovernmental source of funding to recover Canadian species at risk. The organization also produces TV programs, magazines, and books about species and sponsors programs encouraging people to experience nature firsthand.

Center for Biological Diversity
P.O. Box 710
Tucson, AZ 85702-0710
Phone: (520) 623-5252
Fax: (520) 623-9797
Email: center@biologicaldiversity.org
Website: www.biologicaldiversity.org
The Center for Biological Diversity is a nonprofit conservation organization dedicated to protecting biological diversity through science, law, policy advocacy, and creative media. By filing petitions and lawsuits, the Center has obtained endangered species status for more than 500 species.

Center for Plant Conservation, Inc.
P.O. Box 299
St. Louis, MO 63166-0299
Phone: (314) 577-9450
Fax: (314) 577-9465

Email: cpc@mobot.org
Website: www.centerforplantconservation.org/welcome.asp
The Center for Plant Conservation, Inc., is a national network of 39
botanical gardens and arboreta dedicated to the conservation and study of
rare and endangered U.S. plants.

Defenders of Wildlife
1130 17th St. NW
Washington, DC 20036
Phone: (202) 682-9400
Email: defenders@mail.defenders.org
Website: www.defenders.org
Defenders of Wildlife is a nonprofit organization that works to protect
and restore native species, habitats, ecosystems, and overall biological
diversity in North America.

Earth Island Institute
2150 Allston Way, Suite 460
Berkeley, CA 94704-1375
Phone: (510) 859-9100
Fax: (510) 859-9091
Website: www.earthisland.org/index.php
Earth Island Institute sponsors many environmental groups such as the
International Marine Mammal Project, the Urban Bird Foundation, and
Generation Waking Up, which involves young people in creating a sus-
tainable world. It also funds young conservationists and wetland conserva-
tion projects.

Earthjustice
500 California St., Suite 500
San Francisco, CA 94111
Phone: (800) 584-6460
Fax: (415) 217-2040
Email: info@earthjustice.org
Website: http://earthjustice.org
Founded in 1971 as Sierra Club Legal Defense Fund, Earthjustice is a
nonprofit law firm dedicated to protecting nature by working through the
courts. Earthjustice has played a leading role in developing environmental
law in the courtrooms and also in Washington, D.C., where it helps shape
policies and legislation.

Endangered Species Coalition
P.O. Box 65195
Washington, DC 20035
Phone: (240) 353-2765
Website: www.endangered.org
This nonprofit coalition of conservation, scientific, education, religious,
sporting, outdoor recreation, business, and community organizations
works to preserve and improve the Endangered Species Act. Its goals are to

end human-caused extinction of species in the United States, to safeguard animal and plant habitats, and to help endangered populations recover.

Endangered Species International (Headquarters)
2112 Hayes St.
San Francisco, CA 94117
Email: info@endangeredspeciesinternational.org
Website: www.endangeredspeciesinternational.org
This nonprofit focuses on species in the gravest danger of extinction, including those the media often ignores. It conducts scientific research about conservation, uses this research in projects worldwide, and builds relationships between governments, communities, and businesses.

Environmental Defense Fund
1875 Connecticut Ave. NW, Suite 600
Washington, DC 20009
Phone: (800) 684-3322
Website: www.edf.org
One of the world's largest environmental organizations, Environmental Defense Fund addresses Earth's most pressing environmental problems in the areas of climate, oceans, ecosystems, and health. It partners with businesses to craft solutions that help the planet while benefiting people economically.

Environmental Investigation Agency (EIA)
P.O. Box 53343
Washington, DC 20009
Phone: (202) 483-6621
Fax: (202) 986-8626
Email: info@eia-global.org
Website: http://eia-global.org
Environmental Investigation Agency is an international campaigning organization formed in 1989 that is committed to investigating and exposing environmental crime, often working undercover. One of the group's efforts is protecting endangered species by investigating illegal poaching and smuggling.

Fauna and Flora International
Jupiter House, 4th Floor
Station Road
Cambridge, CB1 2JD, United Kingdom
Phone: (202) 375-7766
Email: info@fauna-flora.org
Website: http://www.fauna-flora.org/
Founded in 1903, this British organization attempts to conserve threatened species and ecosystems worldwide, choosing sustainable, science-based solutions that take into account human needs. Its projects often focus on developing countries. It secures endangered species' habitats, monitors species' survival, and raises local awareness about species' impor-

tance. The group also works with businesses, partners with local organizations, and publishes a major conservation journal.

Foundation for Australia's Most Endangered Species, Ltd. (FAME)
P.O. Box 482
Mitcham, SA 5062 Australia
Phone +61 8-8374-1744
Email: fame@fame.org.au
Website: http://fame.org.au/
FAME is the only Australian organization completely focused on saving the more than 300 endangered species in that country. It works with other organizations, wildlife authorities, and private landowners and raises funds from individuals for specific projects, such as saving the mountain pygmy possum and the Tasmanian devil.

International Union for Conservation of Nature and Natural Resources (IUCN)
Rue Mauverney 28
1196 Gland, Switzerland
Phone: +41 (22) 999-0000
Fax: +41 (22) 999-0002

U.S. office:
1630 Connecticut Ave. NW, 3rd Floor
Washington, DC 20009
Phone: (202) 387-4826
Fax: (202) 387-4823
Website: www.iucn.org
An international independent body that promotes scientifically based action for the conservation of nature and for sustainable development. The Global Species Programme and the Species Survival Commission (SSC) of the IUCN publish a Red List online that describes threatened species of mammals, birds, reptiles, amphibians, fish, invertebrates, plants, and fungi.

National Audubon Society
225 Varick St.
New York, NY 10014
Phone: (212) 979-3000
Website: www.audubon.org
Audubon is a national network comprised of nearly 500 local chapters that are dedicated to the conservation and restoration of natural resources and focused on birds and their habitat. The group's work includes restoring habitats, operating nature centers and bird sanctuaries, and encouraging governmental policies that safeguard birds.

National Wildlife Federation
11100 Wildlife Center Dr.
Reston, VA 20190

Phone: (800)-822-9919
Website: www.nwf.org
This group works to protect U.S. wildlife and habitat for future generations, concentrating on safeguarding wildlife and ecosystems in an era of
climate change. It lobbies for environmentally sound policies and educates
the public about conservation.

Nature Conservancy
4245 North Fairfax Dr., Suite 100
Arlington, VA 22203-1606
Phone: (703) 841-5300
Website: www.nature.org
The Nature Conservancy is an international nonprofit organization com-
mitted to preserving biological diversity by protecting natural lands and
the life they harbor.

Oceana
1350 Connecticut Ave. NW, 5th Floor
Washington, DC 20036
Phone: (202) 833-3900
Fax: (202) 833-2070
Email: info@oceana.org
Website: http://oceana.org
Oceana, the world's largest international advocacy group focused solely on
ocean conservation, promotes policies that preserve the ocean's marine life.
Fighting overfishing and ocean pollution, members advocate for science-
based fishery management and restoring the world's oceans.

Wild Aid
744 Montgomery St., Suite 300
San Francisco, CA 94111
Phone: (415) 834-3174
Fax: (415) 834-1759
Website: www.wildaid.org
The goal of Wild Aid is to end the illegal wildlife trade by persuading
consumers not to buy products made from illegally caught animals and by
strengthening enforcement against capturing these animals. Its slogan is
"When the buying stops, the killing can too."

Wildlife Conservation Network
209 Mississippi St.
San Francisco, CA 94107
Phone: (415) 202-6380
Fax (415) 202-6381
Website: http://wildnet.org
Wildlife Conservation Network is a nonprofit that protects endangered
species in 24 countries by supporting independent conservationists with
innovative approaches that focus on work with local communities. The
group trains these activists and brings them together with donors.

Wildlife Conservation Society
2300 Southern Blvd.
Bronx, New York 10460
Phone: (718) 220-5100
Website: www.wcs.org
Founded in 1895 to protect the American bison, the nonprofit Wildlife Conservation Society works to save wildlife and wild places worldwide, managing more than 500 conservation projects. It is the parent organization of the four major zoos and the aquarium in New York City.

Wildlife Preservation Canada
RR#5, 5420 Highway 6 North
Guelph, ON N1H 6J2
Phone: (800) 956-6608
Website: http://wildlifepreservation.ca/
This organization provides direct intervention with specific Canadian animals in grave danger of extinction. Its programs include captive breeding and release, reintroduction of species, nest protection, and other interventions. The organization focuses on preserving specific species, not just protecting their habitats; it relies on well-designed scientific research and hands-on work.

World Wildlife Fund, International (also called World Wide Fund for Nature)
Av. du Mont-Blanc
1196 Gland, Switzerland
Phone: +41 22 364 9111
Website: http://wwf.panda.org/

U.S. office:
1250 24th St. NW
Washington, DC 20037-1193
Phone: (202) 293-4800
Website: http://www.worldwildlife.org/
World Wildlife Fund works to address global threats to wildlife and habitats. The group focuses on six areas: fighting climate change, feeding the world sustainably, conserving forests, protecting freshwater habitats, influencing policy worldwide, and supporting healthy oceans. Local offices exist in many countries, including Australia, Brazil, Canada, Chile, China, Fiji, France, Greece, India, Italy, Japan, Kenya, Malaysia, Mexico, Philippines, Peru, Romania, Russia, South Africa, Tanzania, Thailand, Turkey, United Arab Emirates, and the United States.

The Xerces Society for Invertebrate Conservation
628 NE Broadway, Suite 200
Portland OR 97232
Phone: (855) 232-6639
Fax: (503) 233-6794
Email: info@xerces.org
Website: www.xerces.org

The Xerces Society for Invertebrate Conservation is dedicated to protecting and conserving invertebrates, animals such as butterflies and insects that are often ignored by other conservation groups. It advocates for policies protecting these animals, conducts research, and trains farmers and the public about invertebrate conservation.

Young People's Trust for the Environment
Suite 29, Yeovil Innovation Centre
Barracks Close, Copse Road
Yeovil, Somerset, UK BA22 8RN
Phone: +44 01935 385962
Website: https://ypte.org.uk
This British organization's goal is to help young people understand environmental issues, including wildlife endangerment, climate change, and threats to the ocean and rain forest. Its site includes educational materials, videos, and links.

Movies, Documentaries, and TV Miniseries
Arctic Tale (movie, National Geographic, 2007)
Born to Be Wild (movie, 2011)
Death of the Oceans (documentary, BBC, 2010)
EARTH: A New Wild (National Geographic series, 2015)
Frozen Planet (miniseries, BBC, 2011)
Last Lions (movie, National Geographic, 2011)
Life (miniseries, BBC, 2009)
Racing Extinction (documentary, 2015)

Apps
Endangered Species Finder (Android)
GeoEndangered (Apple)
Project Noah (Apple)
Species on the Edge (Apple)
Survival (game, free, Apple and Android)
WWF Together (Apple, Android, Kindle Fire)

General Index

Italic type indicates volume numbers; **boldface** indicates main entries.
Illustrations are marked by (ill.).

A

Abbott's booby, *2:* **300–2**, 301 (ill.)
Abies beshanzuensis, *3:* **690–91**
Acinonyx jubatus, *1:* **52–55**, 53 (ill.)
Acinonyx jubatus venaticus, *1:* 54
Acipenser sturio, *3:* **648–50**, 649 (ill.)
Acropora palmata, *3:* **605–8**, 607 (ill.)
Addax, *1:* **1–3**, 2 (ill.)
Addax nasomaculatus, *1:* **1–3**, 2 (ill.)
Addra gazelle, *1:* 99
Adelocosa anops, *2:* **277–79**, 278 (ill.)
Afghanistan
    crane, Siberian, *2:* **319–21**, 320 (ill.)
    deer, musk, *1:* **66–68**, 67 (ill.)
    leopard, snow, *1:* 122, **139–41**, 140 (ill.), 153
    markhor, *1:* **152–55**, 153 (ill.)
    pelican, Dalmatian, *2:* **415–17**, 416 (ill.)
    wolf, gray, *1:* **251–55**, 253 (ill.), 259, 261
Africa
    leopard, *1:* 46, 53, **136–38**, 137 (ill.), 153
    See also names of specific countries
African elephant, *1:* **84–87**, 85 (ill.), 88, 89, 90
African painted wolf, *1:* 69
African penguin, *2:* **418–21**, 419 (ill.)
African wild ass, *1:* **10–12**, 12 (ill.)
African wild dog, *1:* **69–71**, 70 (ill.)
Agapornis nigrigenis, *2:* **383–85**, 384 (ill.)
Agelaius xanthomus, *2:* **297–99**, 298 (ill.)
Agelaius xanthomus monensis, *2:* 298–99

Agelaius xanthomus xanthomus, *2:* 298, 299
'Aiea, *2:* 531–32, 534
Ailuropoda melanoleuca, *1:* **191–94**, 192 (ill.)
Ailurus fulgens, *1:* **195–98**, 196 (ill.)
'Akohekohe, *2:* 369
Alabama (USA)
    fanshell, *2:* **541–43**, 542 (ill.)
    manatee, West Indian, *1:* **146–48**, 147 (ill.)
    mussel, ring pink, *2:* **555–57**, 556 (ill.)
    pitcher plant, green, *3:* **713–15**, 714 (ill.)
    sculpin, pygmy, *3:* **635–37**, 636 (ill.)
    woodpecker, red-cockaded, *2:* 398, **474–77**, 475 (ill.)
Alaska (USA)
    albatross, short-tailed, *2:* **293–96**, 295 (ill.)
    bear, grizzly, *1:* **27–30**, 28 (ill.), 33, 254
    bear, polar, *1:* **31–34**, 32 (ill.)
    murrelet, marbled, *2:* **392–95**, 393 (ill.), 398
    sea lion, Steller, *1:* **228–30**, 229 (ill.)
Alasmidonta heterodon, *2:* **544–46**, 546 (ill.)
Albania
    pelican, Dalmatian, *2:* **415–17**, 416 (ill.)
    viper, meadow, *3:* **823–26**, 824 (ill.)
    wolf, gray, *1:* **251–55**, 253 (ill.), 259, 261
Albatross, short-tailed, *2:* **293–96**, 295 (ill.)
Albatross, Steller's, *2:* 293
Alberta (Canada)
    crane, whooping, *2:* **322–25**, 324 (ill.)
Algeria
    cheetah, *1:* **52–55**, 53 (ill.)

Bolivia
- **anteater, giant**, *1:* **4–6**, 5 (ill.)
- **armadillo, giant**, *1:* **7–9**, 8 (ill.)
- **chinchilla, short-tailed**, *1:* **60–62**, 61 (ill.)
- **flamingo, Andean**, *2:* **348–50**, 349 (ill.)
- **jaguar**, *1:* **122–25**, 123 (ill.), 136
- **wolf, maned**, *1:* **256–58**, 257 (ill.)

Bomarea formosissima, *2:* 445
Bombus affinis, *2:* 508
Bombus morrisoni, *2:* **506–8**, 507 (ill.)
Bombus occidentalis, *2:* 508
Bombus terricola, *2:* 508
Booby, Abbott's, *2:* **300–2**, 301 (ill.)
Bornean orangutan, *1:* 180, 182
Borneo shark, *3:* **642–44**
Bos grunniens mutus, *1:* **266–68**, 267 (ill.)
Bos mutus, *1:* **266–68**, 267 (ill.)
Bos sauveli, *1:* **130–32**, 131 (ill.)
Bosnia and Herzegovina
- **salmon, Danube**, *3:* **629–31**, 630 (ill.)
- **viper, meadow**, *3:* **823–26**, 824 (ill.)
- **wolf, gray**, *1:* **251–55**, 253 (ill.), 259, 261

Botswana
- **cheetah**, *1:* **52–55**, 53 (ill.)
- **dog, African wild**, *1:* **69–71**, 70 (ill.)
- **eagle, martial**, *2:* **336–38**, 337 (ill.)
- **elephant, African**, *1:* **84–87**, 85 (ill.), 88, 89, 90
- **hyena, brown**, *1:* **119–21**, 120 (ill.)
- **rhinoceros, black**, *1:* **217–20**, 218 (ill.)
- **vulture, Cape**, *2:* **463–66**, 464 (ill.)

Brachylophus bulabula, *3:* **771–73**, 772 (ill.)
Brachylophus fasciatus, *3:* **771–73**, 772 (ill.)
Brachypelma smithi, *2:* **287–90**, 288 (ill.)
Brachyramphus marmoratus, *2:* **392–95**, 393 (ill.)
Brachyteles arachnoides, *1:* 171, 172–73
Brachyteles hypoxanthus, *1:* 171, 173
Brachyteles spp., *1:* **171–73**, 172 (ill.)
Branching frogspawn coral, *3:* **601–4**, 602 (ill.)
Branta sandvicensis, *2:* **351–53**, 352 (ill.)
Braun, E. Lucy, *3:* 723
Braun's rockcress, *3:* **722–23**
Brazil
- **anteater, giant**, *1:* **4–6**, 5 (ill.)
- **armadillo, giant**, *1:* **7–9**, 8 (ill.)

- **curlew, Eskimo**, *2:* **326–28**, 328 (ill.)
- **ground-dove, purple-winged**, *2:* **357–59**, 358 (ill.)
- **jaguar**, *1:* **122–25**, 123 (ill.), 136
- **macaw, Lear's**, *2:* **386–88**, 387 (ill.)
- **manatee, West Indian**, *1:* **146–48**, 147 (ill.)
- **marmoset, white-eared**, *1:* **156–59**, 158 (ill.)
- **muriqui**, *1:* **171–73**, 172 (ill.)
- **parakeet, golden**, *2:* **400–2**, 401 (ill.)
- **porcupine, thin-spined**, *1:* **202–4**, 203 (ill.)
- **rosewood, Brazilian**, *3:* **724–26**, 725 (ill.)
- **sawfish, largetooth**, *3:* **632–34**, 633 (ill.)
- **tamarin, golden lion**, *1:* **234–36**, 236 (ill.)
- **wolf, maned**, *1:* **256–58**, 257 (ill.)

Brazilian rosewood, *3:* **724–26**, 725 (ill.)
Bridled nail-tailed wallaby, *1:* **244–47**, 245 (ill.)
Bristle-spined rat, *1:* 202
British Columbia (Canada)
- **owl, northern spotted**, *2:* **396–99**, 398 (ill.)

British Virgin Islands
- **anole, Culebra Island giant**, *3:* **754–56**
- **plover, piping**, *2:* **428–30**, 429 (ill.)

Brown bear, *1:* 27, 29, 33
Brown hyena, *1:* **119–21**, 120 (ill.)
Brown-headed cowbird, *2:* 462, 472–73
Brucellosis, *1:* 41
Brunei
- **bear, sun**, *1:* **35–37**, 36 (ill.)
- **dugong**, *1:* **76–79**, 78 (ill.)
- **egret, Chinese**, *2:* **342–44**, 343 (ill.)

Bubalus arnee, *1:* **46–48**, 47 (ill.)
Bubalus bubalis, *1:* 47, 48
Buffalo, *1:* 38, 39
Buffalo, Asian, *1:* 46
Buffalo, Cape, *1:* 39
Buffalo, domestic water, *1:* 47, 48
Buffalo, Indian, *1:* 46
Buffalo, wild water, *1:* **46–48**, 47 (ill.)
Buffy tufted-ear marmoset, *1:* 156
Bufo baxteri, *3:* **595–97**, 596 (ill.)
Bufo houstonensis, *3:* **592–94**, 593 (ill.)
Bukharan markhor, *1:* 154
Bulgaria
- **pelican, Dalmatian**, *2:* **415–17**, 416 (ill.)
- **wolf, gray**, *1:* **251–55**, 253 (ill.), 259, 261

Critically endangered, IUCN (*continued*)
  kouprey, *1:* **130–32**, 131 (ill.)
  lemur, mongoose, *1:* **133–35**, 134 (ill.)
  lizard, Hierro giant, *3:* **781–83**, 782 (ill.)
  louse, pygmy hog sucking, *2:* **529–30**
  marmot, Vancouver Island, *1:* **160–62**, 161 (ill.)
  mink, European, *1:* **163–65**, 164 (ill.)
  muriqui, *1:* **171–73**, 172 (ill.)
  mussel, ring pink, *2:* **555–57**, 556 (ill.)
  newt, Luristan, *3:* **579–81**, 581 (ill.)
  orangutan, *1:* **180–84**, 181 (ill.)
  palm, Argun, *3:* **702–4**, 703 (ill.)
  palm, carossier, *3:* **705–6**
  pearlymussel, little-wing, *2:* **558–60**, 559 (ill.)
  pitcher plant, green, *3:* **713–15**, 714 (ill.)
  possum, mountain pygmy, *1:* **205–7**, 206 (ill.)
  rattlesnake, Santa Catalina Island, *3:* **794–96**, 795 (ill.)
  rhinoceros, black, *1:* **217–20**, 218 (ill.)
  rhinoceros, northern white, *1:* **221–24**, 222 (ill.)
  saiga, *1:* **225–27**, 226 (ill.)
  salamander, Chinese giant, *3:* **585–87**, 586 (ill.)
  sawfish, largetooth, *3:* **632–34**, 633 (ill.)
  sculpin, pygmy, *3:* **635–37**, 636 (ill.)
  silversword, Ka'u, *3:* **731–34**, 732 (ill.)
  spinymussel, James River, *2:* **564–66**, 565 (ill.)
  starling, Rothschild's, *2:* **447–49**, 448 (ill.)
  sturgeon, Baltic, *3:* **648–50**, 649 (ill.)
  tarantula, peacock, *2:* **283–86**, 285 (ill.)
  torreya, Florida, *3:* **735–37**, 736 (ill.)
  tortoise, angulated, *3:* **797–99**, 798 (ill.)
  totoaba, *3:* **654–56**, 655 (ill.)
  tuna, southern bluefin, *3:* **661–64**, 662 (ill.)
  turtle, bog, *3:* **808–10**, 809 (ill.)
  turtle, Central American river, *3:* **811–13**, 812 (ill.)
  vulture, Indian, *2:* **467–69**, 468 (ill.)
  wolf, red, *1:* **259–62**, 260 (ill.)
  wombat, northern hairy-nosed, *1:* **263–65**, 264 (ill.)
Croatia
  gull, Audouin's, *2:* **360–62**, 361 (ill.)

  salmon, Danube, *3:* **629–31**, 630 (ill.)
  viper, meadow, *3:* **823–26**, 824 (ill.)
  wolf, gray, *1:* **251–55**, 253 (ill.), 259, 261
Crocodile, American, *3:* **760–62**, 761 (ill.)
Crocodile, Orinoco, *3:* **763–65**, 764 (ill.)
Crocodylus acutus, *3:* **760–62**, 761 (ill.)
Crocodylus intermedius, *3:* **763–65**, 764 (ill.)
Cross River gorilla, *1:* 108
Crotalus catalinensis, *3:* **794–96**, 795 (ill.)
Crotalus ruber, *3:* 796
Cryptelytrops macrops, *3:* 789
Cryptelytrops rubeus, *3:* **787–89**, 788 (ill.)
Cuba
  crocodile, American, *3:* **760–62**, 761 (ill.)
  mahogany, American, *3:* **695–98**, 696 (ill.)
  manatee, West Indian, *1:* **146–48**, 147 (ill.)
  plover, piping, *2:* **428–30**, 429 (ill.)
Cuban mahogany, *3:* 695
Culebra Island giant anole, *3:* **754–56**
Cupressus dupreziana, *3:* **684–86**, 685 (ill.)
Curaçao
  manatee, West Indian, *1:* **146–48**, 147 (ill.)
Curlew, Eskimo, *2:* **326–28**, 328 (ill.)
Cycad, Natal grass, *3:* **680–83**, 682 (ill.)
Cyclura lewisi, *3:* **774–77**, 775 (ill.)
Cynomys mexicanus, *1:* **208–10**, 209 (ill.)
Cynoscion macdonaldi, *3:* **654–56**, 655 (ill.)
Cypress, Saharan, *3:* **684–86**, 685 (ill.)
Cyprinodon macularius, *3:* **626–28**, 627 (ill.)
Cyprogenia stegaria, *2:* **541–43**, 542 (ill.)
Cyprus
  gull, Audouin's, *2:* **360–62**, 361 (ill.)
Czech Republic
  mussel, freshwater pearl, *2:* **551–54**, 552 (ill.)
  salmon, Danube, *3:* **629–31**, 630 (ill.)
  wolf, gray, *1:* **251–55**, 253 (ill.), 259, 261

D

Da Gama, Vasco, *2:* 420
Dalbergia nigra, *3:* **724–26**, 725 (ill.)
Dalmatian pelican, *2:* **415–17**, 416 (ill.)
Dama gazelle, *1:* **99–101**, 100 (ill.)
Danaus plexippus plexippus, *2:* **512–14**, 513 (ill.)

jaguar, *1:* **122–25**, 123 (ill.), 136

kakapo, *2:* **376–78**, 378 (ill.)

kestrel, Mauritius, *2:* **379–82**, 380 (ill.)

kouprey, *1:* **130–32**, 131 (ill.)

leopard, *1:* 46, 53, **136–38**, 137 (ill.), 153

leopard, snow, *1:* 122, **139–41**, 140 (ill.), 153

lizard, blunt-nosed leopard, *3:* **778–80**, 779 (ill.)

lizard, Hierro giant, *3:* **781–83**, 782 (ill.)

lynx, Iberian, *1:* **142–45**, 143 (ill.)

macaw, Lear's, *2:* **386–88**, 387 (ill.)

magpie-robin, Seychelles, *2:* **389–91**, 390 (ill.)

manatee, West Indian, *1:* **146–48**, 147 (ill.)

mandrill, *1:* **149–51**, 150 (ill.)

marmoset, white-eared, *1:* **156–59**, 158 (ill.)

marmot, Vancouver Island, *1:* **160–62**, 161 (ill.)

monitor, Komodo Island, *3:* **784–86**, 785 (ill.)

monkey, Central American squirrel, *1:* **168–70**, 169 (ill.)

moth, Blackburn's sphinx, *2:* **531–34**, 532 (ill.)

muriqui, *1:* **171–73**, 172 (ill.)

mussel, dwarf wedge, *2:* **544–46**, 546 (ill.)

mussel, fat pocketbook pearly, *2:* **547–50**, 548 (ill.)

mussel, ring pink, *2:* **555–57**, 556 (ill.)

numbat, *1:* **174–76**, 175 (ill.)

orangutan, *1:* **180–84**, 181 (ill.)

oryx, scimitar-horned, *1:* **185–87**, 186 (ill.)

otter, marine, *1:* **188–90**, 189 (ill.)

panda, giant, *1:* **191–94**, 192 (ill.), 198

parakeet, golden, *2:* **400–2**, 401 (ill.)

parrot, imperial, *2:* **403–6**, 404 (ill.)

parrot, thick-billed, *2:* **407–10**, 408 (ill.)

pearlymussel, little-wing, *2:* **558–60**, 559 (ill.)

penguin, African, *2:* **418–21**, 419 (ill.)

penguin, yellow-eyed, *2:* **422–24**, 424 (ill.)

pheasant, cheer, *2:* **425–27**, 426 (ill.)

pitcher plant, green, *3:* **713–15**, 714 (ill.)

plover, piping, *2:* **428–30**, 429 (ill.)

porcupine, thin-spined, *1:* **202–4**, 203 (ill.)

possum, mountain pygmy, *1:* **205–7**, 206 (ill.)

prairie dog, Mexican, *1:* **208–10**, 209 (ill.)

pupfish, desert, *3:* **626–28**, 627 (ill.)

quetzal, resplendent, *2:* **431–33**, 432 (ill.)

rabbit, volcano, *1:* **211–13**, 212 (ill.)

rail, Lord Howe wood, *2:* **434–36**, 436 (ill.)

rat, giant kangaroo, *1:* **214–16**, 215 (ill.)

rhinoceros, black, *1:* **217–20**, 218 (ill.)

rhinoceros, northern white, *1:* **221–24**, 222 (ill.)

rhododendron, Chapman's, *3:* **719–21**, 720 (ill.)

robin, Chatham Island, *2:* **437–40**, 438 (ill.)

rockcress, Braun's, *3:* **722–23**

saiga, *1:* **225–27**, 226 (ill.)

salamander, California tiger, *3:* **582–84**, 583 (ill.)

salamander, Chinese giant, *3:* **585–87**, 586 (ill.)

salamander, Texas blind, *3:* **588–91**, 589 (ill.)

sawfish, largetooth, *3:* **632–34**, 633 (ill.)

sea lion, Steller, *1:* **228–30**, 229 (ill.)

seal, Hawaiian monk, *1:* **231–33**, 232 (ill.)

shrimp, California freshwater, *2:* **490–91**

shrimp, Kentucky cave, *2:* **492–93**

silversword, Ka'u, *3:* **731–34**, 732 (ill.)

snail, Manus Island tree, *2:* **561–63**, 562 (ill.)

spider, no-eyed big-eyed wolf, *2:* **277–79**, 278 (ill.)

spider, Tooth Cave, *2:* **280–82**, 281 (ill.)

spinymussel, James River, *2:* **564–66**, 565 (ill.)

starling, Rothschild's, *2:* **447–49**, 448 (ill.)

stork, Oriental white, *2:* **450–53**, 451 (ill.)

sturgeon, Baltic, *3:* **648–50**, 649 (ill.)

sucker, shortnose, *3:* **651–53**, 652 (ill.)

tadpole shrimp, vernal pool, *2:* **494–96**, 495 (ill.)

tamarin, golden lion, *1:* **234–36**, 236 (ill.)

tapir, Central American, *1:* **237–39**, 238 (ill.)

thrasher, white-breasted, *2:* **457–59**, 458 (ill.)

tiger, *1:* 46, 53, 139, 220, **240–43**, 241 (ill.)

toad, Houston, *3:* **592–94**, 593 (ill.)

toad, Wyoming, *3:* **595–97**, 596 (ill.)

torreya, Florida, *3:* **735–37**, 736 (ill.)

tortoise, angulated, *3:* **797–99**, 798 (ill.)

tortoise, Galápagos giant, *3:* **804–7**, 805 (ill.)

totoaba, *3:* **654–56**, 655 (ill.)

trillium, persistent, *3:* **738–40**, 739 (ill.)

turtle, Central American river, *3:* **811–13**, 812 (ill.)

F

H

S

Sage grouse, greater, *2:* 441
Sage grouse, Gunnison, *2:* **441–43**, 442 (ill.)
Saharan cypress, *3:* **684–86**, 685 (ill.)
Saiga, *1:* **225–27**, 226 (ill.)
Saiga tatarica, *1:* **225–27**, 226 (ill.)
Saiga tatarica mongolica, *1:* 227
Saimiri oerstedii, *1:* **168–70**, 169 (ill.)
Saimiri oerstedii citrinellus, *1:* 170
Saimiri oerstedii oerstedii, *1:* 169–70
Saint Barthélemy
    mahogany, American, *3:* **695–98**, 696 (ill.)
Saint Kitts and Nevis
    mahogany, American, *3:* **695–98**, 696 (ill.)
    plover, piping, *2:* **428–30**, 429 (ill.)
Saint Lucia
    mahogany, American, *3:* **695–98**, 696 (ill.)
    thrasher, white-breasted, *2:* **457–59**, 458 (ill.)
Saint Martin
    mahogany, American, *3:* **695–98**, 696 (ill.)
Saint Pierre and Miquelon
    eagle, bald, *2:* **332–35**, 333 (ill.)
    plover, piping, *2:* **428–30**, 429 (ill.)
Saint Vincent and the Grenadines
    mahogany, American, *3:* **695–98**, 696 (ill.)
Salamander, California tiger, *3:* **582–84**, 583 (ill.)
Salamander, Chinese giant, *3:* **585–87**, 586 (ill.)
Salamander, Texas blind, *3:* **588–91**, 589 (ill.)
Salmon, Danube, *3:* **629–31**, 630 (ill.)
Salvelinus confluentus, *3:* **657–60**, 659 (ill.)
Samoa
    coral, branching frogspawn, *3:* **601–4**, 602 (ill.)
San Joaquin leopard lizard, *3:* 779
Sandhill crane, *2:* 325
Sangoritan'i Belalanda, *3:* 757
Santa Catalina Island (Mexico)
    rattlesnake, Santa Catalina Island, *3:* **794–96**, 795 (ill.)
Santa Catalina Island rattlesnake, *3:* **794–96**, 795 (ill.)
São Miguel bullfinch, *2:* 303
Sarracenia oreophila, *3:* **713–15**, 714 (ill.)

Saudi Arabia
    dragon tree, Gabal Elba, *3:* **687–89**, 688 (ill.)
    dugong, *1:* **76–79**, 78 (ill.)
    ibis, northern bald, *2:* **372–75**, 373 (ill.)
    wolf, gray, *1:* **251–55**, 253 (ill.), 259, 261
Sawfish, largetooth, *3:* **632–34**, 633 (ill.)
Scimitar-horned oryx, *1:* **185–87**, 186 (ill.)
Sclerocactus mariposensis, *3:* 671
Sculpin, mottled, *2:* 545
Sculpin, pygmy, *3:* **635–37**, 636 (ill.)
Sea cat, *1:* 188
Sea cow, *1:* 76, 147
Sea lion, northern, *1:* 228
Sea lion, Steller, *1:* **228–30**, 229 (ill.)
Seahorse, Cape, *3:* 638
Seahorse, Knysna, *3:* **638–41**, 640 (ill.)
Seal, Hawaiian monk, *1:* **231–33**, 232 (ill.)
Senecio, *2:* 506–7
Senegal
    chimpanzee, *1:* **56–59**, 57 (ill.), 102, 106
    dog, African wild, *1:* **69–71**, 70 (ill.)
    eagle, martial, *2:* **336–38**, 337 (ill.)
    elephant, African, *1:* **84–87**, 85 (ill.), 88, 89, 90
    gazelle, dama, *1:* **99–101**, 100 (ill.)
    gull, Audouin's, *2:* **360–62**, 361 (ill.)
    oryx, scimitar-horned, *1:* **185–87**, 186 (ill.)
Sequoia, giant, *3:* **727–30**, 728 (ill.)
Sequoiadendron giganteum, *3:* **727–30**, 728 (ill.)
Serbia
    salmon, Danube, *3:* **629–31**, 630 (ill.)
    viper, meadow, *3:* **823–26**, 824 (ill.)
    wolf, gray, *1:* **251–55**, 253 (ill.), 259, 261
Setophaga kirtlandii, *2:* **470–73**, 471 (ill.)
Seychelles
    dugong, *1:* **76–79**, 78 (ill.)
    magpie-robin, Seychelles, *2:* **389–91**, 390 (ill.)
Seychelles magpie-robin, *2:* **389–91**, 390 (ill.)
Shark, Borneo, *3:* **642–44**
Shark, great hammerhead, *3:* **645–47**, 646 (ill.)
Shiny cowbird, *2:* 299
Short, Charles, *3:* 694
Shortnose sucker, *3:* **651–53**, 652 (ill.)
Short's goldenrod, *3:* **692–94**, 693 (ill.)
Short-tailed albatross, *2:* **293–96**, 295 (ill.)

W